Leonard Bolles Ellis

History of the Fire Department of the City of New Bedford, Massachusetts, 1772-1890

Leonard Bolles Ellis

History of the Fire Department of the City of New Bedford, Massachusetts, 1772-1890

ISBN/EAN: 9783337251888

Printed in Europe, USA, Canada, Australia, Japan

Cover: Foto ©ninafisch / pixelio.de

CUSTOM HOUSE CORNER, BEDFORD VILLAGE, 1815.

(Drawn by C. H. Gifford, from a plan by Wm. Durfee.)

HISTORY

OF THE

FIRE DEPARTMENT

OF THE

CITY OF NEW BEDFORD

MASSACHUSETTS

1772—1890

BY

LEONARD BOLLES ELLIS

NEW BEDFORD:
PRINTED FOR THE AUTHOR BY E. ANTHONY & SONS,
1890.

PREFACE.

This history could not have been written but for the kindly aid rendered by some of my fellow citizens who have been at different times connected with our Fire Department. To all who have in any way contributed material for my use I tender my grateful thanks.

The meagre and fragmentary records of the earlier years of the Fire Department make it impossible to give a complete list of all who have belonged to it. Consequently I have decided to give complete membership rolls for the following years alone: 1834, 1844, 1856, 1867, 1876, 1884, 1890. The names of persons who joined and retired from the Department during the intervening years are not given.

L. B. E.

TO MY HONORED

FATHER

I DEDICATE THIS BOOK.

TABLE OF CONTENTS.

ILLUSTRATIONS.

CHAPTER I.

INDEPENDENCE, NO. 1.

(Drawn from a pencil sketch by Mr. Elisha C. Leonard.)

ONE hundred and eighteen years ago, in 1772, a fire engine was built in London by Richard Newsham. It was bought by Joseph Rotch, one of the original settlers of Bedford village, and was the first engine ever owned here for the extinguishing of fires. It was named "Independence, No. 1.," and was located on the north side of William street, where now stands the building of the New Bedford Safe Deposit and Trust Co. This engine was supplied with double pumps, worked by side-brakes. The water supply was from buckets, which every citizen was expected to have in the house. Generally they were hung in a convenient position in the front hall, in readiness for immediate use. These expectations were not always realized, for these buckets frequently became the receptacles for all sorts of things. Tradition says that one citizen made his the depository for beans; and on one occasion the engine was made useless because this individual, in his undue haste, emptied a quart of them into the pumps.

At a fire the engine was taken close to the building, and water was thrown through a flexible pipe attached to a tower placed over the pumps. Hose had not been invented in those primitive days. This engine was in active service in 1814: for in that year Mr. James Durfee, then a lad of 11 years, remembered very well the engine being brought for repairs to his father's blacksmith shop, then located on North Second street, on the spot now occupied by the building of Messrs. Geo. A. Bourne & Son, directly north of the Institution for Savings. Mr. Durfee assisted his father in the repairs and found a plate on the inside of the tower with the maker's name and the date.

I have found a record book that gives the names of members of Independence, No. 1, from 1820 to 1834, when the fire department was organized under a State act. The list for 1820 was approbated by the Selectmen, Eli Haskell and Roger Haskell:

Captain—Charles Ricketson.
Lieutenant—Zebedee Booth.
Clerk—Isaac Packard.

Henry Ricketson,
Oliver Crocker,
Enoch Norton,
W. H. Leonard,
Jeremiah Macomber,
Samuel Little,
Joshua Doane.
Watson Ellis,
Benjamin T. Sanford,
Pardon Winslow,
Elihu Mosher,
James Delano,
Bezaleel Washburn,
John Foster,
Charles Haffords.

1821.

Isaac Packard,
Lewis Ellis,
Joshua Doane,
John Macomber,
Thomas Nash,
Lemuel Tobey,
Phineas Kenney,
Samuel Bonney, Jr.,
Bethuel Penniman.

1822.

Peleg Clark,
Stephen Freeman,
Samuel James,
Ezra S. Kempton,
Humphrey Alden.

1823.

William A. Wall,
Edward T. Wilson,
Jonathan Russell.

1824.

John H. Chapman,
John Shaw,
George Freeman,
Andrew Brownell.

1825.

Joshua Richmond,
Jonathan Howland,
Edward Dillingham,
William Cook,
William H. Jenney.

1826.

Nathan Reed,
Ephraim Lake.

1827.

Charles Hitch,
Josiah S. Bonney,
George Heath,
Charles Sanford,
Hardy Hitch,
Ichabod Handy,
Sylvanus G. Nye,
Henry Brownell,
Samuel W. Hammond.

1828.

Henry Burbank.

1829.

Asa R. Gifford,
Charles Cushing,
Isaac Bliss.

1830.

Thomas Jouvett,
Edward T. Sherman,
Henry Munroe,
Samuel Ricketson,
Austin Whitehead,
William Carver,
John S. Smith,
Jeremiah Bailey,
William H Stowell,
William Cole,
James M. Gelette,
Thomas Whiting,
Samuel Whiting,
Samuel Watson.

1831.

Samuel Bailey,
Edward Luce,
Alfred C. Briggs.

1832.

Walter Heyer,
Isaac D. Hall,
William A. Munroe,
James H. Munroe,
James M. Cook,
Jonathan Bourne, Jr.

1833.

Shubael Coffin,
Lansing Heyer,
Benj. T. Ricketson,
Joseph E. Reed, Jr.,
Henry Mandell,
William H. Manchester,
Asahel Polley,
Benjamin T. Meader,
E. L. Goddard,
Freeman Snow.

1834.

W. G. E. Pope,
Alexander Wall,
Reuben Nye.

Newsham built in 1730 two engines for the old Dutch burghers of New York. These were operated by a crank.

The next engine, Citizen, No. 2, was built by Philip Mason, of Philadelphia, in 1802, and was purchased by the subscriptions of property owners and presented to the town. At the following town meeting the sum of $325 was asked for to build accommodations for the new engine and also for the hooks, ladders, etc., used in the fire service. This proposition was voted down as a "bad precedent" to increase taxes. The engine was, however, located in a building on the land now occupied by the Custom House.

In 1808 an English engine, built by Richard Newsham, of London, was bought in Boston. It had been attached to a ropewalk at the North end, and was called the "Jolly Ropemaker." When brought to Bedford village it was named Phœnix, No. 4, and located on the south side of William street, near Acushnet avenue. At this time the watch-house was located on the northwest corner of William and North Second streets. The town was under the care of a volunteer night watch, who carried lanterns and announced with stentorian voice the hours of the night: "12 o'clock and all is well."

The first fire-wards were appointed by the town in 1796. William Rotch, Jr., Thomas Hazard, John Howland, Manasseh Kempton, with Jeremiah Mayhew and Abraham Smith, served in that capacity until 1802.

In 1805 Oxford Village, Fairhaven, then a part of this township, purchased an engine (Oxford, No. 2) of Philip Mason, of Philadelphia. The funds were raised by subscription. I give here an exact copy of the bill:

PHILADELPHIA, Sept 16, 1805.

Capt. Constant Norton,

To Philip Mason, Dr.,

To a third-rate fire engine for Oxford, New Bedford, $360.

Received payment in full,

PHILIP MASON.

It was located at first on Samuel Borden's land, opposite the old academy, and at a later period was moved to Oxford village. I present an accurate list of the subscribers and the amounts given :

Reuben Jenne,	$10.00	Allen Crowell,	$5.00
Richard Wood,	15.00	Ellery Tompkins,	3.00
Luther Wilson,	10.00	Seth Allen,	3.00
Gilbert Tripp,	10.00	Jacob Taber,	5.00
Caleb Wood,	5.00	Thomas Nye,	10.00
Constant Norton,	15.00	Job Swift,	4.00
Seth Spooner & Son,	15.00	Josiah Jenne,	3.00
William Severance,	7.00	Thomas Nye, Jr.,	20.00
Joshua Hitch,	3.00	Joseph Terry,	6.00
Seth Mitchell,	5 00	Jabez Sherman,	3.00
Cornell Wilkey,	10.00	Rowland Gibbs,	30.00
Benjamin Sisson,	15.00	Thaddeus Pickens,	15.00
John Taber, 2d,	6 00	Samuel Borden,	30.00
Bartholomew Taber,	5.00	Weston Jenne,	5.00
Nicholas Taber,	7.00	Mayhew Luce,	5.00
Eleazer Allen,	7.00	Alden C. Cushman,	5.00
Zebdiel Sampson,	5.00	Abner Pease,	5.00
Joseph Bates,	15.00	Joshua Howland,	5.00
David Clark,	10.00	Isaac Bates,	3.00
Robert Bennett,	20.00	William Taber,	4.00
John Crowell,	5.00	Joseph Hathaway,	12 00

The following men were chosen members of the engine company, and the list was "approbated" by the selectmen, Bartholomew Aiken and James Taber, Oct. 1st, 1805 :

Bartholomew Taber,	Elisha Taber,
Reuben Jenne,	William Severance,
Bartlett Allen,	Josiah Jenne,
Seth Allen,	Seth Mitchell,
Henry Parie,	Timothy Taber,
Noah Spooner,	John Crowell,
Ellery Tompkins,	Allen Crowell,

Weston Jenne.

Land was given by Rowland Gibbs for the engine house on condition that it be removed at "his pleasure." Whether he ever exercised his rights in the matter is not on record, but the engine itself was moved one day in great haste and secrecy. In the records for Sept. 15th, 1814, I find the following item :

At a special meeting of the proprietors of Oxford engine, held at Nicholas Taber's home, it was voted "that the engine be removed for 'safety,'" and it was done without delay.

The cause of this mysterious action was this: the English sloop-of-war, "The Nimrod," was in the bay, and the inhabitants were quaking with fear that the British might land and loot the town. The people hid their valuable household goods far away in the woods and in other out-of-the-way places. Hence this precaution in moving the engine where it might be safely kept.

George H. Taber, Esq., vividly remembers this occurrence. He says "I was at that time but six years of age and of course easily partook of the terror that prevailed through the town of the probable attack of the English. The cry 'The Britishers are coming,' would have created a panic and would have driven every man, woman and child to the woods. My father's wagon stood in front of the house (where I have lived all my life) loaded with the most important of our goods, ready for a rapid move on the day of the anticipated raid. You can well imagine my fright when I saw this engine, drawn with noiseless tread, pass our house to the barn of our neighbor Howland, where it was stowed away. However, the British didn't raid the town but landed at Wareham where, after seizing several of the most prominent citizens and placing them before their boats on the shore to protect them from being fired upon, they proceeded to burn several ships on the stocks besides committing other depredations."

FLOOD NO. 1.—Fairhaven Lower Village.

(From sketch by Charles H. Gifford.)

The first engine owned in the lower village of Fairhaven was the Flood, No. 1. It was probably bought by the town as early as 1801, for Mr. Edward West has in his possession a bucket with number and date painted on its side. It was a bucket engine, with double pumps and end brakes, and was a valuable machine in its day. I present lists of members for several years, taken from an original record book:

May, 1837.

Foreman—Charles Damon.
First Assistant—Marshall Wilbur.
Second Assistant—John Alden, Jr.
Clerk and Treasurer—John Terry.

Ellis Robinson,
Alden G. Bourne,
Nat'l S. Higgins,
T. G. Bradford,
Franklyn Taber,
Asa Allen,
Richard S. Parlow,
Ebenezer Hitch,
Charles Tobey,
Joseph Damon, 2d,
Alexander Tripp,
Benj. R. Gifford,
Benj. Hammond,
Kelley M. Huttlestone,
Charles C. Allen,
Ira Gerrish,
Henry J. Grinnell,
Josiah R. Howland,
George H. Stevens,
John Damon,
Frederick Williams,
Asa H. Kelley,
Hiram Higgins.

May, 1842.

Foreman—Nathaniel S. Howard.
Clerk and Treasurer—William L. Tilley.
First Assistant Foreman—Amos S. Pierce.
Second Assistant Foreman—Lemuel Martin.

Axemen—Levi Wing, Moses H. Delano.
Torchmen—Jabez H. Wing, Philip A. Bradford.
Hosemen—Franklin Taber, Charles F. Morton.

May, 1845.

Foreman—Ira Lakey.
Clerk and Treasurer—Tucker Damon, Jr.
First Assistant—Lemuel Martin.
Second Assistant—Charles H. Taber.
Axemen—Elisha Fish, Moses H. Delano.
Torchmen—George Sawin, George Wing.

Officers chosen May, 1845-1846.

Foreman—Moses H. Delano.
Clerk and Treasurer—George W. Sawin.
First Assistant Foreman—Lemuel Martin.
Second Assistant Foreman—Amos T. Pierce.
Axemen—James Maxfield, Henry D. Scott.
Torchmen—James F. Swain, William Bowen.
Hosemen—John Gurney, Eleazer H. Wing.

June 9th the company procured uniforms for twenty-two men, and on the coming Fourth they joined in the celebration in our city. The records give expressions of thanks for their kind reception. The following list of officers was chosen May 11, 1849:

Foreman—James I. Maxfield.
Clerk and Treasurer—Charles H. Thompson.
Pipeman—Lemuel Martin.
Assistant Pipeman—Ebenezer Grinneli.
Hoseman—Timothy W. Sanford.
Assistant Hosemen—Alden Burgess, Alden Booth, Benjamin Beetle.
Axemen—Isaac H. Berry, George Miller.
Torchmen—George Bradford, John B. Eldridge.

May, 1850.

Foreman—Ebenezer Grinnell.
Clerk—Alden Burgess.
Pipeman—John Sampson.
Assistant Pipeman—William Burgess.
Hosemen—William Webb, Frederick Cushing.
Assistant Hosemen—Henry Taber, Eli Sherman.
Axemen—George Miller, Steven Leavitt.
Torchmen—Sylvester Parlow, Daniel Eldred.

In 1836 Messrs. Dyer and Richmond, of this city, built for the town of Fairhaven the first suction engine, the Columbia,

No. 3, at a cost of about $1500. It proved to be a serviceable machine, and with the No. 1 and the Oxford engine furnished ample protection for many years, in ordinary fires; but when large conflagrations occurred on either side of the river, all the engines were brought into service.

It was a great feat when either party could get "first water" on their neighbor's fire. This proved especially true of the Lindsey fire in 1811 when the Oxford engine came over from Fairhaven and played "first water." It has been bragged about ever since. It's all right to keep it in remembrance for a reasonable period, but seventy-nine years have passed away since the event, and still the story has a lively existence in the memory of our Oxford friends. One would think they would have forgotten it by this time.

The presence of this engine and the No. 2 at Oxford brought a feeling of safety and reliance, as a story told me by Mr. George H. Taber illustrates. It shows also that there is no real necessity for a man to lose his head at a fire. Mr. Taber's father was walking past a neighbor's house and discovered a fire on the roof of his barn, occasioned by the burning wad from a gun in the hands of a lad who had been shooting squirrels. He rushed in, found the owner walking leisurely about with his hands in his pockets, and a calm, placid expression on his countenance, and said "William! William! Your barn is on fire!" "I knowed it! I knowed it! John's gone for the ingin." Mr. Taber, seizing a pail of water, put the fire out in a moment. It really hadn't occured to the owner that he could have done it himself, but he sent his son John for the "ingin." We must admit he had a strong appreciation of the fire department.

The Bedford Fire Society was formed March 4th, 1807, with Joseph Ricketson moderator and Abraham Shearman, Jr., clerk. A committee was appointed to form rules and regulations, and these were adopted:

RULES AND REGULATIONS OF THE NEW BEDFORD FIRE SOCIETY.

We, the subscribers, considering the danger to which our property is exposed by fire, do agree to form ourselves into a society by the name of "The Bedford Fire Society," for the purpose of assisting, not only each other when in danger, but the citizens at large as far as circumstances will admit, and do agree to be governed by the following articles:

Art. 1. That this society shall consist of a number not exceeding thirty, and shall meet on the Second Day in the first, fourth, seventh and tenth months, at such time and place as the clerk shall appoint; and twelve members shall form a quorum.

Art. 2. A moderator shall be chosen by a hand vote at each meeting, whose duty it shall be to preserve order; and if any member has anything to offer to the consideration of the society he shall address himself to the moderator. While proceeding on business, silence shall be observed by every member except the one speaking.

Art. 3. A clerk shall be chosen annually by ballot at the meeting in the first month, who shall serve till another be chosen, and shall receive such compensation for his services as the society may judge adequate.

Art. 4. The duty of the clerk shall be to transcribe these articles into a suitable book for the use of the society, in order that each member may sign the same in token of his free consent to be governed by them. In this book he is to keep a fair record of the proceedings of the society. He is to notify every member of each meeting by leaving or causing to be left at his dwelling-house, shop or store a notification, on the back of which shall be noted the sum, if any, such member owes to the society. He shall have power to demand and receive all fines and assessments, and to call a special meeting upon the application of six members in writing. He shall call the list in half an hour after the time fixed for the meeting, and if any member be then absent, he shall pay a fine of twenty-five cents; and if absent the whole evening or period of evening, shall pay twenty-five cents in addition thereto, unless he shall be necessarily absent from town or confined by sickness. He shall read the laws to the society at each meeting, and at the end of the year he shall deliver to his successor the records and papers of the society, together with such moneys as may then be on hand belonging to the society.

Art. 5. The clerk shall notify at each stated meeting a committee of three members present, in rotation, to visit the house, shop, store of each member, examine his buckets, bags, etc., and report the state of them at the next meeting. He shall also at some suitable time appoint the day for said visitation, which shall be one week at least previous to each stated meeting of the society, and the time and place for said committee to meet for said purpose. Any member refusing or neglecting to attend to this duty shall pay a fine of one dollar. And if the clerk shall neglect his duty in this or in any of the articles mentioned or hereafter to be mentioned, he shall pay a fine not exceeding one dollar at the discretion of the society.

Art. 6. Each member shall keep constantly in good order, hanging up in some convenient place in his dwelling house, under penalty of fifty cents for each deficiency, two leather buckets and two bags; the buckets to be painted conformably to the orders of the society; the bags to be one yard and a half in length and three-quarters of a yard in breadth, with strings to draw them up. The buckets and bags shall be marked with the owner's name, under penalty of twenty-five cents for each bucket and bag.

Art. 7. At the alarm of fire each one shall immediately repair, with his buckets and bags, to the dwelling-house, shop or store of that member which he believes to be most in danger and use his best endeavors, by the direction of the owner if present, to remove and secure his goods, and to return them to him again free of expense. And for the better preservation of order and the security of property when removed in time of fire, it is agreed that the committee to be appointed by the clerk, in pursuance of the fifth article of these regulations, shall be a committee for the time being, to have the general superintendence and direction in these respects.

Art. 8. The loss of buckets or bags in time of fire shall be made good by the society, provided the owner shall make report of the same to the clerk within a week after it may happen, having the loss previously notified in some public place.

Art. 9. The admission of members shall be by ballot, and three negatives shall be sufficient to prevent any person from being a member of this society.

Art. 10. No person who is not a member shall be admitted to the society's meetings.

Art. 11. Any member who shall absent himself three meetings successively shall on the fourth be particularly notified by the clerk, and if he does not then give or send a reasonable excuse he shall be no longer considered a member, and any one who neglects to pay his fines or assessments after three several applications from the clerk shall be no longer considered a member, and if any member or members shall directly or indirectly disturb or molest the peace and good order of the society such member or members shall without delay be expelled from it, and any member who forfeits his right of membership shall forfeit all his interest in said society.

Art. 12. There shall be a watchword whereby to know each other in time of fire, which shall continue until the society shall see fit to change it; and it shall on no occasion be divulged.

Art. 13. Each member shall have a copy of these articles, with the names of the members annexed, and shall produce the same to the clerk at each meeting in order that any alterations may be inserted.

Art. 14. All questions respecting the affairs of the society shall be determined by a majority of votes, except for the admission of members already provided for, and no member shall leave the society without permission until the business is over, under penalty of twenty-five cents.

Art. 15. If any member shall think that his fine ought to be remitted, for reasons not provided for, he may mention it at any meeting of the society, which fine may be remitted by a majority of the members present.

Art. 16. Nothing in these regulations shall be construed as to interfere with the power or authority of the fire-wards whenever they shall see proper to exert it.

Art. 17. These articles shall be subject to amendment at any meeting of the society by a majority of the members.

Art. 18. Any member who may be duly elected clerk, shall either accept the office or pay a fine of one dollar. It being, however, understood that no member shall be obliged to serve two years in succession.

Joseph Ricketson,	Josiah Wood,
Elisha Thornton,	Francis Taber,
Barnabas Taber,	John Thornton,
Job Eddy,	Peter Howland,
James Allen, 2d,	Joseph Maxfield,
Simpson Hart,	William Ross,
Cornelius Howland,	Gilbert Howland,
Nicholas D. Greene,	Gilbert Russell,
Daniel Taber,	Sands Wing,
Nathan Taber,	Caleb Congdon,
Abraham Shearman, Jr.,	Asa Russell,
Frederick Mayhew,	Benjamin Lincoln,
Caleb Greene,	Freeman Barrows,
Wm. Sawyer Wall,	Pardon Tillinghast,
Jahaziel Jenney,	James Arnold,
William James,	John Howland,

Peter Barney.

From a perusal of the records, faithfully and systematically kept, to the final dissolution of the society in October, 1816, it seems that the members were under strict discipline. I make a few extracts which may possibly prove of interest:

10th mo., 12, 1807.—The committee have examined the state of buckets and bags and find them all in good order, except William Ross, Sands Wing, Benj. Lincoln.

1st mo., 11, 1808.—The society find their bags and buckets all in good order excepting Benj. Lincoln's bags, without strings. This gentleman was fined fifty cents for deficiency.

11th of 4th month, 1808.—The committee report buckets and bags belonging to the society in good order, with the exception of one of Jahaziel Jenney's bags, the strings of which would not draw it up. Abraham Shearman, Jr., Nathan Taber, Fred'k Mayhew, committee.

Jahaziel was fined 25 cents. He was one of the characters of the day, of whom many amusing stories are told. One day when Mr. Thomas Hazard was harnessing for a sleigh-ride, Mr. Jenney coming along, suggested that he be allowed to use the sleigh. "No, Mr. J., you can't have it *now*; but I will give you a sleigh ride next Fourth of July." When Independence day came Mr. J. had not forgotten the promise, though Mr. H. had. Proceeding to the stable, and pulling down the sleigh from the loft, he harnessed up and with a few invited friends scraped through several of the sultry streets with evident enjoyment. History does not record what Mr. Hazard said about it.

Speaking of characters peculiar to the town, I am tempted to relate a story of "George Lecain," a noted wit. The story has no relation to our fire department, but relates how "George was fired out of Newport." He was a noisy, loud-mouthed fellow, often an annoyance to his fellow citizens, and so proved himself to the selectmen of Newport. Once, when on a visit to that town, they threatened him that they would "drum him out of town" if he didn't keep quiet. "Bring on your music," was George's response. He was escorted to the boundary line, followed by a crowd of men and boys. Lifting his hat gracefully, he addressed the company, thanking them for their attention, and remarking, as he closed his speech, that the only difference between George Washington and himself was that George W. was drummed *into* town and George L. was drummed *out* of it.

7th mo. 11, 1808.—Simpson Hart, Job Eddy, Daniel Taber, Peleg Howland, Josiah Wood and Freeman Taber paid fines of 50 cents each for non-attendance at last meeting.

10th mo. 8, 1810.—Peleg Howland's buckets were not hanging agreeable to regulations, and James Arnold's buckets were sitting on the floor without bags. They were each fined 50 cents for the above deficiencies.

1st mo. 13, 1812.—Sands Wing paid fine, 50 cents, buckets and bags not being in their places.

In the records for 3d mo. 13, 1815, a committee reported that they found 230 buckets in the town, about enough to serve efficiently one lane of 400 feet.

The final meeting was held 10th mo., 1816, and I copy the record verbatim:

10th mo., 1816.—On motion made and seconded, voted, That after the rising of the meeting the society be dissolved, each member present engaging that they will continue to keep two good fire buckets and bags ready for use at fires, to which in future they will endeavor to carry them as heretofore. The members present further holding themselves ready hereafter to associate with their fellow citizens in the formation of a similar society or any other measure calculated to provide against the calamity occasioned by fire.

Resolved, That all fines due, together with the assessments last voted, or any other dues be paid by each member to our former clerk.

CALEB GREENE, Clerk.

In 1802 the town was divided into two fire districts, and the board of fire wards consisted of:

SOUTHWEST DISTRICT (New Bedford).

William Rotch, Jr.,
Abm. Smith,
Thomas Hazard,
John Sherman,
Daniel Ricketson,
Cornelius Grinnell,
William Ross,
James Howland.

SOUTHEAST DISTRICT (Fairhaven).

Jethro Allen,
Noah Stoddard,
Nicholas Taber,
Joseph Bates.

These, with Isaac Sherman and Thomas Nye, Jr., served till 1809.

CHAPTER II.

THE board of firewards for 1809 were Caleb Congdon, Cornelius Howland, Seth Russell, Jr., Henry Beetle, Luther Williams, John Alden, Kelley Eldredge, John Delano, Joseph Church, and, with Peter Barney, William Kempton, Peleg Jenney, Benjamin Howland, they served in that capacity until 1814. Abraham Gifford, John A. Parker, James Howland, 2d, Samuel West, Benjamin Lincoln, James Arnold, Charles Church, Zachariah Hillman, Andrew Robeson, Reuben Russell, John Ruggles, Josiah Wood, William James, Edward Wing, Ichabod Clapp, Nathaniel Nelson, Levi Standish, Joseph Bourne and Benjamin Howland served from 1815 to 1821.

In 1811 a fire occurred in Benj. Lindsey's printing office, then located on the east side of Water street, very near what is now the northeast corner of Commercial street. Mr. Lindsey, who celebrated his 83d birthday in 1888, remembered clearly this fire. Though he was but five years of age, his father took him to the office on the afternoon preceding the fire. The smell of smoke caused them to look about, and he helped him to overhaul a lot of old rags in the building. The fire caught, however, from live ashes placed in a wooden barrel in the east part of the building. The fire was first seen from Fairhaven, and the alarm given from there in the night. At this fire a ludicrous incident occurred that will bear relating. A ladder had been placed against the building that was immediately mounted by Mr. William Meader, with an axe, to break in the window. Closely following him was Mr. Timothy Delano, with the pipe and hose of Citizen, No. 2. By accident the pipe was shoved under the trousers leg of the unfortunate Mr. Meader when the order was given to play, and the result was that in less time than I am using in telling this story his clothing was filled brim full with the sparkling liquid.—so full that it gave him the appearance of a bloated aristocrat: so full that he flowed over at the bosom, presenting to his admiring companions a sort of miniature Niagara. It is said that he didn't like it, for some reason; possibly because it was a bitter cold night. People get unreasonable at times.

At this same fire the dwelling house adjoining was in danger. In the confusion, occasioned by the hasty removal of the family with their household goods, the baby was lost. The frantic demonstrations of the parents brought to their aid troops of sympathizing friends, who joined eagerly in the long search for the little one. At last baby was found sleeping quietly in its cradle in Peleg Howland's garden, on the opposite side of the street, where it had been landed, completely enveloped with bed spreads, sheets, etc., and surrounded with furniture and kitchen utensils in a perfect barricade. It seems that the person who removed it did not notice that a child was in the cradle, but piling on it the above mentioned articles had taken "cradle, baby and all" to its place of safety.

Jan. 23, 1819, two tub engines, Nos. 3 and 4, were purchased of Hunneman & Co., Roxbury, for $900, the purchase being made by the following committee: James Howland, 2d, Timothy Delano, Gideon Howland, Jr., John Coggeshall, Jr., John A. Parker. The department now consisted of five engines, Nos. 1, 2, 3 and 4 and the "Jolly Rope Maker." When the first large fire took place on Centre street, Sept. 6, 1820, George H. Taber dares to assert that the Oxford engine came over and played the first water, but James Durfee disputed it with vigor. He modestly admitted that it was true on another occasion—the Lindsey fire. Thus we see the early development of rivalry, not only between the towns, but between the fire companies as well.

I give the account of the first great fire as described in the morning *Mercury* of Sept. 8, 1820: "On Wednesday morning, about half past four, the inhabitants of this town were alarmed by the cry of fire, which originated in the extensive bakehouse of Mr. Enoch Horton, situated on the street leading from the Commercial Bank to William Rotch's (formerly Gilbert Russell's) wharf. In a few minutes the whole building was involved in flames which spread to an adjoining woodhouse, containing a large quantity of dry pine wood, and in despite of the exertions of the citizens, aided by seven engines (these without doubt included the two across the river), which were constantly playing on the desolating element, it spread in almost every direction, consuming in its progress the buildings on the east, west and north of it, until by great exertions it was finally subdued, just as it was communicating to the store of Peter Barney on the south east and the dwelling house, owned by Gilbert Russell, on the west. Had either of these buildings been permanently on fire no human exertions could have arrested its progress until a large part of the town had been laid in ashes, and had there not, fortunately, been an entire calm at the time, we should, in all probability, have had to record a calamity scarcely inferior to those of Wilmington and Savannah. The buildings destroyed were a bakehouse, owned and occupied by Mr. Enoch Horton; a large three-story building, owned and occupied by Mr. John Perkins as a store and paper staining manufactory; a store, owned and occupied by Mr. John Harrisson as a paint store, etc.; a store, owned by Mr. Gilbert Russell and partly occupied by William Card, block maker; a store, owned by Mr. William Tallman and occupied by Mr. Churchill, grocer; two cooper shops, one owned by Mr. Reuben Russell, and the other by Mr. Allerton Delano; a shoe shop, occupied by Mr. James Bosworth; a blacksmith shop, occupied by Mr. Nathan Durfee, and a barn owned by Mr. G. Russell. We understand that Mr. Perkins and Mr. Harrisson are the greatest sufferers: the loss of the former is estimated at about $4000; the latter upwards of $3000; that of Mr. Horton about $1500; and the total at about $12,000. The large three-story wooden building, occupied by the Mechanic Company and Messrs. Hussey & Allen, was saved principally by the judicious, spirited and persevering exertions of the citizens of Fairhaven, attached to the engines from the villages of Fairhaven and Oxford. The manner in which the fire originated has not been ascertained. We hope it will be a warning to a greater caution in the management of fires, particularly in combustible buildings, and that our citizens will see the policy hereafter of building their tenements of brick or stone. It is a mistaken notion that they are much more costly than wood, beside the expense of insurance is abundantly less on a brick or stone building than one of wood."

Exemption from poll tax and military duty was the compensation awarded to members of fire companies during these years. Their organization was of a simple character, their operations at fires being under the supreme dictation of the fire-wards. All citizens were alike under their control, and were expected to keep in their houses fire buckets ready for immediate use. It was an important duty, for we must remember that suction engines were not at this time in use, and the water supply of the engines was dependent upon buckets. To illustrate again how the buckets were often used for other purposes, I relate an instance, given me by Mr. Ambrose Vincent, at the fire of a stable on Second street. The dwelling house of Cornelius Howland, Jr., on the opposite side of the street, was in great danger. It was barely saved by the steady use of the buckets in wetting the roof and sides of the building. Among those passed up was one, the contents of which were not wholly sparkling water, but also a liberal supply of "frozen potatoes," that made themselves known as they went rolling and tumbling down the roof upon the crowd below.

The following citizens were at times members of the Board of Fire-wards during the years from 1822 to 1830:

Jonathan Swift,
William Hathaway,
Sturgis Phinney (22),
Eli Haskell,
William T. Russell (23),
Samuel Rodman,
Richard Williams,
Timothy G. Coffin (24),
Charles W. Morgan,
Jireh Swift (25),
Benjamin Rodman,
Haydon Coggeshall,
Elisha Dunbar,
Lemuel Williams, Jr. (26),
Isaac Case,
Lysander Washburn,
Dudley Davenport,
Charles W. Warren,
Gideon Howland,
William W. Swain (27),
William ——,
John Price,
Elkanah Tallman,
Zachariah Hillman,
William H. Allen,
Ivory H. Bartlett (29).

The Centre street fire caused much uneasiness among the people on account of the limited means of fire protection.

JAMES ARNOLD.

Finally a committee, consisting of James Arnold, Dudley Davenport and Timothy Delano, was empowered to purchase another fire engine. In 1821 the Cataract, No. 6 was received from Philadelphia. The name was changed to Mechanic soon after its arrival. I present a copy of the bill:

THE TOWN OF NEW BEDFORD,
To James Arnold, Dr.,

To one first-class Suction Engine, with 900 feet copper riveted Hose, &c.,	$1,360.00
Freight on same,	15.00
	$1,375.00

Aug. 15, 1821. Received payment by an order on the Town Treasurer.

JAMES ARNOLD.

It will be seen that the addition of this engine to the department was a most important one. It was the first suction machine purchased, though it is stated as a positive fact that the "Jolly Rope Maker" was fitted with the suction apparatus. Its use being unknown, it was cut off.

The No. 6 was a powerful engine, the pumps being the "Perkins patent," then considered an important invention. It had a long and famous career, as will be seen in future sketches. The following is the list of members, Feb. 2, 1826:

Timothy Delano,
Stevens M. Burbank,
Charles M. Pierce,
Gibbs Taber,
Gamaliel Taber,
Lyman Allen,
Benjamin Beetle,
Pardon Potter, 2d,
Samuel Bonney, Jr.,
Frederick Underwood,
Charles V. Card,
Alfred Leonard,
Christopher Slocum,
Charles P. Maxfield,
Marshall Waldron,
Humphrey Manchester,
John Paun,
Joseph Bramhall,
Thomas Peckham,
David Padelford,
Joshua V. Himes,
Christopher Roffer,
Edward Russell,
David Chase,
Stephen Parker,
Nathaniel Crandall,
Obadiah Burgess,
Jonathan Hathaway,
Gifford Taber,
William Crosley,
Humphrey Wood,
David Peckham,
Joseph Congdon.

In 1821, battering rams were ordered by the town meeting for the use of the fire department. They were heavy sticks of timber, about 20 feet long, so fitted and arranged that a number of men could easily handle them in tearing down buildings. They were of considerable importance, for it was frequently the case that buildings were destroyed to stop the progress of fire.

In 1824 a fire occurred, Nov. 17, an account of which I take from the *Mercury* of Nov. 18: "Yesterday morning, between 2 and 3 o'clock, the barn of Mr. Abraham Russell in the town was discovered to be on fire, and was in a short time totally burned, with several tons of hay and other articles which it contained. The fire had made such progress before discovered that any attempt to extinguish it would have been unavailing. An apartment had been fitted up in the building which was occupied by Mr. Abraham Russell, Jr., as a hat manufactory, and in which was a large stock of furs, unfinished hats, etc., not an article of which was saved. Two cows which were in the barn made their escape by some means unknown, one of them badly burnt. The loss sustained by Mr. Abraham Russell, Jr., by this calamity is, we learn, very heavy, and it cannot be doubted but that a liberal and munificent spirit will on this occasion be manifested toward him by our citizens. The citizens of Fairhaven and Oxford Villages are particularly entitled to our thanks for the promptitude with which they offered their assistance on this as well as on all former occasions."

In 1826 a contract was given to Timothy Delano and James Durfee for a suction engine, Columbian, No. 5. It was a bold venture for our resident mechanics to undertake so important an affair. When we remember that John Agnew, of Philadelphia, was the chief builder in the country (his only rival being Hunneman, of Roxbury), we can more readily appreciate the responsibility these citizens took upon themselves.

JAMES DURFEE.
(One of the builders of Columbian, No. 5.)

Columbian, No. 5, was accepted by the town Feb. 28th, 1827, at a total cost of $762. It proved a triumph for the mechanical skill of our own artisans, and it took rank with the best of the Agnew engines. The history of this engine, with that of its contemporary, Mechanic, No. 6, became an interesting part of the fire department annals for the next forty years. Both engines were staunchly built; had they not been they never could have stood the wear and tear of the "runs and races" of the coming years. As they were located in the same house on Purchase street, conditions of rivalry arose that became more vigorous and intense, as the years went by, when the whole department became infected with the same spirit. Poetry alone can do justice to the subject, and so I quote the impromptu verses of a resident clergyman:

Away they went with rush and shout,
  And trumpet blaring high,
Till timid people stood aghast,
  And trembled for the sky.
They trembled for the sky, my dear,
  They trembled for the sky:
The women, too, God bless their hearts,
  Did tremble for the sky.

Each man he did his level best,
  Until the goal was won:
O, it had thrilled your very soul,
  To see those fellows run.
To see those fellows run, my dear,
  To see those fellows run:
O, it had thrilled you to your toes,
  To see those fellows run.

The first engine placed at the Head of the River was in 1821 or 1822. It was a bucket machine and operated with a flexible pipe from the tower, the same as described of Independence, No. 1. At the first trial Foreman Samuel Pierce stood on top of the tower, directing the stream of water at his pleasure, when the pipe burst at the butt, and he encountered the whole force of the water in such a manner as to actually lift him in the air. It is not recorded how many feet the engine played on this trial, but the feat performed proved it to be a powerful machine. It was in service till about 1828, when it was wrecked, accidentally or purposely (the latter quite likely), on the way to the fire of Pardon Nye's barn. The engine was dragged to the conflagration with horses and in some mysterious way it was smashed. This bucket machine was soon replaced by the Hunneman tub, No. 3, from New Bedford.

It was the custom to take out the engine on Saturday afternoons to play, which practice was for some reason an annoyance to Mr. Blank, a resident of the town. One day, when he had dressed in his best Sunday suit, with fine frilled shirt bosom and cuffs, to go to Raynham, he went to the Mill Pond, where the engine was being worked, evidently to criticise and find fault. The stream was being thrown on the cotton factory, and to avoid being sprinkled he took refuge in a blacksmith's shed close by. Now this shed had a poor roof. It was neither fire nor water proof. Many years had elapsed since it had been shingled, indeed it is extremely doubtful if it had ever been at all. It was a poor refuge in a powerful rain storm. It proved to be such to Mr. Blank when the pipemen turned the stream from factory to shed. He indeed presented a sorry sight to his friends when he emerged from the building. The copious supply of water had filtered through the roof and mixed with the collected dust of many years. With this shower he was thoroughly drenched, and his intimate acquaintances could hardly have recognized him. His visit to Raynham was postponed until the next fair day It was an unfortunate accident on the part of the pipemen; for it was quite as much of an accident as the "smash up" alluded to above.

The No. 3 was eventually sold to the town of Fairhaven for $150 and located just across the river. A company was organized and continued in existence until Acushnet was set off as a separate town. The engine remained there for several years afterward, and was finally sold and broken up by Mr. John McCullough.

The Citizen, No. 2, also did long service at the Head of the River, and was replaced June 8, 1860, by Hancock, No. 9. This engine is still in commission, and is the only ready protection of that very important section of our city.

CHAPTER III.

IN 1826, one August day, our village was greatly agitated by the rumor that the dead body of a man had been found in the woods, near a notorious neighborhood called "Hard Dig," on Kempton street, just west of what is now the base ball park. A company of boys, who were picking huckleberries, made the ghastly discovery and hastened into town with the report. Several citizens went out, taking the lads with them for guides. When they reached the spot, the body had been removed, though they discovered unmistakable evidence that the story of the boys was true. The fact of the mysterious disappearance of a ship carpenter at this time (from whom no tidings were ever received), gave color to the report of murder. "Hard Dig" was occupied by the dangerous and vicious classes, and was a constant menace to good order. It was unsafe to travel in that vicinity after dark.

The report of this murder soon came to the knowledge of the whole town and caused great excitement among the people. While the law-abiding citizens would have had this iniquity crushed out by legal measures, others concluded to take the law in their own hands. A mob was organized that evening at Kempton street corner, and, after maturing plans, it proceeded in full force to its work. The first house pulled down was that of Jake Peterson, a leader of the place. Then other buildings were quickly demolished and set on fire. In two hours' time the mob had effectually cleaned out the whole nuisance.

Mr. David B. Kempton lived at that time on County street; and, standing in his yard that evening, he distinctly heard the shouts of the mob and the blows of the axes.

Wild with their success, the proposition to raid the Ark was received with enthusiasm by the mob. It was agreed, however, to postpone it till the next night.

THE ARK. (Burned by a mob in 1826. From a water-color painting by Wm. J. Swift.)

To more clearly understand the Ark riots, our readers must understand that the river front at the foot of High street, at this period, was about two hundred feet east of North Second street, where there was a sort of cove, the south side of which ran due east to the bridge. The Ark stood upon the shore as far as the high tide would permit, and was blocked under the keel to keep it in a firm position. The exact position was just where Charles S. Paisler's brick building on Water street is now located. The Ark was the hull of the old whaler Camillus, with a house built on and entirely covering the deck. A portico or walk about four feet wide was built outside, running the entire length on both sides of the vessel, and was reached by steps from the shore.

It may be interesting to mention how the name "The Ark" came to be given to this infamous vessel. A whaler named "The Ark" was owned and sailed from Nantucket in 1819. She made several voyages and was finally brought to this port to be broken up. Mr. Joseph Wilcox, Jr. remembers when she arrived here, and that she was taken to Rotch's wharf, where she lay for some time before being demolished. The stern board with this name "The Ark" was secured and mounted on the upper deck of the hull in a conspicuous place, and so this bark was called "The Ark." The craft was at first occupied by respectable families in moderate circumstances, but soon came to a baser use and finally was a brothel of the worst character. Its existence was a moral offence to the community, and its removal was earnestly desired by good citizens. It must not be understood that they encouraged riotous proceedings, however much satisfaction they may have felt at the results. And now for the story of Ark Riot No. 1.

The inmates had learned during the day of the proposed raid and, with their sympathizers, had gathered during the day a plentiful supply of stones and other missiles, including bottles of scalding hot water. After dark the crowds began to gather and matters looked ominous. Soon Mr. Timothy G. Coffin appeared and attemped to read the riot act, and probably did so, though it is said he was marched off the ground. Men appeared with hooks and ladders, and the attack commenced in good earnest. Stones flew in all directions and so did bottles of hot water, but the besieged still held the fort till a ship's gun had been brought into position, loaded—all made ready to fire. Then they succumbed and offered to march out. They were allowed to do so. Then the Ark was torn to pieces with axe and crowbar, and was then burned. Now this formidable gun was in fact a "Quaker." When found on an adjoining wharf it was actually filled with mud. Its use never was seriously contemplated. After being drawn in position before the Ark, an imaginary cartridge was rammed home with a stick and the match about to be applied, when the surrender was made. The fire of course called out the engines, but their work principally was to protect the surrounding buildings.

The above facts have been given me by Capt. Joseph Wilcox, Jr., who was present, but not a rioter, and who remembers very clearly the whole proceedings. Possibly a deeper impression was made on him, because he was hit on the shin with a large stone thrown from the Ark. Some fifty citizens were afterward subpœnaed before the court at Taunton, to give testimony of the riot, but they all proved genuine Know Nothings, and so the matter was dropped.

A second Ark soon appeared that became a terror indeed. The hull of this craft was the ship Indian Chief; and it was located further west than the first, and about fifty feet southeast of the red house on the south side of Ark lane. It was occupied by the worst classes and was the abode of debauchery and evil doing. Citizens were in daily fear, not only of their property but of their lives. Any attempt to banish the scourge failed, and it soon became apparent that law was held in effectual defiance.

In the Spring of 1829 the Elm street M. E. church was set on fire, on a Saturday evening. The lower story of the building was stored full of casks of oil. The fire was discovered

LOCATION OF THE ARK. (This building was erected in 1876.)

about 11 o'clock, just in time to prevent a serious conflagration; for it was thought that had the great quantity of oil taken fire, it would have destroyed all the buildings east of it to the river, as the running oil must have spread quickly down the steep hill, carrying destruction in its path. The audience room was uninjured, and the pastor, Rev. Timothy Merritt, preached a sermon on Sunday from the text, "Except the Lord keep the city, the watchman waketh in vain." The general feeling in the community was that some of the desperate characters from the Ark set the church on fire. For this incident I am indebted to Mrs. Josiah Richmond.

The reign of terror continued till Aug. 29th, when the second Ark riot occurred. I am indebted to Mr. James Durfee, Henry R. Wilcox, Rodolphus Beetle, David B. Kempton, Joseph Wilcox, Jr., and others, for valuable material concerning this incident.

The Ark was kept by a notoriously bad character named Titus Peck, a bully and desperado. He and his associates were a menace to the whole town. So strong was their power it was said the selectmen were afraid to interfere with their riotings. For days before the outbreak the streets and workshops resounded with the mysterious words "Jerry," "Jerry keep dark north end," "Keep dark south end," "Jerry is in town." What did all this mean? was the inquiry on every lip. Rumor followed rumor in quick succession; then it became vaguely understood that there was to be a meeting of citizens in the town hall (now Central Police Station) on the following Saturday evening. To the surprise of everybody, everybody else was there. The hall was packed full, more than two hundred men being in and about the building. While there seemed to be no organization, it was evident that well-developed plans were laid. The respectable and influential citizens, among whom were Gideon Howland, Samuel Rodman, Thomas Mandell, J. A. Parker, Jethro Hillman, Zachariah Hillman, Francis Taber and Barney Taber, used their utmost influence to prevent an outbreak. The riot act was read by Timothy G. Coffin, but when the 9 o'clock bell on Dr. Dewey's church rang out, a shout from many throats went up "Jerry is in town. Hurrah for the Ark," and pell-mell went everybody to the vicinity of Ark lane. Here was found the hook and ladder truck, brought there by unknown hands. Then suddenly appeared a company of masked men, dressed in coats turned inside out, trousers covered with white canvas at the knees, slouched hats, etc. On the best authority there were twenty-five of these uniformed rioters. The truck was rapidly stripped of its ladders and hooks, and the destruction of the Ark commenced.

Mr. Coffin, with a lighted lantern in his hand, appeared in the dense crowd gathered near the corner of Middle and Second streets. Somebody paid his respects to the lantern, and darkness came suddenly on. He was good-naturedly hustled about, and it is said to be a fact that he was passed over the heads of the crowd and safely landed where he had more room for himself.

The work of destruction completed, most of the people went home at midnight, but soon were called out by flames streaming from the ill-fated craft, for the torch was not applied till 12 o'clock. The Ark was burned to the water's edge, and when morning broke naught was left but smoking timbers of this dreaded floating hell. Several small houses were burned in the conflagration. The fire department was on hand, and its services were distinguished for what it didn't do. The Mechanic, No. 6, took water at the foot of Middle street, but the leading hose did not reach the fire by fifty feet. After long delay, the position of the engine was changed to Beetle's spar yard, where an incident occurred of which it is not necessary to speak here, but let it suffice to say that the vaulted ambition of several firemen was fully satisfied. I give now the account published in the New Bedford *Mercury*, Aug. 28, 1829: "What happened three years ago has within the last week been reenacted, with little variance of mode or circumstance. From the ashes of the old Ark, demolished and burned

August, 1826, has arisen Phœnix-like, it would seem, Ark the second, transcending as a den of abominations anything that tradition has to relate of Ark the first. On Saturday night last, it met the doom of its ill-omened progenitor, was razed to the ground and consumed by fire. We would not be understood as favoring or advocating in the slightest degree the adoption of forcible measures by lawless assemblages. It is altogether a thing to be deprecated and discountenanced; but there certainly is a difference between the riotous outbreakings of a turbulent spirit, impelling to promiscuous outrage and violence, and operations, although unsanctioned by law, which tend to a specific purpose at least imagined good, and are characterized in the process by as much order and regard for decorum as marked those of Saturday evening. We think that in justice to the character of our town this destruction in the case before us ought to be made. The wanton recklessness and profligacy which gives to a riotous mob its most hideous features was not discernable on this occasion. Still it does not do to say in such an affair that the end can justify the means, as who can predict of lawless measures what the end shall be? And in this very instance, whether the fire was applied to the materials of which the Ark was composed by the hand that demolished it or not, it was a direct and immediate consequence of the act of demolition, and came near spreading the calamity to an extent truly appalling. Nothing but the favorable state of the wind and the admirable management of the firemen prevented a conflagration which might very speedily have extended itself over a good part of the village. As it was, houses owned and occupied by quiet, peaceful citizens, who could ill afford to sustain the loss, were most unfortunately included in its ravages. Here, then, is a solemn warning against all attempts at correcting abuses by violent and lawless means; and as such it ought to be seriously regarded. The truth undoubtedly is that the early and efficacious application of the arm of the civil authority to abate the nuisance would have obviated all the evils of which it has been so fruitful a source. We are glad to learn that energetic measures are now in train for the suppression of other establishments of a like odious and demoralizing description. As with other maritime places, there is a degraded class of population brought within our borders, which can only be kept within the bounds of decency by vigorous police regulations. As the navigation of the port increases, the necessity for such regulations becomes the more apparent, and we have not the least doubt but that, perceiving the need, there will be found both the disposition and ability in those unto whom it legally appertains to second the general wish by adopting adequate measures of prevention in a matter of such growing importance to the community."

The Howard House, on North Second Street, was soon marked as a victim by the riotous elements. It bore a reputation similar to the Arks. Mr. Benjamin Rodman, one of the selectmen, hearing of the proposed raid, notified the people, and when the mob came to do their work they were informed in a speech made by Mr. Rodman that the house was vacated. They saluted him with three hearty cheers. "There are eleven of us," they said as they vanished in the darkness. What the significance of this saying was is unknown. I am indebted to Mr. Thomas R. Rodman for this incident.

On June 30, 1830, a town meeting was held to "see if the town will take into consideration the expediency of adopting measures to prevent the further destruction of property by riotous assemblages, and also to see if the town will think it proper to take any further measures to secure the safety of the town, in consequence of the recent burnings of dwelling houses in the vicinity, agreeable to petition of J. A. Parker and ten others." Samuel Rodman, Jos. Ricketson, D. Davenport, John Howland, Jr., Nathan Hathaway, James B. Congdon, Timothy I. Dyer, Benjamin Rodman, Seth Russell were appointed a committee to take into consideration the subject proposed.

The committee made report: "Your committee are of the opinion that it is highly necessary that measures should be taken by the town in its corporate capacity to indicate its deep reprobation and abhorrence of the riotous proceedings and their attendant crimes, which have recently taken place in this vicinity. Your committee believe that a direct participation in said unlawful acts was confined to a comparatively small number of persons, but that these were countenanced and encouraged by a much greater number of the young, ignorant and the thoughtless who were present, and who perhaps supposed they had an apology for their unwarrantable forbearance in omitting to suppress the disturbance in the degraded character of its victims, which cut them off from general sympathy. These and all others ought to know that the institution of civil government is designed to protect every individual in his rights, and especially to guard the weak and defenceless against the aggressions of the unprincipled and the strong. To the culprit even it guarantees by scrupulous formalities an impartial investigation of the charges alleged against him before it visits upon him the penalty affixed to his crime. Subversive then of all order, of all safety of property and life, not only to the class which have now been the sufferers, but to all, in the spirit of aggression and crime, which marks the late proceedings; and while they stamp the perpetrators as criminals of a flagrant character, on whom if convicted the law would visit its heaviest penalties, all who encourage them by their presence or otherwise are guilty of a misdemeanor against the peace and good order of society, which admits of but slight extenuation from the plea of ignorance or levity. To guard the future against a repetition of such atrocious scenes as have on this and other occasions disgraced our town and vicinity, the resolution appended to this report is herewith respectfully submitted to the consideration of the town."

Voted, To accept said report with the resolution appended: to wit:

Voted, That a large committee be appointed, to consist of persons resident in the different sections of the town, which committee shall be called "The Committee of Vigilance:" and it shall be the duty of the committee to communicate to the selectmen any information which may come to their knowledge of any design on the part of evil disposed persons to injure or destroy the property of any citizen, and to be in readiness promptly to act, under the direction of the municipal authorities, to prevent any threatened outrage; and it shall be the further duty of the committee to communicate to the selectmen any information of which the may become possessed, which may render increased vigilance necessary in order to secure the safety of the town.

SAMUEL RODMAN.
(One of the founders of the Protecting Society.)

The following were chosen a committee of vigilance:

William H. Allen,
James Arnold,
Ivory H. Bartlett,
Joseph Brownell,
Paul Barney,
Joshua Barker,
Thomas B. Bush,
John Coggeshall,
E. N. Chaddock,
Oliver Crocker,
T. G. Coffin,
Peleg Clarke,
Ichabod Clapp,
Zacheus Cushman,
Thomas Cook,
James B. Congdon,
Latham Cross,
Charles Grinnell,
Edmund Gardner,
Benj. Gage,
Cornelius Grinnell, Jr.,
Moses Gibbs,
Hallett Gifford,
William Gordon, Jr.,
Ephraim Kempton,
Manasseh Kempton,
Robt. Luscomb,
E. S. Kempton,
Warren Maxfield,
Stephen Merrihew,
Chas. W. Morgan,
Howard Nichols,
Thos. Pope,
J. A. Parker,
Nat. Perry,
C. M. Pierce,
David Pierce,
Joseph Ricketson,
Thomas Riddell,
Jireh Perry,
Anthony B. Richmond,
Mark B. Palmer,
George Randall,
Samuel Rodman,
W. T. Russell,
Williams Reed,
Wing Russell,
Billings Corey,
Robt. Hillman,
Zach. Hillman,
Isaac Hathaway,
Nathaniel Hathaway,
Jas. H. Howland, 2d,
Eli Haskell,
Cornelius S. Howland,
George Howland,
Ichabod Handy,
T. I. Dyer,
Elisha Dunbar,
D. Davenport,
Paul Ewer,
Alfred Gibbs,
Allerton Delano,
Abraham Gifford,
Alfred Woddell,
Robert S. Smith,
Pardon Tillinghast,
James D. Thompson,
Charles H. Warren,
George Tyson,
Phineas Burgess,
Gamaliel Taber,
Richard Williams,
John P. West,
Lemuel Williams,
Jonathan R. Ward,
Leonard Macomber,
Bezaleel Washburne,
Comfort Whiting,
Bethuel Penniman,
John Woddell,
Dennis Wood,
David R. Greene,
Seth Russell,
Marshall Waldron,
James Wheaton,
James Moores,
Martin Pierce,
Allen Potter,
William P. Grinnell,
Frederick Reed,
Andrew Robeson,
William Phillips,
Frederick Parker,

Richard Luscomb,	William R. West.
Gideon T. Sawyer,	Alex. H. Campbell,
Warren Mosher,	Benjamin Rodman,
William W. Swain,	110 men.

Voted, That it shall be considered by said committee as a special part of their duty to detect any individuals who have been connected, directly or indirectly, with the late outrages, and, if such disgraceful scenes shall be repeated, that the committee shall leave no means untried to enforce upon the criminals the penalty of the law.

A reward of $500 was offered for conviction.

KILLEY ELDREDGE, Town Clerk.

This vigilance committee, organized for the specific object of protecting the town from mob violence, was the parent organization of our present efficient Protecting Society, which has had an uninterrupted career of sixty years, and is the oldest part of the Fire Department. It is a misfortune that the early records cannot be found, for no doubt they would reveal much that is interesting, as this organization has always been one of the most important branches of the fire service.

EDMUND GARDNER.

(Chief of the Board of Firewards, 1830.)

CHAPTER IV.

FROM 1830 to 1835 the following citizens served on the board of firewards:

Name	Year	Name	Year
Edmund Gardner,	1830.	E. N. Chadwick,	1832.
Stephen Merrihew,	1830.	Bethuel Penniman,	1833.
Obed Nye,	1830.	Thomas S. Hathaway,	1834.
Silas Stetson,	1830.	David R. Greene,	1834.
Jethro Hillman,	1831.	Thomas Mandell,	1834.
Joseph Dunbar,	1831.	Jonathan R. Ward,	1834.
Philip T. Davis,	1831.	Charles Covill,	1834.
George Tyson,	1831.	James B. Congdon,	1834.
Wing Russell,	1831.	James D. Thompson,	1834.
Charles Coggeshall.	1831.		

On July 25th, 1830, occurred what may properly be termed "the second great fire." I present the account as vividly portrayed in the New Bedford *Mercury:*

"On Sunday morning last the inhabitants of this town were alarmed by the cry of fire, which proved to be the dwelling house of William H. Allen (now southeast corner of School and Seventh streets) and owing to the combustible material, after a long spell of dry weather, and the citizens being collected in the several churches at distant points, before effective aid could be obtained the whole building was enveloped in flames. The dwelling house of Mr. Gideon Allen adjoining was almost immediately on fire and entirely consumed. As the wind was strong from the west and the position elevated, cinders were wafted from the burning mass in great quantities, threatening destruction to all within their range. The large carpenter's shop of Dudley Davenport, as also a boat builder's shop belonging to Mr. Jethro Coffin, both considerably removed from where the fire originated, the latter three-quarters of a mile at least, were set on fire by these floating flakes of fire and consumed to the earth with the rapidity of magic.

"For a time the aspect of affairs was truly appalling. Several buildings narrowly escaped, which in their destruction would necessarily have involved a widely spread conflagration. But through the untiring and judicious efforts of the fire department and the citizens generally, the further progress of the devouring element was happily arrested. The loss of property is very considerable, and it has fallen upon citizens eminently distinguished for worth and enterprise. Besides the above enumerated, a barn belonging to Tilson B. Denham, and a quantity of oil owned by Abraham Barker, Esq., in the cellar of Mr. Davenport's shop were consumed, the latter insured. Mr. Davenport's loss is estimated at not less than $10,000, being perhaps one-half of the whole amount sustained.

"The efficacy of the newly organized Protecting Society was very strikingly shown on this occasion. Much property was rescued from destruction and much preserved from injury through the well directed exertions of this association. It was an occasion which loudly called for the best efforts of every one; and to the backward in exertion, if such there were, the conduct of the softer sex (ladies were actually seen passing water and furnishing refreshments to the exhausted firemen) must have proved an effectual monition.

"There is no doubt that this fire was occasioned by a lad's inadvertently dropping coals from a shovel. This should be a caution to every one to provide themselves with a covered shovel made for the purpose of carrying fire, which may be had at a small expense, and is perfectly secure.

"We have heard the interminable ringing of bells in cases of fire justly complained of. After the alarm is effectually given, surely no possible advantage can result from keeping up a ringing for hours, and it may be seriously injurious to the sick as well as annoying to near dwellers."

This criticism reminds me of a story told me by Mr. William G. Baker, of a gentleman visiting this town, who, hearing the fierce ringing of the bells, rushed into the street, and seeing the people running quietly in one direction (for it was the prevailing custom to depend on the clanging bells, rather than on the boisterous cry of fire) was led to inquire of a passer-by, what was the matter.

"A fire," was the response.

"A fire? A fire? My dear sir, do they have private fires in this town?" The fact that he heard no voices crying fire led the stranger to ask this question.

At this fire, at the Allen house, one citizen, anxious to do what he could to save property, rushed up stairs eagerly and seized a chair, but seeing a table of more value, dropped the first, took up the second, changed that for another article, and so on, till he actually came out of the house empty handed. Mr. Frederick S. Allen told me this story of himself.

In 1832 several reservoirs were built, and in 1833-4, the Purchase street engine house was erected.

In 1833. Perry Russell's Prussian-blue works, then located on the northwest corner of William and Sixth streets. took fire in the night and burned to the ground. The house recently torn down by the Y. M. C. A. was in great danger. and would have been consumed but for the vigorous efforts of the firemen. One of these, Capt. Humphrey W. Seabury, helped drag one of the engines into the yard, and, finding the well had given out, took the contents of one of the vats to supply the engine. The owner of the house had the satisfaction next morning of seeing his house saved from the flames. and of finding it blossomed out with a new color—a beautiful blue. His feelings were somewhat of the same shade when he saw how hastily and freely it had been applied.

On Wednesday, Nov. 9, 1834, occurred a destructive fire, an account of which I take from the *Mercury:*

"Yesterday morning at an early hour a fire broke out in the building on Water street partly owned (and occupied on the lower floor) by James Wady, as a boot and shoe store. The fire had previously made such progress that the building was almost immediately enveloped in flames, and notwithstanding that our firemen and citizens repaired to the spot with accustomed alacrity, their efforts to subdue it proved unavailing until after several buildings in the vicinity were entirely consumed. A violent gale from the east prevailed at the time, and such was the power to accelerate and extend the flames that the scene presented at one time was truly appalling. Fortunately a rain during the night assisted to prevent the destruction which would otherwise have inevitably ensued.

"The following is an enumeration of the buildings destroyed: On Water street (west side) a valuable dwelling house, owned and occupied by Capt. William Blackmer.

"A two story building adjoining on the south, also owned by Capt. Blackmer, and occupied as a millinery on the lower floor, and by a family in the chambers.

"A three story building also adjoining on the north, owned by Capt. Isaac Vincent and occupied as a dwelling by several families, and in the basement as a victualling establishment by James Carver.

"On the east side, the shop of James Wady, with a stock in trade valued at about $7000, and heavy outstanding accounts.

"A building owned by J. & J. Howland and occupied as a bakery by Messrs. Sayer & Dunham.

"A building owned by John Easton and occupied by him as a store house for casks, etc.

"A building owned by Mr. Thomas Howland and improved as a dwelling house.

"On First street (in the rear of Mr. Vincent's building) a dwelling house, owned and occupied by Capt. Eph. Hathaway.

"Two small tenements owned by Mr. Richard Johnson, and occupied by families; and also another building occupied as a dwelling house.

"We have not been able to ascertain with correctness the amount of property destroyed. It cannot, however, be estimated at less than $20,000. Insurance on a part of the property had been effected as follows: At the Bristol Co. Mutual Ins. Co., by Capt. Blackmer, on dwelling house, $2700; Joseph Wady, on building, $1100; J. & J. Howland, on bakehouse, $2100; at Manufacturer's office, Boston, by James Wady, on stock, $2000; Isaac Vincent, on building, $2000; W. Blackmer, on furniture, $1000; Thomas Howland, on building, $600. None of the properties were fully insured and the loss by several of the sufferers will be felt with severity. To such we hope the benevolence of our citizens will be cheerfully extended.

Some difficulty was experienced in removing a piano from one of the burning houses. The problem was solved by sawing off the legs in order to more easily get the piano through the door and down the stairway. It did not occur to these enthusiastic firemen that the legs could be unscrewed.

From 1835 to 1843 the following citizens served the fire department as firewards:

Andrew Robeson,
C. W. Morgan,
William H. Taylor,
James B. Congdon,
William W. Swain,
Dudley Davenport,
David R. Green,
Geo. Howland, Jr.,
John Baylies,
Thomas Mandell,
Stephen Merrihew,
James D. Thompson,
Edward Gardner,
E. N. Chaddock,
Thomas S. Hathaway,
Alex H. Campbell,
Jeremiah G. Harris,
Sampson Perkins,
Peleg Butts.

1836.

William Phillips,
Henry H. Crapo,
Joseph Grinnell.

1837.

Calvin Staples,
George B. Worth,
Abraham H. Howland.

1838.

James Durfee.

1839.

Shubael H. Gifford,
Z. Hillman,
A. D. Richmond.

1840.

Timothy G. Coffin.

1841.

Edward Merrill,
Matthew Luce,
Samuel Watson.

1842.

Jonathan Smith,
Thomas M. Bush,
William Durfee,
Gamaliel Taber,
Slocum Allen.

1843.

William W. Jenney.

Philadelphia, No. 7, was ordered by the selectmen Dec. 17, 1833, and Mr. William Durfee was sent to Philadelphia to make the contract, the selectmen deeming his experience and advice very important. Through him a contract was made with Messrs. Merrick & Agnew, and in March, 1834, the machine was received. It was built of mahogany, double chamber, $6\frac{1}{2}$ inch diameter, patent pumps, constructed on the lifting and forcing principle, well equipped with pipes, nozzles and suction hose, at a cost of $750. The new engine was stationed on Fourth street, and the company formerly attached to Independence, No. 1, took charge of it, while the latter engine, after being repaired, was held as a reserve.

The first company on record is for 1835:

Foreman, Samuel Watson.

E. L. Goddard,
W. H. Stowell,
Alex. Wall,
William Wilkins,
John Parkhurst,
Peter Brownell,
F. W. Russell,
Nathan Norcross,
Henry Mills,
M. E. Bartlett,
William H. Jenney,
I. C. Parmenter,
Benjamin Irish,
M. G. Sears,
G. W. Church,
William H. Pratt,
William Cushing,
F. S. Dole,
William M. Allen,
Joseph L. Burrows,
William C. Taber,
George C. Coffin,
H. H. Sowle,
John A. Lewis,
Paul Ewer,
Elisha Jennings,
Channing Russell,
James Munroe,
B. S. Perkins,
William Cannon,
John H. Watson,
Luther Simmons,
George Raymond,
Thomas Nelson,
W. H. Manchester,
T. R. Ricketson,
Charles Hitch,
Clement Webster,
William Hall,
James Dunnell,
George W. Chaplin,
Edward S. Cannon,
Daniel Pert,
James L. Barrows,
Robert Luscomb, Jr.,
Seth Martin,
Tilson Wood,
Joseph Devol,
Seabury Pierce,
Philip Bailey,
James H. Perkins,
William Wrightington,
George Wilson,
Ellery Remington,
Nathaniel Shepherd,
Hezekiah Coleman,
William B. Russell,
David B. Wilcox.

An act to establish a fire department in the town of New Bedford was passed by the Legislature on Jan. 30th, 1834. It was perhaps the first formal organization, and though it seems simple in form and of limited scope, in the light of the present thoroughness of system, it was a great advance from the chaotic condition of previous years. The governing power was vested in the board of firewards, who elected three engineers. This board consisted of eighteen members, with full power to appoint engine men, to control apparatus, to establish rules as to carrying of fire, fire brands, lights, matches, etc. To be chosen a member of this board was deemed a great honor, and the long list of distinguished names that appear from time to time emphasizes this statement. Confident that the list of the entire department at this stage of its history will be interesting, I present it in full:

JOHN AVERY PARKER. (Chief Engineer, 1834.)

Engineers—John A. Parker, Andrew Robeson, Stephen Merrihew.

James Arnold,
William W. Swain,
Edmund Gardner,
Thomas Mandell,
Charles W. Morgan,
Timothy G. Coffin,
Ivory H. Bartlett,
Dudley Davenport,
William H. Taylor,
Ebenezer N. Chaddock,
Thomas S. Hathaway,
David R. Greene,
Jonathan R. Ward,
Charles Covell,
James D. Thompson,
James B. Congdon.

Clerk of Board, Killey Eldredge.

Independence, No. 1.

Captain, Charles Haffords.
Clerk, Joshua Richmond.

Charles Sanford,
Samuel Watson,
William H. Jenney,
Nathan Reed,
Isaac Bliss,
Samuel Ricketson,
Aldred C. Briggs,
Jonathan Bourne, Jr.,
William Manchester,
Benj. T. Ricketson,
Asahel Polly,
Isaac D. Hall,
Harvey Mandell,
E. L. Goddard,
William H. Stowell,
Freeman Snow,
Benjamin Wilson,
Henry B. Smith,
Isaac Irish,
Nathan Northrop,
Charles Evans,
William H. Holmes,
Elisha D. Bearse,
Benjamin C. Watson,
John H. Watson,
William H. Hills,
Charles Hitch,
Thomas Jouvette,
Shubael Coffin,
Sylvanus G. Nye,
James H. Cook,
Henry Mills,
Walter D. Swan,
Horatio Bly,
Richard Rau,
Reuben Nye,
William Howland,
James H. Perkins,
John Parkhurst,
James L. Barrows,
Henry Bonney,
Thomas Tobey,
William Pope,
Alexander Wade,
Asa Gifford,
Samuel C. Bishop,
Avory T. Harris,
Benjamin Irish.

Citizen, No. 2.

Captain, Anthony D. Richmond.
Clerk, Edward Munroe.

Edward Cannon,
Peleg Butts,
Edward P. Freeman,
Philip Groves,
Alonzo Cory,
David Weaver,
W. A. Munroe,
A. S. Davis,
A. L. Luce,
W. B. Taber,
D. E. Payson,
Isaac C. Taber,

Henry Walker,
Arphaxed Simmons,
John W. Folger,
Geo. W. Bosworth,
Thomas R. Robinson,
Joseph M. Shiverick,
Albert Tobey,
Edward Howland,
Andrew G. Hayes,
George Perry,
A. S. Cleaveland,
Ichabod S. Holmes,
James Dole,
William D. Burgess,
Sampson Shearman,
A. B. Brownell,
Henry C. Kelley,
Gordon A. Cannon,
William Coffin, Jr.,
John Coffin,
Willard Nye,
I. H. Cheeney,
George Macomber,
Peleg Hall,
W. B. Burdick,
James H. Tallman,
John Wood,
William Watkins,
W. B. Thurston,
Marshall Gilbert,
William Tucker, Jr.,
George F. Barker,
James M. Staples,
Charles S. Macomber,
Seth K. Aikin,
Edward S. Wilcox,
Francis M. Taylor,
J. B. King,
P. Haskins,
Paul Ewer,
Nicholas Davis,
James Simmons, Jr.,
Joseph Seabury,
John H. Thompson,
Samuel Bonney,
Josiah S. Bonney,
Albert D. Hatch,
George Love,
Daniel S. Cobb,
S. E. Nye.

ENGINE NO. 3 (Head-of-the-River).

Captain, Shubael H. Gifford.
Clerk, Jireh Swift, Jr.

Philip T. Davis,
Isaiah Parlow,
Thaddeus M. Perry,
B. Harlow,
Thomas P. Terry,
Samuel Spooner,
Mark Snow,
James Spooner,
William Spooner, Jr.,
Erastus Merrick,
Obed Nye,
Isaac Terry,
Obed Gifford,
R. B. Smith,
Levi Hawes,
Silas Stetson.

PHŒNIX, NO. 4.

Captain, Slocum Allen.
Clerk, Benjamin T. Congdon.

John B. Taber,
Benjamin Lindsey,
W. A. Cranston,
Alfred Woddell,
Zephaniah Pease,
Franklin Tobey,
Samuel Southgate,
Allen Case,
Perry Brownell,
James Brown,
Robert C. Topham,
Richard Williams, Jr.,
Francis Hart,
Benjamin Swain,
James L. Butler,
Zephaniah S. Butler,

Alanson Williston,
Arnold Carr,
T. Howland,
Edmund Woddell,
Samuel E. King,
Charles D. Capen,
Simpson Hart,
William F. Bryant,
Levi N. Goff,
George B. Williams,
Benjamin Popple,
Hiram M. Hammond,
Abner Durfee,
David S. Bradlee,
Andrew J. Bennett,
Harvey Josselyn,
Wright Brownell.

COLUMBIAN, No. 5.

Captain, Zachariah Hillman.
Clerk, Luther G. Hewins.

Thomas R. Bryant,
Francis Bowman,
Joseph Clark,
Elisha W. Kempton,
John Wrightington,
William C. Cannon,
James Foster,
Silas Swift,
Peleg Potter,
Job Bryant,
Ezra Dyre,
Josiah Johnson,
Joseph R. Dunham,
Isaac M. Richardson,
John S. Chadwick,
John D. Handy,
Benjamin F. Spooner,
Merritt Bates,
Ebenezer Tirrell,
Humphrey Shaw,
James L. Martin,
Enoch Burroughs,
Jonathan Smith,
Dennis Smith,
Ellery Willcox,
Leander H. Taber,
Samuel Damon,
Benjamin B. Covell,
Pardon Potter, Jr.,
Uriah P. Allen,
Nathaniel S. Purrington,
Nathaniel Stetson,
John G. Harden,
Henry Sanford,
Fred P. Shaw,
John P. Dunham,
Perry Cornell,
Jonathan D. Howland,
Edward H. Potter,
Nathan Cary,
John Bryant,
Samuel Simmons,
Wilson Drake,
Hezekiah Coleman,
Braddock D. Hathaway,
Henry N. Dean,
Alden G. Snell,
Arvin Smith,
Henry Robinson,
William Dyre,
Smith Jenney,
Ellery Records,
James M. Snow,
Thomas M. Weaver,
James Davis,
Franklin Gifford,
James Drew,
James S. Davis,
James Tripp,
Charles Parker,
Henry Trowbridge,
Lewis Farewell,
Alonzo Hill,
William Whitcomb,
Isaiah Potter,
Alvin Coleman,

Mechanic, No. 6.

Captain, James Durfee.
Clerk, Gamaliel Taber.

William Durfee,
O. B. Burgess,
Stephen Parker,
Gifford Taber,
P. B. Brownell,
Wing Russell,
Ezra K. Delano,
William Bain,
R. H. Gifford,
Corbin B. Lucas,
Anthony Hathaway,
Daniel Pease,
Job Sisson, Jr.,
Benjamin Maxfield,
J. A. Westcott,
Allen Taber,
W. L. Edwards,
Joseph Allen, Jr.,
Isaiah Ellis,
Otis Manchester,
Daniel Wardsworth,
S. G. Edwards,
George Ainslee,
Anthony Gardner,
Micah Eldred,
John Bailey,
George G. Gifford,
Jona. Devoll,
Henry K. Davis,
William G. White,
Otis N. Pierce,
Geo. W. Cushing,
Michael Hathaway, 2d,
Ambrose Vincent,
W. H. Seabury,
C. C. P. Tobey,
James Davis,
W. Francis, Jr.,
John E. Cornall,
Alden Braley,
Hillard Sawyer,
D. M. Baker,
O. G. Pierce,
Caleb L. Ellis,
Joseph H. Wade,
Levi Nye,
Benj. Thompson,
W. H. Shaw,
Benj. C. Watson,
Charles M. Pierce,
Joseph Hicks,
Isaac Kempton,
Othniel Moulton,
John Whitford,
Lemuel T. Pope,
C. A. Davis,
John M. Taber,
A. W. Winslow,
Leonard Taber,
Hervey B. Keene,
C. C. Munroe,
I. B. King,
Timothy Weston,
William Noyes,
W. H. Burgess.

Protecting Society.

Captain, George Randall.
Secretary, John R. Thornton.

James Cannon,
W. T. Hawes,
Zach. Cushman,
Joseph H. Allen,
Robert Bennett,
Alfred Gibbs,
Thomas Nickerson,
Wm. Howe,
Timothy Ingraham,
Robert Gibbs,
Asa Wood,
Lemuel Kollock,
David Silvester,
Mark B. Palmer,
Benj. Russell,
Samuel Little,

Thomas Cook,	Simeon Bailey,
Henry P. Willis,	Jacob Parker,
Francis Taber, Jr.,	Caleb S. Tobey,
W. T. Cook,	Geo. Russell,
B. Thompson, Jr.,	William Knights,
W. A. Wall,	Stephen Potter, 2d,
B. D. Almy,	Jona. Fuller,
Oliver Swain,	Joseph Taber,
Wm. Swift,	Alex. H. Campbell,
Henry Cannon,	James H. Howland,
James H. Collins,	W. R. Taber,
J. H. Crocker,	Wm. Little,
P. Davenport,	Geo. F. Hussey,
Geo. G. Randall,	Joshua E. Gage,
Wing Russell,	Dennis Wood,

L. W. Hawes.

HOOK AND LADDER COMPANY.

Robert Tripp,	Afred Leonard,
A. Tompkins,	John Little,
Henry Dedrick,	Charles P. Maxfield,

Timothy D. Cook.

The first general celebration of the glorious Fourth of July occurred in 1835, in which the fire department appeared for the first time in parade.

The Novelty, No. 8, was built by Mr. William Durfee, and purchased by the town March 23, 1835, for $450. It was furnished with rotary pumps, worked like the capstan of a ship, the men pushing the bars having a jolly "walk around." This was fine exercise on a cold night, but it must have been wearisome in the warm summer days. This was a powerful machine, one of the most useful in its day. While its power of throwing water was moderate, its drawing qualities were immense, and the machine was often used to furnish the water for the other engines.

Why was this engine called the "Old Cider Mill?" Well, I will tell you; and in explaining why this undignified name was given, I must again allude to those dreadful Corsicans across the river, for to them belongs the credit. Mr. George G. Gifford, who was captain at the time, is my authority for the story.

One night a fire occurred at Oxford village, on the east side of the main road, too far from the shore for the Fairhaven engine to draw water. So the Novelty was placed on the river bank and furnished the water supply, while the Fairhaven engine was stationed on the main road, near the conflagration.

WILLIAM DURFEE.

(Builder of Novelty, No. 8.)

Now Capt. G. happened to hear one of the Oxford firemen ask, rather contemptuously., "What thing that was trying to supply water, but which couldn't 'run her over.'" He quietly walked down to the Novelty, held some private conversation with his men, and strolled leisurely back. Pretty soon the water came lively, and in spite of all efforts their engine was deluged. The boys were in sad need of rubber boots, which they didn't have, and so to keep out of the impromptu river, they pulled down a fence and built a platform to stand upon.

GEORGE G. GIFFORD.

(Captain of Novelty, No. 8.)

Finally, one more curious than the rest, went down to the river, and soon returned with his eyes protruding like those of a lobster, exclaiming, "Good gracious, boys, they've got an old cider mill down there that's doing this business." And so ever after the Novelty was known by that name, which was a novelty indeed, only paralleled by the name given to the Jolly Rope Maker.

In 1837, the interest of the citizens began to wane, and the apathy became so alarming as to call for special action on the part of the firewards. It was difficult to obtain members enough to man the engines. A full complement of the fire department called for 490 men, but the whole number enrolled was but 200. At a meeting of the firewards, April 15, 1837, it was voted "That George Howland, Jr., and Thomas Mandell be a committee who shall, through the medium of the newspapers, acquaint the public with the present alarming deficiency in the number of men attached to our engines, and with the necessity which exists that immediate and vigorous measures be taken to fill up the ranks of the different companies, and that said committee be instructed to accept the services of any of the citizens who may volunteer their aid, in the present emergency, until the results of the efforts for filling up the ranks of the companies shall have been determined. William H. Taylor, chairman; Henry H. Crapo, clerk, Board of Firewards." This action produced good effects, and the rolls for the following year showed a marked increase of membership; and in 1839 the department had a full complement of men.

In 1840 the annual report of the board of firewards speaks in satisfactory terms of its condition. At this time there were 15 public reservoirs so situated as to be available in whatever quarter of the village a fire might break out. An apparatus was provided for using powder in blowing up buildings, should occasion require.

In 1841 the hook and ladder company had dwindled in numbers to such an extent as to compel the firewards to furnish horses in dragging the apparatus to a fire. The ladders, hooks, etc., were so large and unwieldly, the weight of the loaded carriage so heavy, that it made the boys tired, and so they left. For a year there was no organized company for the hooks and ladders. This was but a foreshadowing of what became an alarming condition of the whole department, for it soon became thoroughly demoralized. It became difficult to get men to hold membership in any of the companies. In the annual report of 1841 this was the statement of the board of firewards: "That the New Bedford fire department as at present organized has failed to accomplish the design for which it was established."

CHAPTER V.

IN April, 1842, the fire department was reorganized with a force of 378 men, each entitled to $10 a year for his services. This plan was favorably received and its wisdom was soon manifest, for in a short time each company had a full roll.

HENRY H. CRAPO.

(Clerk of Board of Firewards from 1834 to 1847.)

During this year a fire occurred on Elm street, in Ripley's barn. A funny incident happened at this conflagration, related to me by Rev. Samuel Fox, for many years chaplain at our Seamen's Bethel.

On Elm street, just above Second street, and on the southern side, there was a livery stable, a low, one-story affair, with a shallow mow for hay. The hay in the mow was discovered to be on fire about 4 P. M. The horses were safely got out. The flames quickly burned through the roof and ignited the walls of a two-story dwelling house that stood near by. In the lower tenement a lady and her adult daughter were entertaining other ladies who were expected to stay to tea. The conversation had turned upon cookery and various dishes had been commented on, among others apple pot-pie, of which the visitors expressed themselves remarkably fond. To please and surprise them, one of the young ladies had slipped away to the cellar kitchen and commenced the preparation of the pot-pie. With wondrous promptness the fire department subdued the flames. Order measurably restored, ordinary matters again came to the surface, but where was that pot-pie? The concoctor said she had left it on the crane—it was the old fashioned fire-place. Surely no one would take it. However, there was no help for it. Pot and pie were gone, so other tea preparations must be made. Just before sitting down to tea, there was a knock at the door. The damsel who was to have cooked the favored dish answered the door call, and there stood a man with the pot in hand who calmly said: "Here is your pot-pie."

"Why, where did you find it? What does this mean!"

"My dear young lady," was the reply, "I did not find it: you ran into the street with it, and thrusting it into my hands, you said 'For pity's sake, Mr. ———, take care of that.'"

The mystery was solved, but doubtless the pie was spoiled.

July 31, a scorching fire occurred at Alanson Gammons' stable on Elm street. It was very disastrous, several valuable horses perishing in the flames. During this year many fires took place, and the condition of matters became so alarming that the selectmen increased the number of patrolling watchmen and issued a communication to the board of firewards recommending them to increase the number of fire engines, etc. It received their immediate attention, and at the town meeting $3000 was appropriated.

The Philadelphia, No. 7, built by Messrs. Merrick & Agnew had proved so satisfactory that two of their engines were contracted for, and in 1843 Hancock, No. 9, and Franklin, No. 10, were received and placed in commission. I give the roll of their first organizations:

HANCOCK, No. 9.

Foreman, George Perry.
First Assistant, Daniel B. Croacher.
Second Assistant, William L. Edwards.
Clerk, Arphaxed Simmons.

Arvin Smith,
Ansel Landers,
John Wrightington,
Rodolphus Beetle,
Stephen D. Haskins,
Willard Shaw,
Allen Case,
Shubael G. Edwards,
Hattil Kelley,
Lewis Hathaway,
James C. Tripp,
Israel F. Bryant,
John C. Taber,
Peter Peters,
William Bates, 2d,
Wing Spooner,
Lazarus Moulton,
James Drew,
Thomas Sowle,
Asa Gifford,
Tillinghast Tompkins,
Nathaniel S. Purrington,
Henry A. Purrington,
Charles Simmons,
Corban B. Lucas,
John C. Hervey,
Caleb T. Jenney,
Horatio T. Bly,
Sam'l McKenzie,
Henry M. Smith,
Joseph Wing,
Jabez M. Pierce,
Frederick P. Howland,
Levi Salisbury,
Henry P. Nye,
David B. Kempton, Jr.,
William P. Taylor,
Joseph Swift,
Borden Hathaway,
Edmund A. Tallman,
William M. Gifford,
Laban P. Chambers,
William Bly,
Eli Manchester,
Davis Landers,
Hiram Sherman,
James Marble,
Nathaniel Andrews,
Sampson Sherman,
W. R. Barker,
Joseph Sherman,
Joseph Wheaton,
E. L. Foster,
Robert S. Dodge,
Nathan Phinney.

FRANKLIN, No. 10.

Organized in Grove School-house, May 3, 1843.

Foreman, Tillson Wood.
First Assistant, Oliver M. Brownell.

Second assistant, Alanson Williston.
Clerk, Wanton T. Drew.

Lorenzo Pierce,	Sylvanus Churchill,
John Pierce,	Jacob Polly,
Amos Bosworth,	William B. Winslow,
Charles Grant,	Bradford G. Hathaway,
David Nye,	Peter Brotherson,
Henry F. Davis,	George M. Mosher,
Robert C. Topham,	L. S. Jennings,
Seabury Pierce,	Benjamin Durfee,
Albert Reed,	Henry M. Allen,
Samuel Leonard, Jr.,	David Pierce,
Oliver Harding,	Benjamin Popple,
Franklin Perry,	Abijah Cook,
Thomas Albert,	George Jennings,
Henry Parker,	John Butts,
Thomas Murphy,	Alex. Bliss,
C. D. Hathaway,	Benj. W. Spooner,
Caleb Miller,	Gustavus Delano,
Solomon Chadwick,	Hiram Wheeler,
Jeremiah Crapo,	N. S. Booth,
Thomas Nye,	Charles Briggs,
William Gibbs,	A. C. Wilbor,
Elihu Briggs,	Benjamin Davis,
Samuel Fellows,	Robert Sherman.

Membership in these companies was eagerly sought, and among the applicants was a colored man, who desired very much to belong to No. 10. So much did he wish it that he offered Mr. ——— a box of soap if he would secure his election. His name was duly proposed and he was elected. When the company found out that their new member was a colored man a general row ensued, and it was made very uncomfortable for Mr. ———. The prejudice against the colored people in those days was very strong, socially, notwithstanding the reputation of our city as a hot-bed of anti-slavery ideas. Mr. ———, finding himself responsible for such a commotion, and being willing to make some sacrifice in the matter, waited upon the colored gentleman and offered him half a box of soap to withdraw his name. The offer was good, but whether it was accepted or not I am unable to say.

March 19th, 1844, a fire occurred in John C. Haskell's house, northeast corner of County and Bush streets. One of the rooms in the house was finished off as an aviary, and contained over one hundred beauttful birds, all of which were smothered.

Incendiary fires at this period were of freqnent occurrence. Among these were the William street school-house and Charles W. Morgan's barn. At these fires the hose was maliciously cut, thus rendering the engines useless. The situation was truly alarming, and the Selectmen were urged by the citizens to offer a large reward for conviction. This had a salutary effect, for the trouble ceased very soon.

There was a great deal of fun in '43, between the No. 7 and No. 10. Several trials of these engines took place to test their powers, and these were quite sure to be followed by a supper or a picnic. I copy from No. 10's records the following:

The company met at their engine house at 10 o'clock, dressed in uniform, proceeded to the house of Company 7, and being joined by that company, preceded by the firewards, A. H. Howland, Thos. B. Bush and James B. Congdon, escorted by a detachment from the New Bedford Brass Band, through many of the principal streets to Blackmer's Grove, where the company amused themselves with foot ball and other games, etc. They then partook of an excellent chowder, after which the companies again formed and returned to town [Think of it, Blackmer's Grove was located exactly where the Grove street school house now stands!] well pleased with their entertainment.

July 31, 1843.—A silver trumpet was presented by the Philadelphia, No. 7, to their foreman Capt. Seth Russell.

July 31.—The Tremont Engine Co., of Roxbury, visited the town.

Oct. 20.—Philadelphia, No. 7, visited Taunton.

In 1844, the following composed the board of firewards:

Chief Engineer, William H. Taylor.

Zachariah Hillman.
James Durfee.
A. D. Richmond.
Dudley Davenport.
Slocum Allen.
Samuel Watson.
Edward Merrill.
David R. Greene.
George Howland, Jr.,
Abraham H. Howland,
Gamaliel Tabor.
George Perry.
W. H. Jenney.
George G. Gifford.
Jireh Swift, Jr.,
Thomas B. Bush.

Jan. 30th, 1844, a fire broke out at 6 o'clock A. M., in Samuel Leonard's oil works, destroying all the buildings and a large quantity of oil—one of the most destructive fires, the loss being estimated between $50,000 and $70,000. It was bitterly cold weather. Some of the engines froze up, and the

WILLIAM H. TAYLOR.

(Chief Engineer, 1844.)

whole department was much hampered by ice. The Fairhaven engines came across the river on the ice, which was frozen to a great thickness. Men were urged by offers of liberal wages to help save the large quantity of oil; but they refused, unless paid a dollar an hour. Chief Engineer William H. Taylor was highly indignant at these fellows and drove them from the premises. He completely demolished his staff of office on their heads and backs as they retreated. The vigor of the chief was quite as much a surprise to his friends as it was to the objects of his wrath. Several leading citizens offered their services gratuitously under the circumstances, and much property was saved.

The Franklin, No. 10, was the first to reach this fire, and would have taken first water, but the engine was unfortunately out of order, and all efforts to make it work were unavailing. The final attempt to make it take water was to turn up the suction hose and pour in the water, but even this was not a success. A small boy observed the novel proceeding, and noticing the movement of the upturned suction hose, yelled "Elephant," and from that time onward Franklin, No. 10, was called "The Elephant."

The first great parade and festival of the New Bedford Fire Department occurred in September, 1844. I take the following description from the *Evening Bulletin*:

"The different engines of the town met at the Town Hall, each dressed in a holiday suit of wreaths, banners, etc., and drawn by four horses. The procession was formed and under the direction of William H. Taylor and Zachariah Hillman, Esqs., after marching through the principal streets, reached the lot on County street, where a good chowder was served up. After passing an hour in social conversation, the torches were brought, and the procession reforming, commenced its march through the principal streets. The spectacle now was exceedingly brilliant; an array of several hundred torches, blowing in the night air, had a most imposing appearance, and was the theme of universal admiration. After the parade the procession marched to the Town Hall, where addresses were delivered by Thomas Dawes Eliot, Esq., and James B. Congdon, Esq., and an original song, written by a gentleman of New Bedford, was sung by Mr. Bird, the conductor on the railroad, to the tune 'King and Countryman:'

Since here we've met in our beautiful hall,
Give ear to my story, ye citizens all.
I sing the bold fireman, whose true sturdy stroke
Always turns every fire which we have into smoke.

Number One takes the lead with her jolly young band,
She's never caught napping, but always on hand;

Though engine and crew you may think rather small,
You will find she's a pretty great squirt after all.

And the next on the list, sirs, is old Number Two,
Somewhat stricken in years, but still great and true.
"Always ready" her motto, always ready her men,
She has often won the prize and shall win it again.

Number Three, out of town, I can't say much about her,
We have managed to do pretty well without her.
She was one of our line along Number Four,
She might do as well, but she could do no more.

Number Four is the Phœnix, she makes no great show,
With calmness and skill to the fire doth she go.
And just let the "Cider Mill" fill her with water,
To the fiend conflagration she'll show little quarter.

Number Five, the Columbia, and worthy the name,
With a crew who ne'er flinch at the smoke or the flame,
By our brave mechanics constructed and manned
Number Five to the rescue is always on hand.

Number Six, the Mechanic, as firm as a rock,
With her red jacket boys boldly breasts every shock.
Aloft she hangs out her flag of defiance;
In seasons of danger the town's self reliance.

Number Seven, Philadelphia, is never behind,
Not a more gallant crew in the ranks you will find:
And she leaves not a doubt while the fire she is routing,
She can beat e'en a member of Congress at spouting.

And now comes the Novelty, plain and home made,
She will grind at a grist with the best of the trade.
She's a queer one indeed, but yet early or late,
You can depend upon staunch Number Eight.

And next see approach Number Nine of the north,
When the fight rages thickest to plunge nothing loath,
Like her namesake, that sterling brave Yankee of old,
Ever firm as a rock you'll our Hancock behold.

And now last, but not least, comes along Number Ten,
Most worthy the name of our glorious old Ben;
Here's good luck to the Franklin and all her brave crew,
Whose hearts, like their shirts, are always true blue.

Let a peep at the past, a moment engage
When the "Jolly Rope Maker" appeared on the stage;

Though christened the Phœnix,* and robbed of her tail.
If you filled up her tub she would spout like a whale.

But we must not forget the vanguard of our line,
With bags, buckets and bed-screws in order so fine:
All armed and equipped, see them rush through the flame,
'Protection' their motto, protection their aim.

And now, as I close, just a word I would say
Of the corps, the rear guard of our gallant array:
With their axes and ladders and hooks at command,
To strike a bold stroke they are always on hand.

Thus, fellow townsmen, before you displayed,
The thrice gallant band for your safety arrayed;
With such bold protectors no fear will we feel,
With their arms all untiring, and hearts true as steel.

I take the following from No. 7's records:

July 25, 1845.—Took our engine to the North Christian Church for the purpose of playing with No. 10. We played ten feet over the vane above the spire (so said Messrs. James Durfee and Willard Sears), while the No. 10 played just to the vane.

To offset this, I quote from from No. 10's records for June 6, 1843, soon after the engine was received from its makers:

A trial of the power of our engine with Philadelphia, No. 7, took place to-day at the Custom House reservoir, where it was proved that No. 10 beat No. 7, both in throwing more water and at a greater distance.

October 2d, 1845.—Citizen, No. 2, Phœnix, No. 4, and Philadelphia, No. 7, had a grand parade, with the New Bedford Brass Band, and with the firewards and other invited guests, visited Fairhaven and partook of a chowder. Amused themselves during the afternoon with foot-ball and other games. After dark they took up the line of march through the principal streets of Fairhaven and New Bedford. The procession was liberally supplied with flaming torches and made a fine display.

At this great parade the department was in uniform for the first time. It would be more satisfactory could a complete description of their uniforms be given. It is impossible to do so, for until 1853 there are no records of Companies Nos. 2, 3, 4, 5, 6,

*The old Phœnix, now defunct, had, it is said, a suction, which, as its purpose was not known, was *cut off*.

and 9, and all I may give in relation to them is wholly traditional. I am indebted to Messrs. James Taylor, George G. Gifford, William R. Palmer, Joshua B. Ashley and Robert C. Topham for what I am able to present.

Independence, No. 1.—Blue frocks, trimmed with white; red trousers with black leggings, close-fitting cap with adjustable cape.

Citizen, No. 2. — Highland shirts, black trousers, belts, caps, etc.

Head of River, No. 3.—White shirts, red belts, dark trousers, etc.

Phœnix, No. 4.—Scotch plaid shirts, with Highland scarf and black trousers.

Columbian, No. 5.—White flannel shirts, trimmed with blue, black trousers, blue caps, visor, with figure 5.

Mechanic, No. 6.—Red shirts, black trousers, belts, caps, etc.

Philadelphia, No. 7.—Red shirt with large collar to turn over ten inches, wristbands four inches wide, duck trousers without suspenders, belt of black leather. Hat with round top, broad brim, wide on the back, narrow on the front, with "Philadelphia" painted around the crown in gilt, with the figure seven in front.

Novelty, No. 8.—Green jackets, velvet collars, blue trousers, yellow stripes trimmed with fringe, glazed cap, gilt figure 8.

Hancock, No. 9.—Red shirts, dark trousers, belts, tarpaulin hats.

Franklin, No. 10.—Blue shirts, trimmed with white, dark trousers, white suspenders, forming the letter X, on the back, tarpaulin hats.

Hook and Ladder Co.—Shirts, dark trousers with double and diagonal stripes at the sides, forming a ladder.

I now present the full register of our Fire Department for 1844–1845. It is my purpose to publish the official membership for every ten years. Of course many names will not appear of those whose terms of service may have ceased during these periods.

GEORGE HOWLAND, JR.

(First Assistant Engineer, 1844–45.)

1844–1845.

Chief Engineer, William H. Taylor.
Assistant Engineers, George Howland, Jr., Zachariah Hillman.

FIREWARDS.

James Durfee,
Jonathan Smith,
George G. Gifford,
Abraham H. Howland,
Seth Russell,
Ezra K. Delano,
Slocum Allen,
Philip Groves,
George Perry,
E. W. Kempton,
Gamaliel Taber,
Tilson Wood,
Dudley Davenport,
W. H. Jenney,
Jireh Swift, Jr.,
Edward Merrill,
Edward Cannon.

A red staff was the distinguishing badge of the engineers. The other firewards carried trumpets painted red, with the word "Fireward" in gilt letters upon a black ground, placed on the bowls.

INDEPENDENCE, No. 1. (100 North Second street.)

Foreman, Joseph H. Fuller.
Pipeman, Charles M. Spooner.
Assistant Pipeman, George D. Davis.
Clerk, Edward D. Reed.

Alban Crowell.
Horatio A. Braley.
Rufus Randall.
John E. Brown.
Charles F. Paine.
John Burke,
William Bosworth.
George Taylor.
Edward Blandell.
Daniel Chappell.
W. H. Pullen.
Charles Davis.
William Champlin.
Charles B. Russell.
George Underwood.
Moses G. Davis.

CITIZEN, No. 2. (65 Purchase street.)

Foreman, Philip Groves.
Assistant Foremen, Edward S. Wilcox, George Hinckley.
Clerk, George C. Gibbs.

Charles C. Moore.
Albert R. Paulding.
John N. Barrows.
Peleg Allen.
Lewis G. Carpenter.
John Matthews.
Perez Jenkins.
Frederick Underwood.
Benjamin Gage.
Chas. H. Underwood.
George W. Brockman.
John Waldron,
James D. Driggs.
Samuel P. Raymond.
John P. Nash.
Peter M. Vaughn.
Charles Wilcox.
Richard Curtis.
Benjamin F. Spooner.
Charles R. Tobey.
William H. Cook.
B. Penniman, Jr.,
Nathaniel Milliken.
Henry Bates.
Joseph M. Shiverick.
John A. Ruggles.
Henry R. Stewart.
Alfred Briggs.
Stephen Wing.
James S. Browning.
George Young.
C. O. Churchill.
C. M. Vaughn.
Zenas Knapp.
Gamaliel Wardworth.
S. W. Reed.
Oliver N. Wing.
Charles H. Walker.
William Nutter.
William H. Sherman.
Israel B. Bolles.
Alden Pope.
Isaac Sherman.
Elihu Allen.
Isaac N. Vaughn.

ENGINE NO. 3. (Head of Acushnet.)

Foreman, Thomas P. Potter.
Clerk, Silas Stetson.

Mark Snow,
Amos Braley,
Philip T. Davis,
Silas Braley,
Augustus Harrington,
A. B. Grinnell,
Peter Taber,
Simeon Hawes,
Lemuel Terry,
Nathaniel Spooner,
George T. Russell,
A. B. Richardson,
Charles McArthur,
Edwin Payson,
Levi Shorey,
Borden Spencer,
Bartholomew Lund,
Warren Parker,
Rufus Williams,
John Mansfield,
Joseph Spooner,
W. R. Caswell,
James Wilbor.

PHENIX, NO. 4. (42 Fourth street.)

Foreman, Robert C. Topham.
Assistant Foreman, Benjamin Durfee.
Clerk, Edwin R. Russell.

Franklin Tobey,
Francis Vinal,
C. P. Maxfield,
Ebenezer Parlow, Jr.,
S. A. Eupolen,
C. D. Macomber,
Benjamin C. Munroe,
Isaac Brownell,
Isaac Sherman,
John G. Gorham,
Fred. H. Vinal,
George Young,
George Tynan,
William Holmes,
Doane Damon,
Samuel Gabriel,
Solomon L. Damon,
Joseph Taber,
Gideon Vinal,
William White,
Ezra Bisbee,
Abraham Taber.

COLUMBIAN, NO. 5. (102 North Second street.)

Foreman, Henry R. Wilcox.
Assistant Foremen, Ebenezer Tirrell, Samuel Damon, Israel T. Bryant.
Clerk, Rodolphus Beetle.

Peleg Potter,
Ezra Dyer,
Benjamin Hayes,
Joseph W. Cornell,
W. J. Spooner,
Andrew G. Hayes,
John W. Spooner,
Richmond B. Wood,
Henry Walker,
John W. Nickerson,
Samuel S. Paine,
James Foster,
Loring G. Hayes,
Harry J. Leach,
T. R. Bryant,
Joseph Bowman,
Joseph D. Hall,
Jabez Gibbs,
Isaiah D. Foster,
William Walker,
John D. Hillman,
Nathaniel Jenney,

John Warren,
John A. Sawyer,
Henry N. Dean,
Ebenezer Keen,
H. S. Tower,
Philip Simmons,
William Whitcomb,
Allen Stoddard,
Nathan Adams,
Henry Peirce,
John D. Childs,
Elihu H. Gifford,
Artemas Redland,
Thomas W. Sowle,
John Hoxie,
H. F. Ripley,
David C. Hathaway,
Thaddeus Burgess,
James Drew,
William B. Pierce,
Giles S. Fales,
Charles D. Hathaway,
William Gates,
Daniel T. Daggett,
Josiah C. Burbank,
Michael Hathaway,
Consider Smith,
James M. Cranston,
William Bly,
William Hersey,
William Bisbee,
Edward Spooner,
Hattil Kelley.

MECHANIC, No. 6. (61 Purchase street.)

Foreman, Ezra R. Delano.
Assistant Foremen, Joseph Hammond, John P. Crosby.
Clerk, Henry F. Thomas.

Levi Nye,
Thomas C. Allen,
Nathan Barker,
John Wooden,
Jeremiah M. Morris,
William F. Nye,
George Y. Nickerson,
George Howland, 3d,
Hiram Shearman,
Stephen Parker,
Alex. P. Dyer,
Caleb L. Ellis,
William Wilbour,
J. R. Rogers,
George Warren,
Walter H. Thomas,
Wellington Bucklin,
Obediah Keene,
Peleg B. Clark,
Stephen Waite,
William Hammond,
Isaac Sanford, Jr.,
R. W. Raymond,
Isaac McFarlin,
William M. Cowen,
David C. Gifford,
Oliver Peckham,
Uriah Mayo,
Benjamin Besse,
John H. Davis,
A. J. Vaughn,
John Wright,
William Sowle,
Jona. W. Whitney,
Edwin Luce,
Chas. H. Taber,
Shipley W. Bumpus,
John Lowe,
William James,
Charles E. Brownell,
Whitman Vinal,
John H. Young,
Ebenezer Kempton,
Charles Kempton,
Bowers Hathaway,
W. H. Farrington,
John A. Smith,
Ezra Pope,
Henry Palmer,
James Haffords,
Job Almy,
John Burrill,
B. C. Wardsworth,
Freeman C. Luce,
Hervey Hammond,
George James.

PHILADELPHIA, No. 7. (40 Fourth street.)

Foreman, Seth Russell.
Assistant Foremen, George Wilson, Edward S. Taber.
Clerk, Freeman P. Bartlett.

James T. Paul,
Charles H. Leach,
Marshall B. Bird,
John S. Davis,
Chauncey Russell,
T. B. Denham,
John F. Vinal,
O. T. Sherman,
H. M. C. Denham,
Rodney Howland,
John O. Wilmarth,
E. S. Corson,
Wing Russell,
S. G. Ricketson,
H. K. Oliver,
Stephen A. Tripp,
N. T. Brownell,
George Barney,
William F. Brown,
H. M. Jackson,
Silas T. Sears,
W. H. F. Clapp,
Seth Hathaway,
Josiah Coggeshall,
Cyrus W. Chapman,
Wm. H. Willis,
Nath'l Shepherd,
Charles Parker,
Gideon Cornell,
John H. Thompson,
Albert Brightman,
S. P. Chamberlain,
Joseph Swift,
David S. Robinson,
William M. Howard,
John Britnell,
Asa L. Smith,
Peter Y. Flynn,
Martin Haskins,
Abm. S. Taber,
John H. Webster,
N. C. Lewis,
Darius Bosworth,
Edw. Slocum,
R. H. McLaughlin,
Benj. R. Watson.

NOVELTY, NO. 8.

NOVELTY, No. 8. (Mechanics Lane.)

Foreman, George G. Gifford.
Assistant Foreman, Joseph Allen, Jr.
Clerk, James Bates.

C. C. P. Tobey,
Joseph G. Dean,
Silas N. Richards,
William Durfee,
John Russell,
W. P. Newell,
Charles M. Pierce,
George Gooding,
Phineas T. Drew,
Otis Manchester,

Leonard Dorr,
Thomas P. Swift,
Andrew Wilbour,
Isaiah C. Gage,
Joel L. Burrell,
Fred. Brownell,
Lot Tripp, Jr.,
Seth Bryant,
Benj. Manchester,
James S. Chase,
Samuel Amsden,
Ephraim H. Wade,
G. N. Carpenter,
Enoch Bearse,
Josiah Johnson,
Samuel Small,
Robert Luscomb,
Rufus Russell,
Ira C. Pierce,
Willard Tripp,
M. C. Swift,
Richard Luscomb, Jr.,
Abram M. Gifford,
Job Wilcox, Jr.,
Pembroke Rich,
James Porter,
Joseph S. Taber.

HANCOCK, NO. 9. (Foster street, near North.)

Foreman, George Perry.
Assistant Foremen, D. B. Croacher, L. Hathaway, S. G. Edwards.
Clerk, Arphaxed Simmons.

Arvin Smith,
Ansel Landers,
Caleb T. Jenney,
Horatio Bly,
John Wrightington,
Stephen Haskins,
Willard Shaw,
Allen Case,
James C. Tripp,
John C. Taber,
Peter Peters,
Lazarus Moulton,
Tillinghast Tompkins,
H. A. Purrington,
N. S. Purrington,
S. McKenzie,
H. W. Smith,
Fred. P. Howland,
Levi Salisbury,
William Gifford,
James Marble,
W. R. Barker,
Charles Simmons,
Joseph Wheaton,
Corban B. Lucas,
John C. Hervey,
Nathan Phinney,
E. L. Foster,
Henry C. Hathaway,
Nathaniel Moulton,
Horace French,
I. H. Mandell,
Isaiah Potter,
Thomas Croacher,
George A. Cornell,
Francis W. Heath,
Joseph M. Hatch,
Aaron Davis,
Newell Raymond,
Otis Leach,
Robt. Croacher,
John Gifford,
John K. Potter,
Benjamin Covell,
Joshua Shearman.

FRANKLIN, NO. 10. (Third street, head of Griffin.)

Foreman, William M. Allen.
Assistant Foremen, O. M. Brownell, Isaiah W. Churchill.
Clerk, James Taylor.

George W. Jennings,
Thomas Albert,
L. S. Jennings,
Thomas Lowe,

Charles Briggs,
Moses H. Bliss,
Isaac Bliss,
Sylvanus Churchill,
Solomon Chadwick,
Zenas F. Chadwick,
Ezra B. Chase,
Nathan Chapman,
Alonzo L. Cory,
Fred. A. Chace,
Edw. Cavenaugh,
Henry T. Davis,
Benjamin Davis,
Nathan S. Davis,
L. R. Eldridge,
C. D. Foster,
William Gibbs,
C. L. Watkins,
T. F. Haffords,
C. F. Gifford,
B. G. Hathaway,
Caleb Miller,
Thomas S. Nye,
David P. Pierce,
Benjamin F. Popple,
Henry Parker,
Daniel Pollock,
Jos. M. Robinson,
R. A. Sherman,
M. G. Sears,
H. R. Tripp,
Barton Wilbour,
Hiram L. Wheeler,
Alex. C. Wilbour,
Elbridge G. Wood,
Holmes Winslow,
Watson Thomas,
Elihu Briggs,
Gilbert Wordell,
Abiel Westgate,
Martin L. Wheeler,
James McKenny.

HOOK AND LADDER CO. (63 Purchase street.)

Foreman, Benjamin Tripp.
Clerk, William Davenport.

Ambrose Vincent,
P. B. Brownell,
Thomas R. Pierce,
William Chambers,
Edmund Doty,
William Earl,
David Thomas,
Jethro Daggett,
Watson Thomas,
William H. Pitman,
Alex. O. Nelson,
Rodolphus Mosher,
J. H. Leonard,
James K. Robertson,
Wm. F. Hayes,
Hadley Brownell,
Nathan Stetson,
Ephraim Landers,
Alfred Weaver,
George Morse,
G. E. S. Bly,
George W. Howland,
Henry Peets,
Edw. Williams,
Stephen Skiff,
William G. Allen,
Joshua Ashley.

PROTECTING SOCIETY.

Place of meeting, Town Hall.
Annual meeting, Third Monday in October.
President, William Hathaway.
Vice-President, Joshua Richmond.
Secretary and Treasurer, Reuben Nye.

Directors,

George O. Crocker,
John A. Standish,
Dennis Wood,
Asa R. Nye,

W. P. S. Cadwell,
George A. Bourne,
James H. Howland,
Henry P. Willis,
William T. Cook,
William A. Wall,
Pardon Tillinghast,
William P. Field,
Ferdinand Vassault,
John Kehew,
Edward D. Mandell,
Francis L. Parker,
William C. Pierce,
Francis Taber, Jr.,
Horace Gushee,
Charles Taber,
George H. Dunbar,
Joseph T. Hunter,
Josias H. Coggeshall,
Andreas T. Thorup,
Joseph F. Dearborn,
Loum Snow,
Charles D. Swift,
Samuel G. Hudson,
Jonathan Bourne, Jr.,
Samuel Southgate,
Sylvanus G. Nye,
J. B. King,
H. G. O. Gwyneth,
Charles S. Randall,
Edward S. Taber,
Augustus J. Eaton,
Edmund Rodman,
Henry C. Kelley,
Edward Russell,
Revilo A. Swain,
George F. Barker,
Charles D. Cushman,
Isaac C. Woods,
Charles Chandler,
John Hopkins,
William L. Gerrish,
Charles O. Wilson.

Engine company No. 1, twenty men; No. 2, fifty; No. 3, twenty-five; No. 4, twenty-five; No. 6, sixty; No. 7, fifty; No. 8, forty; No. 9, fifty; No. 10, fifty; Hook and Ladder Company, thirty; Protecting Society, fifty.

The following citizens served as firewards from 1845 to 1848:

William H. Taylor,
Z. Hillman,
James Durfee,
George Perry,
Jonathan Swift,
E. W. Kempton,
George G. Gifford,
Gamaliel Taber,
Ezra K. Delano,
W. H. Jenney,
Slocum Allen,
Jireh Swift, Jr.,
Edward Cannon,
Philip Groves,
Edward D. Mandell,
Geo. Howland, Jr.,
A. H. Howland.

1846.

Joseph Allen, Jr.,
O. M. Brownell,
Robert C. Topham,
Nathaniel Kelley,
J. H. Mendall.

1847.

Shubael H. Gifford,
Dudley Davenport,
Edward J. Wilcox,
Samuel Watson,
Ambrose Vincent.

1848.—Sampson Perkins.

AMBROSE VINCENT.

(Member of the Board of Firewards, 1847.)

In 1846, Oregon, No. 11, was ordered of Merrick & Agnew. This was a fine engine, and was of about the same capacity and power as No. 7. This engine was located on the south side of Middle, just above County street, and was entered in the fire department for 1847, with the following company, organized under the direction of Fireward Ambrose Vincent:

Gibbs Taber,	Gideon Sherman,
Isaac Brownell,	P. B. Brownell,
Ambrose E. Luce,	W. D. James,
Otis Manchester,	A. Merrick,

Lewis G. Carpenter,
Israel Bolles,
William Gifford,
William Davenport,
Nathan Gifford,
George A. Wilson, Jr.,
Simeon Webb,
Tillinghast Kirby,
Benj. Maxfield,
Jesse W. Dyer,
W. C. Howland,
David E. Chase,
Edward Manchester,
Jonathan Devoll,
Thomas P. Swift,
W. B. Cole,
A. A. Thomas,
James Taber,
Stephen McFarlin,
Gifford Taber,
Silas C. Sherman,
Charles Searell,
John H. Chapman,
Chas. Simmons,
George Allen,
Job Wilcox,
Ezra Dyer,
Seth Bryant,
Francis H. Vinal,
R. W. Raymond,
Samuel Johnson,
Charles B. Gifford,
George Gooding,
N. W. P. Cobb,
Calvin A. Paine,
Henry S. Little,
Isaac S. Thomas,
George Lee,
William Cox,
C. P. Russell,
Daniel P. Devoll,
Lewis Manchester.

Sept. 12, 1846, the Independence Co., No. 1, on invitation of Capt. Philip Davis and other citizens of Acushnet village, visited that place and had a jolly time. They were accompanied by the Citizens' Band. They were served with a fine collation and, as their record says, were received with great kindness. After passing the afternoon in an agreeable manner, they marched through the village during the evening in torchlight procession, returning home at 9 o'clock, well paid for their visit. For these acts of kindness the inhabitants of Acushnet village will never be forgotten by Independence Co., No. 1.

Records of Independence, No. 1, Sept. 26, 1846:

> The Independence, No. 1, with the Fairhaven Engine Co., No. 1, accompanied by the New Bedford Brass Band, went to Holmes' Hole on an excursion, where they received many courtesies. The people of Edgartown extended an invitation to visit their town, but they were obliged to decline.

The records of this company as kept by the clerks, Messrs. Edward D. Reed, George P. Underwood, Southward Potter, 2d, Gideon B. Spooner and E. J. Richmond, are models of neatness and are interesting for the information they give of all matters connected with the company.

The town became a city April 29, 1847, amid great rejoicings on inauguration evening. The event of the birth of the new city was signalized with the usual demonstrations of public joy, such as national music by the Citizens' Band, ringing of bells and firing salutes.

Dissatisfaction with the amount of annual payment of the firemen became manifest, and soon developed into a fierce discussion in the City Government. It resulted in the voluntary disbandment of the companies, August 7th, attached to Nos. 4, 5, 6, 7, 8, 10, 11, and the Hook and Ladder Co. The practical result of this action was that the fire department became thoroughly paralyzed, and the city was left unprotected for a time. Soon, however, new companies were obtained for Nos. 7, 10 and 11, and finally the whole department was reorganized, the dissatisfied members withdrawing from membership. During the interim occurred a fire at the Prussian-blue works, on Court street, August 16th. The condition of affairs in the city may be seen from the account published in the *Mercury* at the time:

> "The fire department was on hand, all but No. 6. Many of our venerable citizens were seen 'swinging at the brakes' like veterans. Among them we noticed our deservedly esteemed member of Congress, Mr. Joseph Grinnell, who proved himself, as he has often done in the House of Representatives, 'a good spouter.'"

May 18, 1848, occurred the Dudley Davenport fire, which destroyed about $30,000 worth of property. The fire commenced about 10 o'clock in the evening and was one of the fiercest ever experienced in our history. Mr. Davenport's steam planing mill, lumber yard, grocery store, dwelling house belonging to William Rotch, and other buildings were burned. A vast amount of property in the vicinity, including the candle works, oil, etc., was rescued from destruction only by the spirited and hearty exertions of the firemen and citizens. Several of the engines were worked for five hours without intermission. A more severe or more satisfactory test of the capabilities and efficiency of the fire department as then constituted can hardly be imagined. The firewards furnished a fine breakfast for the department when the flames were finally subdued.

Among the buildings saved from destruction was one owned by Matthew Luce. Mr. George M. Eddy found in the upper story a barrel of lime, and, using his broadbrimmed hat for want of a shovel, he spread it freely upon the roof, and by this novel means was successful in keeping the fire fiend at bay. His services were gratefully recognized the next day by Capt. Luce by the presentation of a new hat.

At this time a fire occured in Oxford Village that furnished an opportunity for sweet revenge. The Mechanic, No. 6, went over and played first water. William H. Sherman held the pipe and proud he was, and is to-day, of the event. This balanced the first water of the Oxford engine at the Centre street fire in 1820.

June 9, 1847, occurred a large fire at the Head-of-the-River, destroying hotel, bowling alley, stable and several dwelling houses. The bowling alley and appendages were regarded in the community as a nuisance. The origin of the fire was considered not wholly accidental, as the *Mercury* intimated in its notice of the event. The firemen of our city repaired to the scene, and their exertions were highly commended. There was a great scarcity of food the next day, for the hungry firemen were liberally fed by the grateful citizens.

The next day at 3 P. M. a dwelling house on the farm of Mr. Gideon Nye, Jr., was burned. One of the victims of the fire on the day before, Mrs. Margaret Hathaway, had moved into it with what household goods she had been able to save, only to have them all destroyed in the second fire.

ZACHARIAH HILLMAN.

(Chief Engineer, 1848-1850.)

CHAPTER VI.

THE following citizens composed the Board of Engineers for the year 1848:

Zachariah Hillman, Ambrose Vincent,
William H. Taylor, Samuel Watson,
Edmund Gardner, Oliver M. Brownell,
Sampson Perkins.

1849.

Zachariah Hillman,
Wm. H. Jenney,
O. M. Brownell,
Philip S. Davis,
Robert C. Topham,
Caleb L. Ellis,
Benj. B. Covell,
Samuel Watson,
George Perry,
Alanson Williston,
Ezra K. Delano,
Philip Groves.

1850.

Z. Hillman,
E. K. Delano,
W. H. Jenney,
George Wilson,
George Perry,
B. B. Covell,
C. L. Ellis,
T. B. Denham,
Joshua B. Ashley,
Thomas P. Potter,
Tilson Wood,
Asa R. Nye.

1851–2.

Ezra K. Delano,
Z. Hillman,
Robert C. Topham,
George Perry,
Elisha W. Kempton,
Tilson Wood.

July 4, 1847, the Philadelphias made an excursion to Nantucket and had a grand reception on their return. If I glean more frequently from the records of Nos. 7 and 10 than from those of other companies, it is for the reason that they were kept with great care, and everything of interest found mention in their pages at this time.

The Relief engine, No. 5, built by John Agnew, of Philadelphia, was received in Oxford Village, Fairhaven, in September, 1849, and the following company was organized that year:

Captain, Benjamin D. Coombs.
First Assistant, Paschal Allen.
Second Assistant, William H. Davis.
Clerk and Treasurer, William H. Hoeg.
Hosemen, Elisha B. Stevens, A. K. Bowen.

John P. Winslow,
James M. Allen,
Squire S. Stevens,
Oliver Wilcox,
James A. Cannon,
Andrew Wilcox,
Charles Savery,
William H. Hoeg, Jr.,
Thomas W. Nye,
Frank Bates, Jr.,
John W. Smith,
E. K. Jenney,
John Lawton,
Ebenezer Aiken, Jr.,
Timothy Sanford,
Davis Landers,
Charles Coombs,
Ebenezer G. Grinnell,

Dexter Jenney,
William Burgess,
George F. Neil,
D. K. Hathaway,
E. S. Jenney, Jr.,
James Braley,
Isaiah West,
Joseph N. Peck,
Edward Winslow,
Ezra B. Briggs,
Watson Nickerson,
Edward West,
Robert Bennett,
John Kendrick,
Alden Davis,
Jeremiah West,
George Davis,
Benj. Drew,
Amos Rogers,
Ansel D. Bourne,
John A. Peck,
Eli Sherman,
John West,
Loring Boomer,
Elihu Wood, Jr.,
Joseph H. Burgess,
James H. Taber,
William H. Davis,
Jason Spooner,
Asa West,
Andrew W. Hart,
Philip Wilcox.

The company, arrayed in uniform caps and mourning badges, joined the procession in New Bedford on the occasion of the obsequies of President Taylor, in August, 1850.

The Relief, No. 5, continued in effective service until 1879, when it was condemned and retired. It was succeeded by the Alert, No. 4, of Taunton, built by Button, of Waterford, N. Y. The old name and number, Relief, No. 5, was retained, and this engine continued in service until 1886, when it was taken out of commission. The following company was attached to it at this time:

Foreman, Marcellus P. Whitfield.
First Assistant, Joseph C. Jenney.
Second Assistant, James K. Paull.
Clerk, Charles P. Maxfield.

Amos Rogers,
Wm. H. Bates,
Wm. H. Norris,
Charles Coombs,
Wm. H. Eldred,
Thomas Wrightington,
James M. Allen, Jr.,
Charles H. Coombs, Jr.,
Henry Wilson,
Robert Campbell,
Edw. L. Besse,
Geo. Carpenter,
Oliver H. Wilcox,
Edgar C. Taber,
Lorenzo F. Wilde,
Wm. K. Rogers,
Oliver S. Gurney,
Seth Shaw,
Albert Charey,
Thomas W. Nye,
Albert Eldred,
Henry B. Gifford,

James Cannon,	H. T. Wilde,
Wm. H. Dunham,	Edward C. Earley,
James A. Gammons,	Fred. J. Vaughn,
James C. Chapman,	Arthur Harrington,
Benj. W. Kempton,	Stilman Ryder,
Herman H. Hathaway,	Courtland Shaw,
John J. Hammond,	Nathaniel Dunn,

William Aston.

For a "used-up engine," the Relief made a surprising exhibition in the hand-engine trial, July 4, 1890. Of this performance I shall speak again.

On Jan. 28, 1850, a disastrous fire occurred in Tallman's block, on Union street, Messrs. George M. Eddy & Co. being burned out. A sad event at this conflagration was the death of Mr. Timothy Tallman, an aged and well known citizen. He occupied a room in the upper story, and was smothered by the dense smoke. Messrs. William Neal and William H. Sherman were the first to enter the room and rescue the body; but life was extinct. A favorite dog, "Wallace," belonging to Mr. Eddy, met the same fate. He was a powerful mastiff and a valuable watch dog.

Wallace had a fine reputation, gained principally through an incident which I will relate. In the yard of the house was kept a swill barrel, which was regularly emptied by a poor neighbor, rich in pig stock. Much to his annoyance, it was frequently found empty when he made his regular calls. These occurrences came so often that a sharp lookout was kept, but without success. It was concluded finally to let Wallace take a part in the investigation, and so he was left out of doors for the night. The family retired at the usual time, but before sleep had come to the eyelids the short, sharp, significant growl of Wallace was heard on the night air. Mr. Eddy concluded not to get up; for if anybody was in the yard not intent on mischief, the dog would do him no harm. Should it happen that any person was on the premises engaged in unlawful pursuits, he was confident that Wallace would attend to the business faithfully. In the morning the barrel was found lying on the bilge, and the dog, with his head close to the open end, was comfortably taking his ease. On close investigation a a plump, good-sized colored boy was found in the barrel with his head toward the lower end. Wallace was sent into the house to partake of his morning meal, and the lad crawled out. He acknowledged that he was the thief. On being asked to explain matters, he said that he had turned down the barrel to scoop out the contents when he heard the dog coming. Becoming suddenly frightened at the situation, he crawled in for safety's sake, and the dog coolly lay down and looked at him in calm contemplation. Any movement looking like a desire to depart was greeted with a suggestive growl. No doubt it was an edifying spectacle for the dog. As to the boy, he concluded to stay all night, as his parents wouldn't be very anxious about him. Suffice it to say that the regular scavenger had no further trouble in getting the weekly supply for his pigs.

The Philadelphia records give this item for July 4, 1850:

"The engine was taken to Market square, drawn by a pair of beautiful black horses, provided by Mr. N. O. Tripp, a member of the company. We then had a trial with Nos. 5, 6, 9, 10, 11, and the No. 5, of Fairhaven. It was admitted by everybody that No. 7 'beat the crowd.'"

I find the following "Song to the Firemen" among the records of the Philadelphia, No. 7, and I presume the poet was inspired to write it in praise of this engine. It is written to the tune of "Lucy Long:"

Now comrades pay attention
While I rehearse the fame
Of a pretty little engine
We always love to name.

Chorus.

O, break her down, my hearties,
My hearties, stout and strong,
O, crack her down, my hearties,
To the tune of "Lucy Long."

This little one's a snorter,
A hardened case indeed,
And the way she throws the water
Is a caution to the breed.
Chorus.

Her lungs are made of copper
And her limbs are clothed in brass,
And she runs, the young jade hopper,
Like a snake among the grass.
Chorus.

She's no rum soaking sinner,
Her drink is from the wells,
And you'd think the deuce was in her
When she hears the ringing bells.
Chorus.

The saucy little vixen
Is fire's deadliest foe,
And the way she puts the licks in
When she comes to the scratch ain't slow.
Chorus.

The strife she's ever after,
She always holds out game,
So long as smokes a rafter,
So long as flares a flame.
Chorus.

Where'er the fire is hottest
You'll find her on the spot,
Then toast the saucy varmint
In cups of ":" coffee hot."
Chorus.

On July 4th, 1851, engine companies Nos. 5, 7, 9 and 10 spent the day in Providence, participating in the grand parade in that city.

The rivalry between the fire companies at this period took a most singular turn. Among the performers belonging to the Forbes Dramatic Co., of Providence, then playing in Liberty Hall (the old wooden structure, burned Nov. 10th, 1854), were two talented actresses, Miss Evangeline Hathaway and Miss Kate Newton. These ladies were very popular with the firemen, Miss Hathaway being the favorite of Nos. 5 and 7, and

Miss Newton of Nos. 6 and 11. How this sort of thing came about nobody knows, but all the enthusiasm of the rivalry was fully developed in this mad craze. Every benefit night, (and they occurred almost weekly in the season) the companies would parade in uniform, accompanied by music, and attend the performances of these actresses, showering upon them

EZRA K. DELANO.

(Chief Engineer, 1851–1852.)

wreaths, bouquets of flowers, and purses liberally filled with money. "Anything to beat Grant," seemed to be the spirit underlying this whole transaction, and the greatest wonder is that this foolishness continued as long as it did.

The year 1851 developed a strange and alarming condition

of things, that spread alarm among our citizens. The frequency of incendiary fires was disturbing enough, but the fire apparatus was tampered with, the hose was cut, and other malicious acts were committed. The No. 6 was mutilated, and also No. 3. Several large rewards for conviction were offered by the Board of Firewards.

The interest in the Fire Department at this time was simply wonderful. Every one had his favorite company. He was a weak-minded youth or a comparatively new resident in the town who had attained the age of eight or ten years, and didn't "blow" for Nos. 5 or 7, or Nos. 6 or 11. So contagious became the racing spirit that it was a common sight during the summer evenings to see boy companies with miniature engines, built from large shoe boxes, mounted on a set of condemned wheels, bought at a close bargain from some block-maker. The sides of these elegant creations would be covered with hieroglyphics containing the information that it was No. 5 or 6 or 7: that it was "Always ready," that it "Strives to conquer," or "Our duty done our aim accomplished."

With these instruments of fun the boys would have race after race, night after night, unless good fortune broke the spell with the frequent false alarms calling out the bigger boys with their apparatus. What days they were! Let the reader be gentle in his criticism of this sport, and remember that we were boys then, with boyish fancies, boyish aspirations, and brimful of enthusiasm for that which our fathers were identified with and preferred; and so we lifted our voices and shouts in praise of our favorite.

I wonder if any of my readers remember the Juvenile Engine Co., No. 12, of which Charlie Collins and Henry Howe were captains. Among the members were Zach. Cushman, Nathan D. Maxfield, Gen. George Worth, Fred. Wood, William Howland, John D. Howland and others, making about twenty-five in number—all scholars at Bush street school. We had for an engine a tiny garden machine, with end brakes. It belonged to Edward S. Taber, Esq., who kindly loaned it to the boys, and it is still in Mr. Taber's possession. He was for five years a member of Oregon, No. 11, and was captain of the company when he withdrew from membership. in 1854. He was presented with a silver trumpet during his term of service, the presentation being made by Mr. William G. Taber, in behalf of the Oregons.

Our uniform consisted of white shirts, red stripes on our trousers and bright bands on our caps. What grand parades we used to have on Saturdays! Bright, happy days they were; that is, most of them. One lovely summer day our company started out with drums beating and banners flying for an excursion to Fort Phœnix. We paraded through our own streets first, dragging our little engine, beau-

JUVENILE ENGINE, NO. 12.

tifully decorated with flowers, wreaths, and gaily colored ribbons. After permitting ourselves to be admired by our own citizens first, we took passage in the staunch ferryboat Union, bound for Fairhaven. We had a delightful passage, and landed in safety and in good health. None were seasick, but all were homesick before the day was over. We marched into the town with great pomp, and we received a warm reception from the youth of the village; very warm indeed. Before we had reached the centre of the town every native-born had "scented the battle from afar." And we were soon surrounded with a large and enthusiastic following. They became very demonstrative, they became close friends, too close for comfort, they did their best to amuse us by tossing pebbles at us. They hustled us about good and ill naturedly. They wanted very much to see how our engine looked bottom side up. Now all this didn't furnish any real fun for us, and so boy-like we got mad and, singular as it may seem, that made fun for them.

This sort of entertainment continued until we got tired. The fact was there was too much of it and too long continued to be thoroughly enjoyed. Fort Phœnix seemed to be far, far away, and the day was passing so rapidly that we finally concluded to go home. They generously furnished us escort. When we turned down the street and had a straight course, we took a double quick and went on board the ferryboat as if we had been shot from a mortar. Pleasant social remarks passed between us as we sailed out upon the river.

There used to be a little ditty, familiar to all in those days, which we might have sung on this occasion:

Corsica jigs put on your wigs,
And over to Bedford come:
New Bedford boys put on your hats,
And make the Corsicans run.

If I remember correctly, our future excursions were confined to Howland's Grove and Clark's Point, which were much preferred to Fort Phœnix because of better protection from violent winds and sudden storms.

At this time there was a juvenile company, No. 13, Captain Records, at the north part of the city. The company had uniforms and appeared frequently on the streets in parade. They made almost as fine an appearance as the No. 12s, but they couldn't put on such airs as we did, for they hadn't been to Fairhaven. Besides, the No. 12s had the distinguished honor of actually joining in the torchlight procession with Franklin, No. 10, on the evening of Oct. 4, 1851. The occasion was the escorting of Columbian, No. 5, and Philadelphia, No. 7, from the station on their return from a visit to the Protectors, of North Bridgewater.

The Active, No. 2. was a little bucket machine belonging to Mr. George M. Eddy, on Third street It had an organized company, and among the boys were Abram T. Eddy, George M. Eddy, Jr., Fred. Smith. Rodman Tripp, William Cobb, Frank Taber, William Bryant, Charley Knights, "General" George Worth (he must have been an enthusiast, for he also belonged to No. 12), Fred. Barker, Jake Johnson and others. In their parades the dog Wallace appeared with a blanket suitably adorned.

The Board of Engineers from 1853 till Aug. 21, 1854:

George Wilson, Chief.

George G. Gifford,	Caleb L. Ellis,
Benjamin B. Covell.	Tilson B. Denham.

1854.

Joshua B. Ashley, Chief.

Oliver M. Brownell.	Tillinghast P. Tompkins,
Israel T. Bryant,	George Hinckley.

1855.

Zachariah Hillman. Chief.

James Durfee.	George Perry,
George G. Gifford,	Robert C. Topham.

The Ohio, No. 3, was received from its builders. the Agnews, of Philadelphia, early in 1850, and placed in the North Second street engine-house. It was esteemed a valuable and powerful addition to our fire apparatus and gave satisfaction to the authorities. Their pleasure took the form of complimentary resolutions. passed by the Board of Firewards, speaking in flattering terms of all engines built by the Agnews for our city. The resolutions were spread upon the records and published in the newspapers.

Singular as it may seem. more than six months passed before any attempt was made to provide a company for the new engine. Then Mr. Henry R. Wilcox took the matter in hand and completed the organization with the following officers:

Foreman, Henry R. Wilcox.
First Assistant. Nathan Johnson.

Second Assistant, Frederick P. Chase.
Clerk, George W. Paine.

A substantial brick house was built on Purchase street, just north of Maxfield, and the engine was moved to the new

JOSHUA B. ASHLEY.

(Chief Engineer, 1854.)

quarters Jan. 2, 1855. The company made a parade through North Second, Union and Purchase streets to the house, where the engine was worked, taking water from the cistern under the new building.

I give my readers the full roll for 1852, which we are assured by Capt. Wilcox is substantially the same as when organized in 1850:

OHIO ENGINE CO., NO. 3. (North Second street.)

Foreman, Henry R. Wilcox.
First Assistant, Nathan Johnson.
Second Assistant, Frederick P. Chase.
Clerk, George W. Paine.

Josiah Coggeshall,
W. F. H. Clapp,
James C. Devine,
James McKenney,
Samuel Johnson,
Edward Hicks,
James Durfee, Jr.,
William Lavers,
Joseph M. Shiverick,
Patrick Mead,
W. H. Damon,
Michael Ryan,
Thomas Cross,
Michael Devine,
Patrick Devine,
Charles J. Place,
W. B. Hathaway,
Samuel Haven,
Lemuel R. James,
Thomas Cranston,
James Warren,
Maltiah J. Bourne,
Richard T. Durfey,
Enoch Crocker,
James Conway,
Gorton Aessey,
Cornelius Smith,
Joseph Hoyle,
James H. Hood,
Valentine Francis,
Leander Manchester,
Bernard McGurk,
Michael H. Elliot,
George G. Peck,
Jacob Moores,
Benjamin Tripp,
George Young,
Charles Westgate,
Job Slocum,
Benjamin Crocker,
Ezra Tew,
David P. Devoll,
Richmond M. Taber,
Benjamin R. Brownell,
Andrew Harper,
Timothy Blanchard.

On the evening of June 30, 1851, a fierce conflagration occurred on Purchase street, in Albert Shaw's looking-glass and picture frame manufactory. The combustible nature of the materials made a fire of fearful intensity, and the entire structure, with contents, was quickly destroyed. At this fire an unpleasantness occurred between the Chief Engineer and Franklin Co., No. 10, growing out of a misunderstanding of an order. Considerable feeling was stirred up, but the matter soon subsided without any serious consequences. At this fire the Ohio, No. 3, was used for the first time. Mr. William Durfee acting as pipeman.

In November, 1852, a serious difficulty arose between Columbian Engine Co., No. 5, and the Board of Engineers, which resulted in the disbanding of the Columbians. The occurrence took place at the period when false alarms were raised, many of them no doubt to furnish an opportunity for a race. One evening Nos. 5 and 6 started north on Purchase street at a tearing pace, when the Chief appeared on the scene and ordered the No. 5 to stop. In their zeal and excitement they failed to obey his command, and seizing the headrope, he took a turn around a lantern post. This would have been successful if a ready knife hadn't left some twenty feet in the hands of the Chief, as the Columbian still pursued its course. The affair, of course, resulted in an investigation, and a demand was made by the Board of Engineers that the captain of No. 5 should furnish a list of the names of the disobedient members. This was refused and the company disbanded, only to be invited to return to the fire department the following year.

Sept 18, 1852, the Franklin Engine Co., No. 10, went on an excursion to Newport. On their arrival at Fall River they were met by Capt. Buffington and Mr. Wrightington of the Niagara, No. 4, and escorted to the Exchange Hotel, where they enjoyed a substantial breakfast, provided by the Niagaras, a handsome compliment, and one that found due appreciation from the Franklins. (I find numerous instances on record where our fire companies were the recipients of the generosity and courtesy of the Fall River firemen.) At 9 o'clock they took passage on the good steamer Canonicus, arriving in Newport at 11, where they were cordially received and generously entertained by Protection Engine Co., No. 5. After several hours of enjoyment in the town, they took a return steamer to Fall River. The company were again met by the Niagaras, and, after being escorted through the principal streets, they took the train for home. On their arrival another agreeable

able surprise was in store for them, for the Columbian, No. 5, with full ranks, awaited them with cordial greeting. After a short parade the Columbians escorted them to the Mansion House, where a sumptuous banquet was prepared and fully enjoyed. Toasts, speeches and music followed, and the festivities of the day closed with their being escorted to their house, and the fun was over. Clerk Charles D. Tuell records it as being one of the pleasantest excursions ever had in this country or "any other." A card of thanks was prepared by a committee consisting of Charles D. Tuell, Robert C. Topham, John P. Taylor, George R. Hurlburt, and George H. Jennings and published in the home newspapers and in Fall River and Newport.

At this time the rivalry between the engine companies developed many false alarms of fire—raised to give an opportunity for another race. Almost every evening found them racing through the streets as if the fate of the nation depended on the result. An unusual smoke from some chimney was sufficient cause to yell "fire" and raise the alarm. The record books of the companies show it to have been a common occurrence to have three or four alarms in a week. A genuine fire was a surprise, so frequent were these alarms.

I am tempted to give a story bearing upon the subject. A large congregation had assembled to hear a strange preacher of some note. Soon after he had introduced his subject the cry of "Fire! Fire!!" in the street, very much disturbed the congregation, and many were about to retire, when an elderly brother arose and said: "If the congregation will be composed I will step out and see if there is any fire, and report." The congregation became composed and the minister proceeded. Taking advantage of the occurrence, he called attention to a fire that would consume the world, a fire that would burn forever in the lake that is bottomless; and had just concluded a sentence of terrible import, and not without manifest impression on his audience, when a voice from the other end of the church, as if in flat denial of all he had said, bawled "It's a false alarm." The effect was ludicrous in the extreme. The old man had returned, but his inopportune response spoiled the force of the eloquent appeal from the pulpit.

March 28, 1853, a destructive fire occurred which destroyed the oil and candle works of Sanford & Howland on Water street, just north of Middle street and in the rear of Parker's Block. Owing to the combustible nature of the material, the extensive wooden buildings were quickly enveloped in flames and speedily destroyed. The loss of property was about $50,000. The fire communicated with Wilcox's lumber yard, which, with buildings, was destroyed, entailing a loss of $20,000. Engines were present from Fairhaven and Head-of-the-River and rendered valuable service.

The cooper-shop on the east, belonging to Mr. Caleb L. Ellis, was in constant danger and would have been destroyed but for the generous aid of a host of citizens, who, with buckets of water, kept the fire from making headway, though it caught on three sides of the building. The lofts were filled with new casks, and as there was no insurance on them, the loss would have been a grievous one. "Thereby hangs a tale," which I cannot refrain from telling. Grateful to his friends for their arduous and successful labors and knowing they must feel exhausted, Mr. Ellis requested one of his men to get hot coffee for them. The messenger returned after a prolonged absence, saying he couldn't find any hot coffee, nor could he get anybody to make it. He was sent away the second time with orders to *get it*, get *something hot* anyway, and something hot he did get. "Two buckets of whiskey punch," was what the bill [from Lindgreen] said next morning. As Mr. Ellis was at the time a candidate for alderman on the temperance ticket, the transaction was embarrassing, but the bill was paid. On questioning the messenger (now one of our most successful business men) how he came to do such a thing, he replied that he obeyed orders. As he couldn't get hot coffee he got what was equally hot. The lecture he received on this ocasion was of about the same temperature.

August 11, 1853, a company was organized in anticipation of the new engine, Young Mechanic No. 6, which had been ordered of John Agnew, of Philadelphia. The old engine was put in commission until the new one arrived.

CALEB L. ELLIS.

(Assistant Engineer, 1853-54.)

Sept. 9, 1853, the great fire on Pearl street, corner of Purchase, occurred. It commenced in the stable of Eleazar Phillips, spreading quickly to the Franklin House, Farmers' and Mechanics' Hotel, a dwelling house, Exchange Hotel and stable. Seven buildings were destroyed with $10,000 loss. The *Morning Mercury* says:

> "The buildings destroyed, though designated as hotels, were not strictly such, but occupied for a variety of purposes, which rendered their reputation rather doubtful. Most of the furniture was saved. One hundred barrels of liquor, belonging to Mr. Phillips, were consumed by—fire (?)."

The Mechanic, No. 6, was manned by volunteers, as the company was in Newport at the celebration of Perry's victory on Lake Erie. They had taken their departure on the 8th, and, in passing through Fall River, were entertained by Niagara Engine Co., No. 4. On their arrival at Newport they were warmly welcomed by their hosts, Protection, No. 5, "The Honey Bees," and were escorted to the Ocean House, where a sumptuous banquet was in preparation. Three hundred plates were laid and a most enjoyable time followed. Music and speeches made the occasion one long to be remembered by every participant.

In the grand parade, on the following day, the company was assigned a prominent position and under most favorable circumstances to get the full benefit of a tremendous rain storm that prevailed during the morning. They were the recipients of many attentions from the citizens, and the royal entertainment provided by "The Honey Bees" was fully appreciated. We believe it is traditional with the Mechanics that this Newport excursion was the finest of any in their history.

At about this period an incident occurred at a fire in the suburbs of the city, the truthfulness of which is vouched for by one of our veteran firemen, whose statement would not be questioned should I mention his name. To reach effectually the burning stable the firemen were obliged to enter an adjoining dwelling house and fight the fire from the attic windows. They were appalled to find in the upper story a closed coffin, a ghastly find under any circumstances, especially so in this instance, as it was carefully shoved under the bed and in a manner suggesting that it was intended to be carefully secreted. Curiosity finally overcome their fears, and throwing off the cover they found the coffin, to their agreeable surprise, filled with apples. Apples ripe, apples red, apples rosy, and like Eve of old they were tempted. So they helped themselves and treated the crowd below. It was afterward ascertained that the owner of the house had lost a member of his family, and finding that he could purchase two coffins much cheaper in proportion to the price of one, he invested, and stowed the spare one in the attic for future use, using it in the mean-time as an apple bin.

JAMES B. CONGDON.

(Member of Board of Firewards in 1835.)

CHAPTER VII.

THE "red letter" day for the Young Mechanic Engine Company, No. 6, came into existence much like any other, and to the general world it probably had no significant features, but to the enthusiastic adherents of the "Sixes" the morning of Sept. 27, 1854, did seem to be unusually bright and cheery, and the atmosphere had the exhilarating effect of a Fourth of July.

The day had come, and with it the new machine from Philadelphia. For twenty years the Agnew firm had furnished every engine for our fire department, and they had in every instance given the highest satisfaction.

The company met at the engine house at 7 o'clock, arrayed in a new uniform of red shirts, faced and trimmed with blue, belts, blue caps, and black trousers. The New Bedford Brass Band put in an early appearance and entertained the assemblage with fine music, winding up with "Auld Lang Syne," as the company, 47 strong, rolled the veteran machine from the house. After parade through our principal streets, they took the Mechanic to the house on North Second street, which had become a sort of sepulchre for the old apparatus of the fire department, giving the faithful and venerable machine three hearty cheers as a parting greeting. The line of march was then taken for the freight depot.

All expectations were fully met when the new engine was drawn from the car and brought to the gaze of an admiring crowd. It was built on the well known model of the Agnew make, 8-inch cylinder, length of stroke 8½ inches, and furnished with all the modern appliances then known. The engine was a double-decker, with extension brakes, a powerful suction, and seemed to have all the qualities of a first-class engine. It was elegantly mounted with polished brass, and painted in excellent taste. On either side of the tower appeared the name "Young Mechanic," with the motto of the company, "Always Ready," and that of the State, "Ense petit," etc., hanasomely wrought.

A new hose carriage had been built by Messrs. Gray & Barker, the iron work being done by Messrs. Joseph Brownell & Co. It was a fit companion for the new engine. The apparatus was taken to the Pope street reservoir and then to the house. The company then proceeded with the band to "the ploughing match," near Rodman's farm, where they were welcomed in a hearty speech by Hon. J. H. W. Page. When the festivities of the day were concluded the company returned to their hall and were dismissed.

The company's record of the day closed with these words, "May the course of the Young Mechanic be as glorious and her end as pleasant as those of its namesake." The price paid for the new engine was $1850.

NATHAN BARKER.

(Captain Young Mechanic Engine Co., No. 6, 1853-54.)

I now give the full organization of the Young Mechanic, No. 6, at this date and for the year 1854:

Captain, Nathan Barker.
First Assistant, Joseph Hammond.
Second Assistant, Charles W. Dyer,
Third Assistant, J. Augustus Brownell.
Fourth Assistant, Joseph W. Lavers.
Clerk and Treasurer, Sanford Almy.

William E. Watson,
James D. Jenkins,
John C. Paul,
John D. Murdock,
Warren G. Pierce,
Thomas C. Allen,
Charles G. Kempton,
Freeman C. Luce,
Joseph R. Watson,
William A. Church,
William McKimm,
Seth C. Chase,
Thomas Paul.
Moses C. Vinal,
Ira W. Hathaway,
Gus. H. Cushman,
Thomas Dowden,
Fred. A. Plummer,
William H. Sherman,
George T. Sears,
Fred. Underwood,
C. H. Underwood,
Abm. I. Davis,
Roland W. Snow,
Charles H. Bourne,
Jireh W. Clifton,
C. E. Wheaton,
Roland Crocker,
Wm. Ricketson,
Isaac Quinnell, Jr.,
Leonard Doty,
William Hackett,
Sylvanus Baker,
Calvin G. Fisher,
William C. Nichols,
Thaddeus Betz,
Michael Kennedy,
Henry Koenig,
John McCoy,
John Nutter,
Matthias C. Pease,
Jos. N. Landers,
William Kent,
George Devoll,
Andrew Lincoln,
Bradford Potter,
Charles Barnard,
L. T. Manchester,
Frank J. Bourne,
James Green,
William Crowell,
Pardon G. Thomson,
Alex. H. Sowle,
Jireh Tripp,
Thomas C. Allen, Jr.,
William H. Allen,
John Francis,
Jesse Chase,
Samuel Hinckley,
John E. Brown,
G. N. Maxfield,
John B. Gifford,
Horatio N. Durfee,
H. O. Brown,
Clarfaus Vansant,
John P. Noble,
Edwin Betz,
Christian Betz,
M. H. Elliot,
Peter Donley,
Thomas Cranston,
Nath'l R. Pierce,
James Champion,
James Hemenway,
David Chadwick,
James Dooley,
Henry Stowe,
Hiram Randall,

Henry Klads,	Jesse Allen,
John C. Jones,	J. J. P. Zettick,
Fred. Weyler,	B. F. Hinckley,
Charles A. W. Oesting,	Warren W. Parker,

Richard Luce.

Henry Hazzard, } Torch-boys.
Leonard B. Ellis, }

The supreme satisfaction at first manifested soon became modified and grew gradually into a positive dissatisfaction with the new machine. When put to the regular work it failed to accomplish what was expected and promised by the builders. Finally Mr. Agnew visited the city May 21st, 1856, and, after an examination, the company worked the engine under his instruction. His verdict was, "all right at all points," and that settled the matter so far as the builders were concerned.

Not so with the Board of Engineers, however, nor with the company. The dissatisfaction was kept at a boiling heat. The boys finally, Aug. 7, 1856, petitioned the Board to return them the old engine they had laid away with such imposing obsequies. The petition was laid on the table; but prompt action was taken by the authorities, and a contract was made with William Jeffers & Co., of Pawtucket, to put new works in the engine. The old engine had been put in thorough repair and christened with a new title, "The Veteran, No. 1," and was held as a reserve engine. It was placed in commission in the hands of its old friends, and did service till the remodelled machine was received, March 4, 1858. When this arrived it was taken to the reservoir near the Custom House and subjected to a most rigid test, under the direction of Mr. Jeffers, and in the presence ot the full Board of Engineers—Tillinghast Tompkins, Chief; John Mathews, Moses H. Bliss, George Hinckley, Thomas P. Swift, Assistant Engineers. The result of the trial, which proved satisfactory to all concerned, was as follows:

1 stream, 1 inch nozzle, 100 feet hose, 185 feet.
1 stream, 1 1-4 inch nozzle, 300 feet hose, 146 feet.
1 stream, 7-8 inch nozzle, 300 feet hose, 171 feet.
2 streams, 7-8 inch nozzle, 300 feet hose, 140 feet.

YOUNG MECHANIC, NO. 6,

(On Purchase street, returning from a fire, 1855.)

The verdict pronounced was that Jeffers & Co. had fulfilled their agreement and had made of the engine a first class machine. It was put at once in commission. At a trial, Aug. 1, 1858, it played 210 feet through one inch nozzle and 100 feet hose, and 192 feet through $1\frac{1}{3}$ nozzle.

July 10, 1855, our city was visited by the Dirigo Engine Co., No. 8, of Portland, accompanied by the magnificent Chandler's Brass Band, of the same city. The company numbered 40 men and were arrayed in undress military suit with white stripes. Their caps were very handsome. The company made a good appearance in parade and were a fine looking body of men, splendid representatives of the Pine Tree State. They were received at the station by the Young Mechanic, No. 6, Capt. Nathan Barker, and Capt. Robert C. Topham of the Board of Engineers. The "Sixes" were accompanied by the East Stoughton Band, then deemed one of the best in the state. Cordial greetings were exchanged with the visitors, then the line of march was taken up, and a parade was made through the principal streets. At an early hour in the evening a banquet was served in Sears Hall. After this was disposed of, song, speech and sentiment ruled the hour. This part of the entertainment opened with a selection by the "Harmonions," an organization of gentlemen whose reputation for fine singing was of the best. This was followed by a duet by Messrs. Thurston and Shaw, of the Casco Glee Club. The *Standard* said: "The rich, musical voices added a rare feature to the occasion. It is seldom our good fortune to hear better singing." Speeches were made by Chief Engineer Davidson, of Portland, and by others of that and of our own city. Music was rendered by the Chandler and East Stoughton bands. The next day the firemen took an excursion to Holmes Hole, in which occasion the Ohio, No. 3, participated; and the festivities concluded with a grand ball in Mechanics Hall.

During the "fifties" the Young Mechanics had a fine excursion to Nantucket, and were entertained by the Fountain Engine Co., No. 8, Capt. Mitchell. This visit was returned at a later period, and the Nantucket firemen received the cordial attention of the Young Mechanics and Oregons, on a Fourth of July celebration. The Young Mechanics also entertained the Protection, No. 5, of Newport, and Niagaras, of Fall River, during these years.

The old engine, the "Mechanic," which had done such long and faithful service, was stationed in the North Second street house, and an organization was formed, Dec. 21, 1854, called the Veteran Association of Firemen. It was composed entirely of fireman who had seen five years of service in our fire department. They were attached to this engine, the name of which had been changed to the Veteran, No. 1. I give below the complete membership, for which I am indebted to Mr. Charles S. Paisler:

Wm. H. Taylor,	Zacharaiah Hillman,
Samuel Watson,	George Wilson,
W. L. Edwards,	Edward S. Taber,
James B. Congdon,	Ezra K. Delano,
Thomas Sanford,	Nath'l Kelley,
George Howland, Jr.,	Jos. Allen, Jr.,
Ambrose Vincent,	Abraham Delano,
John Mathews,	Jos. Chase,
Peleg Potter,	Thomas N. Allen,
James Wheaton,	John N. Barrows,
Ebenezer Keen,	John H. Chapman,
Gideon T. Sawyer,	Moses H. Bliss,
Wright Brownell,	Caleb T. Jenney,
E. E. Shepardson,	Tilson B. Denham,
Arvin Smith,	Allen Case,
Wm. H. Jenney,	Ebenezer Ryder,
E. W. Kempton,	Isaiah Wood,
Oliver P. Brightman,	Squire Sanford,
Simpson Hart,	Chas. M. Pierce, Jr.,
George G. Gifford,	John Wrightington,
Wm. H. Knights,	W. H. Willis,
Benj. C. Ward,	Wm. Whitton, Jr.,
Otis N. Pierce,	David E. Chase,
Charles W. Morgan,	Andrew G. Pierce,
Pardon Potter, Jr.,	James Durfee,
Asa R. Nye,	Rodolphus Beetle,
David B. Kempton,	Caleb L. Ellis,

Nathan P. Brightman,
Peleg Butts,
A. D. Richmond,
Levi H. Sturtevant,
Bethuel Penniman, Jr.,
J. B. Hadley,
Frederick Homer,
Ellery Records,
Benj. Gage,
Martin Pierce,
Willard Shaw,
Charles Sanford,
Charles M. Pierce,
Phineas White, Jr.,
Wm. G. Taber,
Benj. B. Covell,
Charles C. Tobey,
James Drew,
Charles H. Leach,
Henry V. Davis,
Gamaliel Taber,
James H. Mendell,
Lazarus S. Moulton,
Isaiah H. Potter,
Joseph G. Dean,
Francis W. Hatch,
Nicholas Davis.

The intervening years between the reception of the remodelled machine and the date of the disbanding of the company, Oct. 8, 1860, were distinguished by intense strife with their neighbors, the Columbians, this competition often assuming phases neither orderly nor creditable. As a rule, however, it was of a good natured sort. A few extracts from the records of No. 6 will reveal the nature of this emulation:

No. 6 Records.

Oct. 21, 1854.—Alarm of fire at 8.30 P. M. Burning of bushes at Head-of-the-River. Six out first, with Five close after her. Went as far as our limits to give our neighbors a good chance to go ahead of us, if they could. Five stopped first two squares behind.

Feb. 5, 1855.—Fire at 6.30 P. M, from the North Christian Church, opposite the Parker House. Damage slight. Six out first and first water.

June 4, 1855.—Fire at piano manufactory on William street. Six out first and Five first water.

July 3.—Fire at 10.30 P. M., North Christian Church. Five out first. Six first water.

Aug. 25.—Fire at Mountain Brow, Perry's Neck. Five out first. Six passed her and led more than two squares in going to Rodman's farm.

10th mo., 15th, 1854.—Alarm, caused by burning of a barn near the railroad crossing. Six out first, but being stopped by the Chief Engineer, Five passed us. Upon the Chief being convinced that there was a fire, he gave word to go ahead. Went up Purchase street in good style and passed No. 9 (she showing fair play); overtook No. 5. The men holding the tongue seemed to be laboring under some complaint that caused a dizziness in the head to judge by the way they managed their engine; for, though the Six came nearly alongside two separate times on two separate sides, we were unable to pass her, as they meandered in most beautiful style from one curbstone to the other.

Oct. 11, 1855.—Fire at Kempton's lumber yard, Foster street. Five out first and first water.

Nov. 30.—Met this morning at 9.30 o'clock for a trial at Custom House reservoir, with Ohio, No. 3, and we got most woefully beaten, considering the size and capacity of our engine.

April 30, 1855.—Donated to the Dorcas Society and Ladies' Aid Society each $37.66.

July 22, 1859.—False alarm of fire at 9.30 o'clock P. M. Five out first, Six passed her on Fifth street. Five, in attempting to pass the Six, locked wheels, so that she was under the necessity of taking off one of her wheels to get out of the mess.

Oct. 30.—False alarm of fire at 7 P. M. Five out first, with full complement of men on the drag ropes—bound to keep ahead or burst.

I frankly admit that all this was undignified—that it was boys' play. I don't pretend to defend all that occurred in those palmy days of the hand-engine; but it was fun for the boys, and even our elders were not altogether disinterested as to which got first water or won the race. When, however, the common enemy took hold upon the homes and property of our citizens, then to the credit of the firemen be it said that all animosity was laid quickly aside, and harmoniously they worked together in conquering the fire fiend. Early and late they strove to stay the progress of its devastation.

Speaking of late hours gives me an opportunity to relate a story told me by my friend, James Taylor. Few citizens were better known in their day than Col. John Baylies and Joshua B. King, both noted wits and famous story tellers. Their homes were close together at the head of Bedford street; they were warm friends and sought constantly each other's society. It was their custom to go down town together evenings to the post office, and sauntering homeward, they would stand in front of the colonel's gate and chat till a late hour. This became very annoying to Mrs. B., and the colonel pretended that he also disliked to be kept from his rest by the loquacious tongue of his friend.

One afternoon in early winter the colonel came home and asked his wife to lay out for him his heaviest underclothes, an extra pair of stockings, his gloves, and a muffler. He proposed to give his friend King all the time he wanted that night and see if he couldn't freeze him out. So, dressing himself throughout with a double suit of clothing, he put himself in condition to be warm enough to spend a season in the Arctic. Meeting his friend down town, the two went to the post office, and called at the Eagle Hotel (then situated where now stands Ricketson Block), to hear the news. Starting homeward, they arrived at the colonel's gate soon after 9 o'clock. It was a bitterly cold night, and Mrs. Baylies flattered herself that the colonel would come in at an early hour. Alas for human expectations! 10 o'clock: 11 o'clock: 11½ o'clock: 12 o'clock,—it was well past that hour before the colonel came into the house.

"Almost sorry I came in," was the response to the tender inquiries of his wife.

"Why so?" she gently inquired.

"Old King had just commenced a new story," was his answer.

The winter clothing was laid away for a more inclement season.

After the difficulty with the Board of Engineers had been settled by the disbanding of the Columbian Engine Company, No. 5, Oct. 25, 1852, the Ex-Five Association was formed Nov. 1, with the same officers, and held meetings in a room in the rear of the Columbian Club room, in the second story of the Nathan Chase building, recently removed from the lot now occupied by the Wing building on Purchase street. The organization continued in vigorous existence till May 21, 1853, when the members were invited to resume their places in the fire department. At the meeting when the company voted to accept the invitation, the discussion gave rise to many spirited remarks by Messrs. Cook, Hyde, Palmer, Weaver, "Friend" Perez Jenkins, and Sanford. The last named gentleman wound up his eloquent speech with the following quotation altered to fit the occasion:

> "This was the winter of our discontent
> Made glorious summer by late events,
> And all the clouds that o'er the exiles frowned,
> Were in the bosom of ocean drowned."

In 1853 the Columbians accepted an invitation to visit the Atlantic Engine Co., No. 10, of Providence. Clerk Fales, in his report, said:

"We were hospitably received and made welcome. As firemen they know how to greet their friends and brothers who toil for the public good."

Nov. 28, 1853, the Columbians presented a nice chandelier to the Cannonville church. The gift was gratefully received and acknowledged in a courteous letter from the pastor, Rev. Mr. Greenwood.

The Columbian, No. 5, was reorganized May 28, 1853, with the following officers:

Foreman, Israel T. Bryant.
First Assistant, George Hinckley.
Second Assistant, John B. Hyde.
Clerk, Giles Fales.

June 27, Mr. William Brownell presented the company with an elegant copy of the Bible, and a vote was passed that one chapter should be read from it at the opening of each meeting. This was done regularly for many years, the clerk, Mr. Fales, performing the duty. It is fair to suppose that the members listened carefully and attentively. And yet it is said that Mr. Fales read the same chapter for thirteen consecutive meetings without having the fact discovered. Mr. Perez Jenkins, a good Methodist brother, "caught on" to the situation and suggested that for variety's sake it would be well for Mr. Fales to make other selections. The Bible reading continued with a more extended choice of chapters.

COLUMBIAN, NO. 5.

Built by L. Button & Co., Waterford, N. Y. This picture is also a good portrait of the Relief No. 5, of Oxford Village, Fairhaven.

In 1854 Capt. Israel T. Bryant resigned the command, having been elected a member of the Board of Engineers. He was succeeded by James L. Borland, who soon resigned on account of ill health. John B. Hyde was elected captain, and held that position till 1861; and I think that his officers, Messrs. Sherman, Weaver, Hart and Fales, were associated with him during this long term of office. Capt. Hyde was very popular with his command, and this may be said of all the officers.

Feb. 15, 1855, the Board of Engineers voted to contract, for the sum of $1650, with Messrs. L. Button & Co., Waterford, N. Y., for a first class fire engine and hose carriage for Company No. 5, the engine to be "32 man power," and of the following dimensions and finish:

> "The engine box to be built of mahogany and hung on half elliptic springs, with wheels 43 inches in diameter forward, and 45 inches behind. A crane neck, so that the wheels can turn completely under, pumps 10 inches in diameter, with a stroke varying from 5 to 9 inches: three outlets for as many streams, with three discharge pipes and eleven nozzles; brass corners to the box, and cut-offs to the outlets, with 29 feet suction hose, 21 feet of it to be carried in a tube over the engine. The brakes to be 22 1-2 feet long, all the iron work, including the scrolls and crane work to be polished. A bell, weighing 18 pounds, to be suspended to the tube by a handsome scroll. The whole to be finished, painted, varnished, and all the brass work silver-plated."

This description I have copied from the records of the Board of Engineers.

The engine was warranted to throw a stream, one inch nozzle, 180 feet. The company agreed to furnish a substantial hose cart, without silver plating. How well the builders fulfilled their contract was soon tested, for the engine arrived in town on the morning of July 20, 1855. The company, dressed in a new uniform, turned out in the afternoon to receive the new machine, accompanied by the New Bedford Brass Band. The full membership for 1855, as taken from the records of the company, is appended:

JOHN B. HYDE.

(Captain of Columbian, No. 5, 1854–1861.)

Foreman, John B. Hyde.
First Assistant, Pliny B. Sherman.
Second Assistant, Benjamin Weaver.
Clerk, Giles S. Fales.

George D. Bisbee,
Charles W. Keen,
Samuel C. Hart,
Thomas Cross,
Horace King,
John F. Wood,
Eugene Gifford,
Charles Morgridge,
Perez Jenkins,
Thomas W. Cook,
Thomas Hilliard,
Otis Wilcox,
William A. Russell,
Charles H. Bisbee,
Nathan D. Maxfield,
Benj. F. Hayden,
Henry A. Wilcox,
George T. Sears,

Francis T. Tuite,
Henry B. Covell,
Thomas Garvy,
Alfred Wordell,
Edwin Gage,
George Gifford,
Frederick Morse,
Edward S. Jenkins,
Stephen H. Shepherd,
Joseph Gifford,
John Harity,
Judson Tozier,
William S. Maxfield,
James F. Chase,
Adoniram Myrick,
Henry Morse,
Seth Wilcox,
David L. Hathaway,
James L. Wilbur,
James H. Hood,
Hiram A. Davis,
Charles Gifford,
William Gammell,
Christal Licht,
Robert N. B. Doane,
Seth R. Thomas,
Robert N. Wing,
Charles H. Booth,
Peter Gobell,
Henry I. Strong,
William H. Holmes,
George Hinckley,
Andrew T. Wood,
Allen Raymond,
James Smith,
William Peckham,
William Love,
John Duffy,
Caleb A. Thomas,
Joel B. Arnold,
George R. Maxfield,
Israel T. Bryant,
Silas Wordell,
Daniel Catternach,
Charles M. Corson,
James O. Thompson,
Luthan J. Greene,
Benjamin P. Crocker.

During the parade, made before proceeding to the station to receive the new engine, the boys honored Mayor Rodney French with a round of hearty cheers as they passed his residence. The same compliment was extended to the newspaper offices. The new engine fully met the fondest expectations of the company. Built on so different a model from the Agnew machine, which for a generation had been the only style bought for our city, its appearance was a genuine surprise, and a gratifying one at that. To be sure the jealous boys gave it the title of "the hay cart," because of the long upturned side brakes, which made an outline suggestive of that useful farmer's wagon: but all acknowledged the engine to be of graceful form and beautiful in finish. The Columbians were deservedly proud of the machine, and when they manned the ropes, and, preceded by the band, marched down town, they presented a fine appearance, which won them the plaudits of the crowds lining the streets. The engine was taken to the School street reservoir and submitted to its first trial, which gave general satisfaction. It played 168 feet, though hampered by the foliage. It then played through 675 feet of hose, up School street, 115 feet, and, through the same hose, 20 feet above the observatory. The steep elevation of School street made this trial a very gratifying exhibition of the power of throwing water. The last trial was to send three good streams over the steeple of the Trinitarian church. The next day the new engine played a solid stream of 186 feet. The following is taken from the *Evening Standard*, of the 21st:

After the trial the company, with a few invited guests, sat down to an elegant dinner at the Parker House. Messrs. Blaisdell and Wing furnished all that could be desired and illustrated their excellent practical knowledge in the gastronomic department.

Mr. William A. Russell furnishes me with a copy of the bill of fare on this occasion. It is a double-paged circular, elegantly printed in gold and highly decorated. I am sure that many of the "Fives" will enjoy seeing a list of the viands discussed that day:

Dinner for the Columbian Engine Co., No. 5, at the Parker House, July, 1855:

BILL OF FARE.

SOUP.

Oyster.

FISH.

Salmon, with Anchovy Sauce.

BOILED.

Leg of Mutton and Caper Sauce.

Corned Beef. Chicken and Pork. Corned Tongue.

ENTREES.

Stewed Oysters. Macaroni a la Creme.

Sword Fish Fried in Crumbs.

Rice Croquettes. Lobster. Potted Pigeon.

ROAST.

Beef. Ham, Champagne Sauce. Chicken.

Lamb, Mint Sauce. Duck. Mongrel Goose.

Veal, Stuffed. Turkey.

VEGETABLES.

New Potatoes. Turnips. Mashed Potatoes.
Squash. String Beans. Beets.
Green Peas. Onions. Cucumbers.

PUDDINGS AND PASTRY.

Bread Pudding.
Apple Pie. Custard Pie. Berry Pie.

DESSERT.

Almonds. English Walnuts. Raisins.
Pine Apple. Ice Cream.

The *Evening Standard* says:

"The admirable justice which was done to the eatables by the company was the most flattering encomium that could have been bestowed upon the banquet. Short, neat, spicy and telling speeches were made, and sentiments offered at the table by Hon. Rodney French, L. Button, Esq., manufacturer of the engine, R. C. Topham, Esq., of the Board of Engineers, J. B. Ashley, Esq., ex-Chief Engineer, Mr. Foreman John B. Hyde, Mr. Assistant Benjamin Weaver, Mr. M. A. Covell, C. W. Brown and others. An extremely pleasant half hour was spent in this species of 'playing away,' when the company retired with three cheers for the New Bedford Fire Department, for the builder of the new machine, Mr. Button, for the band, for the Parker House, and for the ladies 'who were obliged to wait for their tea' until the company had got through their dinner.

In the evening as large, happy and merry a company assembled at city hall as was ever gathered within its walls. There was as bright an array of beauty as the most cynical old bachelor could have wished to look upon, and the whole affair passed off in such a way as to reflect the highest credit upon the Columbians, by whom the ball was given in compliment to their friends. The management was admirable, and no effort was omitted by the "Fives" to contribute to the happiness of their guests. No pleasanter, more social or better managed party was ever given in our city. The dancing was continued into the small hours, when the party separated, satisfied that in all which constitutes genuine hospitality, courtesy, and gentlemanly bearing, the Columbians cannot be surpassed The music was by Smith & Hawes' Band, and was, as usual, excellent. The supper was got up in good style by Tilden. We heard many encomiums passed upon the company during the parade in the afternoon. Everybody concurred in the opinion that it was as handsome a turnout of firemen as ever occurred in this city, and that the purchase of so handsome a machine for so good an organization 'served 'em right.'"

I give a song, dedicated to the Columbian Engine Co., No. 5, by Frank Easy—the *nom de plume* of Mr. Mayhew A. Covell:

When flames so bright illume the night,
  Or shame the lustrous day,
Our duty calls where falling walls
  And crackling embers lay.
But naught we fear, however drear
  And desolate the night,
We ne'er forsake the engine's brakes,
  But work with all our might.

CHORUS.
Then Wake her! Wake her!! Now my boys!
  As through the streets we fly,
And when we reach the fire, my boys,
  Then "break her down" 's the cry.

And since our "tub" has given the rub
  To others once so bold,
We'll swell the fame of "Button's" name
  And feel we've not been sold.
For she, our pet, can throw her jet
  As far as the eye can see;
And all do say that none can play
  And claim a rivalry.

And she's our pride, both far and wide,
  We'll sound her praise abroad,
The name she bears a charm it wears,
  To nerve the listless crowd.
Then let us strive that Number Five
  May never disgrace her name,
And let us stand, a fearless band,
  To fight the raging flame.

Our Foreman's plan is: Every man
  Shall at his post be found.
His heart is stirred whene'er he's heard
  "We're first upon the ground."
Then as we rear our standard here,
  O, may we ever thrive,
And while we live we'll ever give
  "Three cheers for Number Five."

Sept. 25th, 1856, the Columbians went on an excursion to Salem, where they were received by the Adams Engine Co., No. 10, of that place. They took their new machine with them; and what was done on that occasion is well told by the Salem *Register*, in its mention of the visit and performances of the Columbian Engine Co., No. 5. It said:

"On Friday, in Chestnut street, the engine threw an inch stream horizontally 193 feet and perpendicularly over the vane of the South Church steeple, about 170 feet. The steeple stands 166 feet high, and the position of the engine was in the street, near the cistern, considererably lower than the base of the steeple. The band meanwhile struck up 'Pop Goes the Weasel,' and as the stream mounted higher and higher under the force applied, the gratified spectators cheered the successful efforts of the company to the echo. The power of the engine and the skill of the company were well tested and gave great satisfaction to all who witnessed the exhibition. We take pleasure in noticing the orderly and commendable deportment of the Columbians, which was generally observed and appreciated. They were not only a remarkably fine looking body of young men, but their courteous demeanor on parade in the public streets and in the stores elicited many compliments, and was so marked as to attract more than ordinary observation. Our New Bedford friends have not only gained credit for themselves by this course, but also for the department with which they are connected, and for their beautiful and enterprising city; and they have thereby given to this community great pleasure by their visit. The Columbians numbered 50 men and were officered as follows:

Foreman, John B. Hyde.
First Assistant, Pliny B. Sherman.
Second Assistant, Benjamin Weaver.
Third Assistant, Samuel C. Hart.
Clerk, *pro tem*, Albert A. Bolles."

On their return home the men were welcomed by the Hook & Ladder Co., Capt. R. A. Dillingham, who had prepared an elegant collation for them.

On the evening of Sept. 5, 1857, a beautiful silver trumpet was presented to Capt. Hyde by the company as a token of the esteem in which he was held. He has it still in his possession, and it occupies a prominent place in his home in New York city.

The firemen occasionally attended church by companies, and during the great revival of 1857–8 I find record where several of the companies attended divine service on the Sabbath. The Columbians in 1858 attended, by invitation of the Trinitarian Church, with other firemen, a service specially prepared for them. A discourse was delivered by Rev. Wheelock Craig, one of the purest and kindest of men, who is still held in precious memory by many of our citizens. The Columbians' records of the event speak in highly respectful terms of the service and of the preacher. During the same year the Philadelphia, No. 7, attended a service at the Elm Street Methodist Church, Rev. H. S. White, pastor.

At the annual meeting, in 1859, Mr. Giles S. Fales, the much respected clerk of the company, who had performed long and faithful service, resigned his position. He had been a member of the department since 1834, when he served in the capacity of torch boy. He was succeeded in office by Mr. Robert H. Taber.

On the evening of Jan. 17, 1859, there was a large assemblage at the Columbians' hall, on the occasion of a presentation of an American standard by the lady friends of the company. The address was made by Miss Mary A. Raymond, and was well delivered. Capt. Hyde responded in a good speech. Brief addresses were made by Hon. Rodney French and others, interspersed with music. A collation followed.

A large frame containing the photographs of the fifty volunteer members was presented by them to the company, Mr. Eugene Gifford making the speech for the givers. The inscription will tell the story: "Presented to Columbian Engine Co., No. 5, by the volunteers, Feb. 14, 1859."

The continued difficulty with the city government finally led the Columbians to disband Sept. 24, 1860. A new company was formed Oct. 1, 1860, with the following:

Foreman, L. W. Davis.
First Assistant, Allen Almy.
Second Assistant, John Colwell.
Clerk, Charles H. Bisbee.

Sylvester Paul,	William R. Palmer,
John W. Footman,	William H. Welch,
George W. Hunt,	Robert C. Topham,
Clarfaus Vansant,	Charles Thomas,
Edwin Dugan,	Frederick B. Davis,
Alfred Weaver,	Isaac H. Barrows,
James H. Hood,	Nathan Brooks,
Charles Brightman,	George M. Ennis,
Charles Parker,	Lewis H. Coble,
W. F. Howland,	John W. Ennis,

John Duffy,
Rufus Randall,
Peter Gobell,
Patrick McDonald,
Hugh McDonald,
John E. Bowen,
Richmond M. Taber,
Patrick Carroll,
Patrick Murphy,
Barney Kenney,
Joseph Vincent,
Luther Brownell,
Jesse V. Lake,
Giles G. Barker,
Thomas F. Clarke,
Henry Stephens,
Benjamin Sowle,
Edwin Cavenor,
Daniel B. Standish,
David Pollock,
Allen G. Ashley,
James F. McKenney,
Alonzo B. Tripp,
Alvin C. Smith,
George W. Farnum,
W. G. Reynolds,
Michael Dugan,
John Coote,
James O'Brien,
John Butman,
William S. Wilcox,
Charles W. Hunt,
Peleg R. Thurston,
Simeon Bailey.

The ex-Fives Association continued its existence for many years, the annual meeting consisting of a reunion celebration, with a grand dinner.

The relations between the Columbian, No. 5, and the Young Mechanic, No. 6, were of such a character as to develope a rivalry, intense and uncompromising. Alike ambitious to be ahead of the other, either in getting first water or winning the race at a false alarm, this rivalry resulted often in considerable ill feeling, kindred to that shown in the political strife of the day. As citizens, however, the members were among the most energetic and prominent, and were harmonious and progressive in all that advanced the interests of our city. When the city was threatened with a riot the authorities were glad to fall back upon the firemen as a reserve force. Quickly did they respond to the call, and they were sworn in ready for duty. Our readers may judge from this confidence that the firemen were in more ways than one the protectors of our city.

The new company attached to the Columbian, No. 5, continued in service till Feb. 28, 1866, when it was disbanded by the Board of Engineers, and the engine taken out of commission. It was soon afterwards sold to the town of Galesburg, Illinois.

CHAPTER VIII.

SEVERAL fires have occurred in our city where the loss of property was far greater than that of Horatio A. Kempton's lumber yard on the night of Oct. 18, 1854, but never in our history one that created such terror and consternation. To fully comprehend this great conflagration, our readers must understand the location and its surroundings. The entire section lying between North and Hillman, Foster and Pleasant streets, was occupied as a lumber yard, with the exception of the north side of North street, which was lined with dwellings. Situated in the heart of the city, with all intersecting streets densely occupied with wooden structures, the yard itself was lined on its outer edges by immense piles of lumber that skirted in unbroken line the Foster and Hillman street fronts, the Pleasant street side being occupied with a long shed filled with dry and therefore highly inflammable building material. Within the enclosure were two wooden buildings, one a carpenter shop, occupied by Mr. John K. Cushing, the other as an office by Mr. Kempton, and both situated near the Pleasant street entrance. In the central portion of the yard were hugh piles of flooring timber, here a mass of joists, there piles of laths and floor boards, staked with air spaces between them, while the unoccupied ground was littered with shavings and refuse timber. The engine located at the nearest point on Foster street, Hancock, No. 9, had been taken apart for repairs only a few days before, and on this night was still in pieces. Surely there were favorable conditions for a fierce conflagration. So thought the incendiary, no doubt, as he secretly entered the premises and applied the torch, which soon brought such terrible results. He was seen emerging from the yard half an hour before the flames burst forth.

The alarm rang out at 11 o'clock, and soon the whole city was brilliantly illuminated from the burning timber. It seemed to ignite in a moment, for when the engines arrived the whole mass was in flames, and, aided by a strong southwest wind, was quickly transformed into a seething furnace, sending out intense heat and making it an impossibility for the firemen in any way to control it. All efforts to check the raging element was unavailing, and though the surrounding streets had become well nigh impassable the firemen turned their efforts to save the houses. But the merciless flames soon crossed the streets, and, one after another, the buildings on Pleasant and Hillman streets were burned. At this moment it looked as if the whole north section of the city must be destroyed. The stores on Purchase street and the dwellings at the northeast were being emptied of their stock and goods. To add to the intense apprehensions, the water gave out in the reservoirs one after another in quick succession, leaving, for a time, the engines without supply. This was, however, partly remedied by sending an engine to the river, which pumped into another and thus gave a limited supply of water. The Wilcox Building, on the northwest corner of Foster and Hillman streets, was miraculously saved by the use of wet blankets and carpets, as was the house on the northeast corner of Pleasant and Hillman streets. Had this building been burned it would probably have led to a greater destruction of property, for the fire would have passed beyond control. As it was the following persons were burned out on Pleasant street: Two-story house southeast corner of Hillman and Pleasant streets, occupied by Gilbert Howland and Andrew J. Dam: house next south, occupied by Captain Philip Sherman and Andrew Hayes; house next south, occupied by Thomas A. Howland and Mrs. Edward Howland. While these houses were being destroyed, the flames communicated to the building on the northwest corner of Hillman and Pleasant streets, occupied by Robert Hillman, then to house next west, occupied by Mrs.

Mary West and Mrs. Kempton, and next to house on northeast corner of Foster street, occupied by Mr. Aaron Upjohn. The estimated loss was $40,000.

It was a sad spectacle that greeted the eyes of our citizens the next morning, when the whole immense area was a mass of smouldering ruins and falling chimneys. The streets were filled with household furniture, kitchen utensils and such things, which told the story of desolate homes.

One of the most painful incidents of the great fire was the fatal accident to one of the most useful and highly respected citizens of his day, Mr. Jethro Hillman, a member of the well known firm of ship builders, Messrs. J. & Z. Hillman, who, the *Evening Standard* said, had constructed some of the most substantial ships that ever floated. Their shipyard was located on the corner of Hillman and North Second streets, directly in the range of the fire, and the sky during the night was filled with floating embers that carried destruction in their course. The brothers were engaged in throwing water upon the roof of a shed to prevent its taking fire, when he fell from a ladder, striking his head on a stick, breaking his skull and injuring him in such a manner that he died the following evening at 9 o'clock. His untimely death was regretted by a large circle of friends.

Our readers may well imagine that the years 1855 and 1856 were the palmy days of our fire department. It was during these years that the highest point of interest was reached. Already "steam" loomed in the distance, though subjected to scoff and ridicule, both in and out of the department. The funeral of the hand engine service commenced on the day the first steamer landed in the city. But more of this later on. We are in the midst of the most exciting years of the fire department life and we must make the most of it, for with them went out much of the poetry and personality peculiar to the hand engine service.

The new engines for the Young Mechanics and Columbians

were now in full commission. Both companies were at their best, and so were all the other organizations,—alert, vigorous, and full of enthusiasm. Two more hand engines were added to the service, and then the record ceases. Soon the department entered upon a new era.

The old engine, Columbian, No. 5, built by Messrs. Durfee & Delano, in 1827, was put in good repair and the name and number changed to Acushnet, No. 4. It was stationed at Mount Pleasant in the Sepulchre, which had been moved from North Second street to the corner of Mt. Pleasant and Durfee streets.

A company was formed Feb. 2, 1857, as follows:

Foreman, Joseph W. Cornell.
First Assistant, Peleg W. Blake.
Second Assistant, Octavius C. Smith.
Clerk, George W. Maker.

Gideon P. Tripp,
James Beetle,
Charles F. Tripp,
Samuel Driscoll,
George Kennerson,
Sylvanus Gifford,
Phineas Reynolds,
Barjona D. Tripp,
James C. Hathaway,
James M. Tripp,
Albert Booth,
James S. Manchester,
Holder A. Brightman,
Benj. R. Wordell,
Daniel Hathaway,
Nathaniel Manchester,
Sumner M. Faunce,
Ebenezer Andrew,
George Macomber,
Luthan Blake,
George Albro,
Curtis T. Gammons,
Thomas Childs,
Benjamin Reynolds,
John W. Manchester,
Abiathar Rogers,
Paul B. Warren,
Isaac Manchester,
William Coggeshall,
Frederick Collins.

The company continued in active service till about 1867, when it was disbanded.

The spirit that thrilled the fire department animated the youth of the city: and one of the practical results of this enthusiasm was the organization of the Young America, No. 8. A company of young men, 25 in number, raised among themselves and from some of our public-spirited citizens $300 for the purchase of a fire engine. Among the contributors were

Thomas Nye, Jr., Samuel Rodman, Ivory H. Bartlett, Benjamin Rodman, and many others whose names I do not recall. An organization was completed, and the company sent a committee to Pawtucket to complete the purchase of the Young America, No. 8. No army contractor ever felt more important in closing a contract than did the committee in closing a bargain with the proprietor of a jobbing wagon to drag our engine to the station. We were anxious to get it to New Bedford that night, for the state of Rhode Island wasn't big enough to hold us and give sufficient breathing room. The boys were well pleased with the appearance of the machine. On the test trial it played 140 feet, through 100 feet of hose. This engine was of about half the size of the ordinary hand engine, with side brakes, and suction pumps, and was as well and thoroughly equipped for actual fire service as the best of them.

The board of engineers placed us in the Second street house, and we entered upon our career as a full-fledged fire company. We did valuable service on many an occasion, often getting first water. In running to a fire we frequently took our engine on the sidewalks, thus getting a decided advantage in easier travel.

I give the membership of the Young America company, taken from the original records. These have been since 1857 in the possession of Mr. W. H. Peacock, of Chicago. During the great fire in that city, in 1872, they were packed in his safe, which lay for three days on the bottom of the Chicago river. Mr. Peacock has now given these records to our Fire Department:

Captain, L. B. Ellis.
First Assistant, Matthias C. Pease.
Second Assistant, James W. Lawrence.
Third Assistant, James D. Kent.
Clerk, A. M. Osgood.

James C. Hitch,
George Walden,
Alex. H. Ellis,
William H. Peacock,
Ephraim Kempton,
Otis N. Pierce,
Preserved Rider,
Barney Cox,

B. F. Lowden,
C. A. Perry,
Roland B. Murphy,
Benj. F. Lewis,
Edward B. Wilson,
Haile R. Luther,
William B. Allen,
Charles E. Maxfield,
George W. Allen,
Joseph C. Austin,
Edward T. Wilson,
James A. Smith,
George Homer,
Andrew Hayes,
Simeon Potter,
Gideon Underwood,
William Mann,
Horatio Bly,
Ezra Howland,
C. E. Wardsworth,
Newton F. Barrows,
Joseph Dean,
H. M. Snow,
John Davis,
Ira Negus,
Philip Topham,
Thomas Brotherson,
Benjamin Hayes,
Joseph Knowles.

A song, dedicated to Young America, No. 8, of New Bedford, by Alexander H. Ellis:

Come citizens, attention give, a story I'll relate
About a little engine, we call her Number Eight:
We keep her upon Second street, and when duty may require,
You'll ever find us on the ground—playing on the fire.

Chorus.

Wake her, shake her, now my boys,
And let us have a sing:
We'll let you know the Eights are 'round
When the bells begin to ring.

She is an independent tub, the first one in the town,
And when the alarm of fire is given you'll always find her 'round.
To throw the first stream on the fire will always be our aim;
We'll do our duty while we're there, and gain a noble name.
Chorus.

Our new machine is Jeffers' make, one whom every fireman knows;
She'll play one hundred forty feet through one hundred feet of hose.
A side-brake machine is she and takes water in behind;
She is as saucy a machine as you will ever find.
Chorus.

Young America is her name and she will do her best,
When the fire is raging most, to put her to the test;
We know she is a small machine, but then she'll put out fire,
And we'll try to save the property of all who may desire.
Chorus.

Our foreman and officers are faithful to their trust,
  And when we hear them give command we work without a fuss;
Our hosemen they all know their place, and the boys who man the brakes,
And when they halloo "Strike her, boys," she's always sure to take.
Chorus.

Our tub she'll go to the reservoir and put her suction down;
The boys they'll man her brakes and commence to brake her down.
The water'll come with lightning speed and through her hose will skate,
And soon will come the welcome sound, "First water," Number Eight.
Chorus.

By day or night we'll be on hand, in sunshine, fog or rain.
You'll find us promptly at our post, smothering the flame;
And when we've done our duty there, and made the water foam,
We'll take her up and man the ropes and drag our engine home.
Chorus.

We thank our generous citizens for lending us a hand,
And if their houses get on fire, we'll save them if we can.
We'll try to fill a fireman's place, we'll mind our brakes and hose,
We'll do you all the good we can in conquering our foes.
Chorus.

The Young America was in constant service until 1857, when the company was disbanded and the engine was sold to the city and placed in reserve. It was subsequently sold to Hon. Weston Howland, and was in constant use for 18 years at his Fish Island factory.

The *Evening Standard* of Nov. 9, 1854, contained the following:

At five o'clock this morning Liberty Hall building was discovered to be on fire. The fire department was immediately on the spot, but their efforts were unavailing to save the far-famed "temple of liberty," within whose hallowed walls freedom for all men has so frequently been proclaimed, and from whose tower the note of warning to the poor, trembling fugitive from oppression has so often sounded. At about 7 o'clock the structure was destroyed. It had fretted away its short term of existence and witnessed its last exhibition of impressive tragedy and mirth-provoking farce. The actors have positively made their last appearance. The fire caught from a lamp in a transparency in front of the restaurant, in the lower part of the building, that had been left burning all night. From thence the flames were communicated to the building, and thence ascended to the upper portion, between the wall and ceiling, and were consequently invisible for some length of time.

Being out of reach of water until it had gained strong headway, it was impossible, from the combustible character of the building and the scenery attached to the theatre, to stay the progress of the flames. The occupants of the building were as follows: E. C. Leonard, carpet store; Bourne & Perry, shoe store; City liquor store; Davis & Allen, merchant tailoring establishment; Isaac Quinnell, restaurant; Uncle Tom's Cabin, a restaurant of long standing, owned by Thomas T. Allen: Charles E. Hawes, daguerreian rooms; Mechanic, No. 6, club-room; Telegraph office, Benoni R. Paine, operator. The Grotto restaurant, west of the building, and Eli Haskell's house, on the north, were repeatedly on fire, badly charred and scathed by the fiery element and drenched with water.

We but express the concurrent opinion of all sensible men when we say that no department in the world could have exhibited more indisputable evidence of skill, efficiency and manly effort than ours that morning. To Chief Engineer Joshua B. Ashley and his efficient corps of assistants and the members of the fire department, collectively and individually, our citizens were indebted for the safety of that portion of the city in the vicinity of the hall. Let the proper meed of praise be given."

A thrilling accident occurred during the progress of the fire that came near costing the life of Mr. Pliny B. Sherman, an officer of Columbian, No. 5. He was on a ladder, well up on the south side of the building, with the pipe, when the burning jet fell, striking him as is came down. He was thrown violently from his position, and, without doubt, would have been instantly killed but for the fall being partially broken by his striking against an awning frame and being caught in the arms of Mr. George D. Bisbee, who, seeing the accident, leaped from the lower rounds of the ladder and caught him as he fell. A few minutes' rest and he was back again to his work. He never did know when it was the proper time to go home; and Bisbee always had the reputation of being in the way when wanted.

I have gathered from various sources some facts about this building which will prove interesting to our readers. The tract of land on which this building was located (northwest corner of Purchase and William streets) was given by William

Rotch, in 1795, to the First Congregational church, and a building was erected during the years 1795-6-7 by Manasseh Kempton, Jr., and Eastland Babcock. It was occupied by the society for public worship some time before its completion. It is said that one of the pew holders was so anxious to occupy his pew on the following Sunday that he gave a carpenter a quart of brandy to saw open the pew door. It was, however, long before the Maine law was projected and while temperance movements were in their infancy.

The famous bell was purchased Feb. 18, 1796, of Capt. Silas Jones, of Nantucket. The money, $255, was raised by subscription, the largest amount, $10, being given by Thomas Pope, and the next largest $6, being given by a colored man named Aaron Childs. It was a bell of remarkable tone and clearness. In the November fire it was melted in the flames. The metal was gathered from the ruins, and several of our townsmen had tea-bells and articles of ornament made from it, which are still held as valuable relics of the old liberty bell.

During the excitement that thrilled the nation following the passage of the infamous fugitive slave law, in 1851, and at the time Thomas Simms was arrested and sent back into slavery from Boston, a rumor became current in that city that the United States marshals were planning to visit our little Quaker city by the sea in J. H. Pearson's brig Acorn, accompanied by United States marines, to recover certain fugitive slaves that were supposed to be in hiding, awaiting transit to Canada by the underground railroad. The news was brought into town by Mr. S. P. Hanscom, the New Bedford express rider, who rode all night, arriving Sunday morning with the startling intelligence. It was not long before the warning notes of the Liberty Hall bell rang out and said in thunder tones to the affrighted colored people that their enemy was near. The immediate cause for the alarm was that a strange vessel was reported to be in the bay, and Mr. Rodney French ordered the bell to be rung. Some of our readers will vividly remember the excitement that followed, for everyone, especially the colored people, felt that real danger was at hand. No officers, however, made themselves known, and it is not certain whether they entered the city or not. One thing is sure, that the reported presence or the vessel was a mistake. The marshals would have assuredly met with a warm reception had they put in an appearance. This is but one of many interesting episodes that occurred during those days when it cost something to be an anti-slavery man. To illustrate the work going on in the interest of the slave during that eventful period, I quote the following from the *Morning Mercury*, April 21, 1851:

"EXTRADITION EXTRAORDINARY.—We are pleased to announce that a very large number of fugitive slaves, aided by many of our most wealthy and respectable citizens, have left for Canada and parts unknown, and that more are in the way of departure. The utmost sympathy and liberality prevails toward this class of our inhabitants.

At the completion of the elegant stone church corner of Union and Eighth streets, in 1838, the old building was sold and became "Liberty Hall," and was used for lectures, political meetings and entertainments. From time to time several additions were made to the building on the west end, and about 1846–7 stage and scenic properties were added, and the hall became the principal place for theatrical representations, etc. It became chiefly noted as the place for lyceum lectures and for lectures by the distinguished advocates of the cause of the slave. The mere mention of the names of William Lloyd Garrison, Wendell Phillips, Frederick Douglass, Stephen Foster, Theodore Parker, Parker Pillsbury, and Henry Ward Beecher will call up recollections of an era in our history that was pregnant with results affecting the extinction of slavery in the United States, and it was in this hall that these orators poured forth their torrents of eloquence, argument and invective.

Charley Rhodes once astonished the audience at a local political meeting in this hall, when our home orators were called to the platform to speak upon the vital issues of the hour. Several citizens had been through the ordeal when Charles saw from the gallery Mr. Nancecawen, a well known citizen, enter the hall and take a back seat. In voice loud and strong, in notes full and prolonged, he shouted: "N-a-n-c-i-e-cowen," with an emphasis on the last syllable and a continued stretch on the first two. It is needless to add that the audience was taken by storm, and so was Mr. N., who was obliged to respond with a speech to satisfy his admiring citizens.

Stephen D. Jordan, an old fireman, gives me the text for another true story about the bell. One night the bell-ringer put in an early appearance to ring the 9 o'clock, and while waiting for the hour, fell asleep while sitting on the upper stair. Time rolled on and still he slept, calm and undisturbed. The deep tones of the clock in the adjoining church was tolling the hour of midnight when the bell-ringer was startled from his nap, and grasping vigorously the bell-rope, rang out his 9 o'clock at 12. In a moment the whole town was in commotion. The other bells took up the refrain; the fire engines were flying through the streets; citizens dressed and half-dressed were scudding through the thoroughfares, anxious to lend a helping hand against the fire fiend. But it was not the night for him to be abroad, it was only a false alarm—the price paid for that comfortable nap.

CHAPTER IX.

THE first hook and ladder truck belonging to our fire service was stationary, and was located on the land now occupied by the post office. It consisted in part of the stone wall near the engine house, then standing on this land and occupied by the Citizen, No. 2. On this wall were fastened several horizontal bars connected with an equal number of upright posts. This arrangement served as a repository for the ladders, and the hooks were hung upon brackets—sometimes. It is said that when the firemen were in very much of a hurry for them they usually explored the ground first, and as a rule found them there.

This structure had a roof, not altogether a tight one, but a roof nevertheless. It served splendidly to catch a good proportion of the rain and snow, and its open-work character made it successful in keeping the ladders and hooks moist and slimy in summer, and in winter everything would be locked in an icy embrace. This served to keep the ladders at home during the winter season, for they were not in condition to be borrowed.

Our modern truck is mounted on wheels, and the whole apparatus goes to the scene of conflagration. Then, when a fire was raging in any part of the village, and a ladder or hook was wanted, it was sent for. There was some economy in all this, for the unused apparatus was not subjected to the wear and tear incident to the average fire.

Among the implements belonging to this branch of the service in those primitive days was the "battering ram." When a fire was very obstinate and likely to prove dangerous to the neighboring houses, these long sticks of solid timber were brought out, manned with sufficient power, and the whole thing pushed flat to the ground.

I have already given a list of the members attached to the Hook & Ladder Co. in 1835. At that time the company manned a carriage built by Mr. Nathan Durfee, father of James Durfee, in 1800, that was equipped with the ordinary means of service, and fully met the requirements of the day. It was stationed in the house on Purchase street and was in commission till 1855, when a new truck was built by Joseph Brownell & Co. This carriage did royal service till 1872, when great improvements were made. Among these was a system of rollers, arranged so that the heavy ladders were moved with greater freedom. The carriage was fitted at this time to be drawn by horse power. In 1861 the truck was moved to the engine-house on Market street. This building was formerly occupied by the Hancock, No. 9. on Foster street: and when it was moved in March, 1861, the company held their monthly meetings in the house while it was being moved on the rollers.

July 4, 1865, our city celebrated with great pomp, and the fire department, as usual, was an important feature in the parade. The Pioneers made a beautiful show, the truck being decorated with flowers and flags. Two boys, dressed in appropriate costume, were placed in prominent positions on the carriage—one a representative of the Revolutionary army, and the other of the navy—while under a high canopy in the centre were two lovely figures. the Goddess of Liberty and the Soldier of the Rebellion. The whole decorations were in fine taste and gained the admiration of the great concourse of people who thronged the streets. The company spent $100 on this feature of the parade.

The battle axes taken from the pirate Georgia. were presented to the company by Austin S. Cushman, Esq., in recognition of the patriotic zeal of the Pioneers in honoring the return of veterans of the army and navy.

In June, 1872, the Pioneer Hook and Ladder Company returned to their old station at the Central Engine-house. A few extracts from the records may prove interesting to members and their friends:

Nov. 26, 1873.—The company made a public parade, having the Volunteer Hook & Ladder Co., of Taunton, as guests; and on Sept. 9, 1874. the Pioneers made a return visit to their Taunton friends.

They seem to have had a close fellowship with the Volunteers, for we find record that on Oct. 7th they again visited our city and had a public parade and a general good time.

Feb. 8, 1875.—Mr. John H. Judson, 1st assistant, was elected assistant engineer.

Oct. 15, 1875.—The Pioneers visited Taunton again, and were presented an elegant trumpet by their hosts—the Volunteers.

Jan. 31, 1876.—After 20 years' faithful service, Mr. Martin L. Hathaway withdrew from the company and was presented an elegant testimonial.

July 4, 1877,—The Pioneers received as a prize a silver pitcher and salver, given by the citizens, through the solicitation of Mr. Charles S. Kelley, now president of the Protecting Society. The trial was as follows: The truck starting from the corner of Pleasant and Market streets, ran to the north of Mechanics Hall, took a 30-foot ladder from the carriage, placed it against the building, one of the members mounted to the top, returned, and the ladder replaced on the truck in 42 seconds.

Aug. 13, 1877.—The Pioneers took an excursion to Rocky Point, as guests of Reindeer Hook and Ladder Co., of Fall River. Took with them, as guests, Assistant Engineer Judson and L. G. Hewins, Jr., Clerk of Board of Engineers.

Aug. 23.—Moonlight excursion to Mattapoisett, with the Reindeers and Steam Fire Engine Co., No. 4, of Fall River, and Contest, No. 3, of Fairhaven.

Aug. 4, 1877.—The new carriage, built by Joseph T. Ryan, of Boston, was received and put at once into commission. [It cost $1800 and is still in active use. The old apparatus was sold to the town of Middleborough.]

Jan. 24, 1883.—Mr. Charles H. Walker resigned his membership after a long service. [Mr. Walker was presented with a token of esteem. In 1862, September 1st, he resigned his position as foreman to go to the war, and was escorted to the station on the morning of his departure, Sept. 19, by the Pioneers.]

This branch of the fire service has always been an important one, and its record for usefulness is equally creditable with that of any other organization belonging to our fire department.

I mention a few happenings during these eventful years:

March 9, 1855.—Occurred the burning of Taber & Grinnell's rivet factory. Loss $6000.

July 3, 1855.—The Ohio, No. 3, records 186 feet as the result of a trial of the engine.

July 4, 1855.—During the morning, just as the grand procession had been formed, a fire broke out in the dwelling of the widow of the late George Howland, corner of Sixth and Walnut streets. It immediately communicated to the adjoining barns of Charles Taber and Capt. Robert Gibbs. A lively blaze ensued. The Tremont Engine Co., of Roxbury, who were in our city as guests, took their apparatus to the reservoir corner of Walnut and Sixth street, and worked like tigers, until the water gave out, when their position was changed to the Friends' Academy reservoir.

The following description of the engine trial, July 11, 1855, is from Mr. George B. Wilbour's records of Franklin, No. 10:

July 11, 1855.—The postponed trial of engines, appointed for the 4th of July, came off this morning in the presence of a large crowd of spectators on Market square. The exhibition was spirited and exciting, but was conducted with great harmony and with the best of feeling.

The first company that played was the

Ohio, No. 3.

1st trial—170 ft. 2d trial—170 ft., 10 in. 3d trial—172 ft.

Young Mechanic, No. 6.

1st trial—147 ft., 2 in. 2d trial—133 ft., 9 in. 3d trial—not played.

Hancock, No. 9.

1st trial—167 ft., 8 in. 2d trial—168 ft. 3d trial—166 ft., 4 in.

Franklin, No. 10.

1st trial—169 ft. 2d trial—170 ft. 3d trial—163 ft.

Oregon, No. 11.

1st trial—157 ft., 5 in. 2d trial—168 ft., 3 in. 3d trial—176 ft., 8 in.

Final results and best distances were decided to be in the following order:

Oregon, No. 11,	176 feet,	8 inches.	
Ohio, No. 3,	172 "	4 "	
Franklin, No. 10,	170 "		
Hancock, No. 9,	168 "		
Young Mechanic, No. 6,	147 "	2 "	

The engines drew their own water and played a horizontal stream through 150 feet of hose. The size of pipe used was about 13-16ths of an inch, except No. 6, she being larger than the others and was restricted to one inch stream. After the trial the companies adjourned to the City Hall, where the presentation of city plate was made by the municipal committee of the 4th of July. The first prize, a silver speaking trumpet, valued at $100, was presented to No. 11. The second prize, a silver trumpet, valued at $75, was given to No. 3. The third prize, a silver cup and salver, valued at $65, to No. 10. The fourth, a silver trumpet, value $55, to No. 9. The fifth, a silver pitcher, value $45, to No. 6; and to Pioneer Hook and Ladder Co. a silver pitcher, valued at $35, was presented. The whole affair passed off very pleasantly and satisfactorily to all concerned.

Jan. 7, 1856.—The oil and candle works belonging to Lawrence Grinnell & Co., were burned at 4 p. m. The streets were well-nigh impassable with huge drifts of snow, and the firemen experienced great difficulty in getting the machines to the scene.

Feb. 25, 1856, occurred the fire at Gifford & Topham's Copper Foundry, on Front street.

In order to curb and break up the racing spirit between Nos. 5 and 6, the Board of Engineers felt compelled to adopt the rule that only one of these engines should respond to an alarm, the other to wait until it was ascertained that its services were actually needed. The rule provided that they should alternate monthly in this arrangement. As might be expected, this movement did not prove popular. An amusing result of its enforcement, not anticipated by the authorities, was that whenever either engine was rolled from the house the opposition company would hook on to the Pioneer Hook and Ladder truck, and the racing was kept up. It wasn't quite so enjoyable but it was better than nothing.

The Pioneer enjoyed a reputation for awhile of having a very large and enthusiastic company. Some of my readers will recollect when this new side show came near proving a serious matter. It was on a Sunday afternoon when the No. 6 and the Hook and Ladder truck were returning from an alarm of fire in Fairhaven. The Pioneer, returning to the house (it occupied the centre, as the boys will recollect), ran up and by the building preparatory to backing in (having the right of way) as if nothing were there; but there was something there, it was No. 6, and vigorous pushing resulted in the rear end of the truck being lifted on top of the engine. The excitement at this moment was intense, and a vast concourse of people filled the street. It looked like a row, but it didn't come. Chief Engineer Ashley, aided by City Marshal Ingraham, soon brought the affair to a close, and the engines were housed in good order, barring a few scratches. The incident, however, was not without results, for its occurrence made many advocates for the steam fire engine, and was one of the many causes that brought about the change.

I present the full membership for 1856, in which year the hand-engine service was perhaps at its best:

Fire Department, 1856.

Chief Engineer, Zachariah Hillman.

Board of Engineers, George Perry, Robert C. Topham, James Durfee, George G. Gifford.

A fair picture of Citizen, No. 2.

Citizen, No. 2. (Acushnet Village.)

Foreman, Reuben Washburn.
Clerk, Edward P. Lund.

James S. Howard,	James Terry,
James Butler,	John McCagh,
Lemuel A. Washburn,	Howard Pittsley,
Thomas S. Potter,	L. M. Emerson,
Charles H. Potter,	George L. Hathaway,
Valentine Luce,	A. B. Grinnell,
Charles A. Cushman,	Arthur Ricketson,
Rodolphus S. Nye,	Samuel P. Burt,

Edward Spooner,
Francis Spooner,
George Collins,
Augustus Hathaway,
Seth Howard,
B. Ritter,
H. Matthews,
Charles D. Reynolds,
William Chase.

OHIO, NO. 3. (Purchase street.)

Foreman, Frederick P. Chase.
First Assistant, Albert M. Tallman.
Clerk, George W. Paine.

Warren Moore,
Henry B. Almy,
William H. Records,
Isaiah Wilson,
Augustus G. Shorey,
David Almy,
Ebenezer Pierce,
D. Barbour Angell,
Corban B. Lucas,
Joseph R. Hathaway,
George Mahan,
Samuel Hawes,
James Warren,
Timothy Blanchard,
John T. Sherman,
George Haskins,
Frederick P. Spooner,
Abner T. Case,
Franklin Taylor,
Isaac H. Barrows,
Albert Chadwick,
Richard T. Durfey,
John Barnett,
Abraham Bolles,
Edward Raymond,
William Carter,
Franklin Hammond,
Isaac Burgess,
Isaac Kenniston,
Andrew R. Turner,
Benjamin N. Luce,
James Gillespie,
Erastus Remington,
Alfred Spencer,
Sylvester Parlow,
Daniel V. Smith,
Edward S. Thomas,
Frederic Wood,
William Cower,
John Cook,
Samuel W. Richmond.

COLUMBIAN, NO. 5. (Purchase street.)

Foreman, John B. Hyde.
First Assistant, Pliny B. Sherman.
Second Assistant, Benjamin Weaver.
Clerk, Giles S. Fales.

George D. Bisbee,
Charles W. Keen,
Samuel C. Hart,
John F. Wood,
Eugene H. Gifford,
Charles A. Morgridge,
George T. S. Sears,
Joseph F. Gifford,
Perez Jenkins,
Henry B. Covell,
Thomas W. Cook,
Thomas Hilliard,
Christal Licht,
Otis Wilcox,
William A. Russell,
Charles H. Bisbee,
Nathan Maxfield,
Benj. F. Hayden,
Henry A. Wilcox,
Robert N. B. Doane,

Thomas Garvey,
Alfred Wordell,
Edwin P. Gage,
George G. Gifford,
Thomas Cross,
Francis Tuite,
Horace King,
Frederick Morse,
Edward S. Jenkins,
John Harrity,
Judson Tosier,
James F. Chase,
Adoniram Myrick,
Henry Morse,
Seth A. Wilcox,
David L. Hathaway,
James L. Wilber,
James H. Hood,
Hiram A. Davis,
Charles H. Booth,
William Gammell,
Peter Gobell,
Henry G. Strong,
William H. Holmes,
George Hinckley,
Andrew T. Wood,
Allen Raymond,
James Smith,
William Peckham,
William Love,
John Duffy,
Caleb A. Thomas,
Joel B. Arnold,
George R. Maxfield,
Michael Vhay,
William Gifford.

YOUNG MECHANIC, NO. 6. (Purchase street.)

Foreman, Nathan Barker.
First Assistant, Charles W. Dyer.
Second Assistant, J. Augustus Brownell.
Third Assistant, John Murdock.
Clerk and Treasurer, Sanford Almy.

William E. Watson,
William A. Church,
Thomas C. Allen,
Thomas C. Allen, Jr.,
Benj. R. Watson,
Joseph Hammond,
Thomas Dowden,
Jireh Tripp,
Jos. A. Landers,
Benj. F. Hinckley,
Roland R. Crocker,
Martin J. Lewis,
Clarfaus Vansant,
John J. P. Zettick,
Charles H. Underwood,
James M. Dooley,
Wm. H Sherman,
David Chadwick,
Warren G. Peirce,
Freeman C. Luce,
John McCoy,
Wm. Ricketson,
Wm. H. Allen,
Fred. A. Plummer,
Thaddeus Betz,
Christian Betz,
Edwin Betz,
Thomas Paul,
Wm. G. Denham,
William McKim,
James Patterson,
Daniel Ripley,
Bradford G, Potter,
George B. Devoll,
Warren Potter,
Gustavus H. Cushman,
Fred. Underwood,
Wm. D. Smith,
Edwin R. Baker,
Alex. McKenzie,
William Winslow,
Charles Perry,
William Neal,
Roland W. Snow,
S. A. Pierce,
Ira Milliken,

Henry Hazard,
Lorenzo D. J. Sears,
George M. Young,
Moses C. Vinal,
Charles G. Kempton,
Abm. S. Davis,
John E. Jones,
Thomas A. Cranston,
Leander T. Manchester,
James Munroe,
Andrew R. Lincoln,
Fred. Macy,
Benj. F. Soule,
William P. Sowle,
William H. Nichols,
Isaac W. Benjamin,
Hallett Hamblin,
Joseph H. Lawrence

PHILADELPHIA, NO. 7. (Fourth street.)

Foreman, Thomas L. Clark.
First Assistant, Daniel S. Eaton.
Second Assistant, Joseph Burt, Jr.
Third Assistant, Charles F. Brightman.
Clerk, George S. Bowen.

Robert T. Barker,
John C. Maul,
Allen Raymond,
Thomas Almy,
Thos. S. Palmer,
James Maguire,
David W. Wardrop,
Nathan Ellis,
Cornelius B. Tripp,
Stephen Robinson,
Benjamin Cole,
Albert Gray,
Leander F. Pease,
Wm. B. Cook,
Adam Brown,
Holder R. Tripp,
James A. Davis,
George Baylies,
John Sweeney,
Geo. H. Chase,
Benj. C. Warren,
Daniel McDonald,
Charles G. Jones,
Roland T. G. Russe
Robert McKay,
Fred. N. Stearns,
Wilson Pierce,
Nathaniel Pierce,
Jos. Allen, Jr.,
Henry Russell.

HANCOCK, NO. 9. (Foster street, near North.)

Foreman, Tillinghast P. Tompkins.
First Assistant, Samuel H. Mitchell.
Second Assistant, William James.
Clerk, Lazarus S. Moulton.

George A. Pool,
Joshua Bowman,
Amos F. Lovejoy,
Edwin Luther,
Joseph A. Parker,
John P, Caswell,
Robert Luscomb,
Lot Tripp,
Davis Johnson,
Nathaniel Jenney,
Silas Taber,
Henry Shiverick,
Wm. Huddy,
J. C. Haskins,
Hiram E. Small,
Samuel White,
Daniel Besse,
Joseph Hoyle,
Wm. F. James,
James Lowther,

Horatio N. Bly,
Charles Crocker,
Wm. C. Bassett,
Gilbert Winslow,
John Wrightington,
Abiel Winslow,
William Card,
William Hubbard,
George W. Perry,
Daniel D. Perry,
Mitchell Lowther,
Richmond Macomber,
Hervey H. Fish,
Joseph Lawton,
Benj. Crocker,
Charles H. Luther,
Allen Wilcox,
Richard Luce,
Warren W. Parker,
James H. Pease,
Geo. F. Lucas,
Edward Reed.

FRANKLIN, NO. 10. (Third street, head of Griffin.)

Foreman, Marshall G. Sears.
First Assistant, George W. Jennings.
Second Assistant, Andrew J. Jennings.
Clerk, George B. Wilbour.

William Gibbs,
L. S. Jennings,
W. H. Eldredge,
N. B. Colyer,
Robert S. Cornell,
Benj. F. Sowle,
Zach. Booth,
Albert W. Taber,
James M. Tripp,
Henry Moore,
William Booth,
L. W. Baker,
Elias Tripp,
Nathan Sears,
Job. W. Heath,
B. R. Jennings,
George Wilson,
Samuel Eldredge,
J. S. Conway,
George H. Tripp,
F. M. Chadwick,
E. L. Dexter,
Francis McShane,
Isaac C. Booth,
W. H. Jennings,
Bradford Sowle,
S. A. Colyer,
Stephen Haskins,
Charles H. Griffin,
Charles Russell,
Jesse V. Luke,
Charles M. Dedrick,
Gamaliel Moore,
John Allen,
Daniel Eldredge,
James Pike,
J. O. Fisher,
Charles Shields,
Benjamin W. Allen,
Bradford L. Church,
W. A. Dunbar,
S. H. Jennings,
W. H. Lothrop,
George Burger,
Gifford Haskins.

OREGON, NO. 11. (Middle street.)

Foreman, Henry H. Fisher.
First Assistant, W. J. Chadwick.
Second Assistant, Samuel S. Gifford.
Third Assistant, James S. Chase.
Clerk, Thomas P. Swift.

Gibbs Taber,
Richard W. James,
Franklin Nye,
Andrew Devoll,

William A. Weeden,
Joseph F. Roberts,
John H. Gray,
Daniel McLaughlin,
Alden Lawton,
George Shaw,
David Shepherd,
Luther Lemunion,
Thomas Peirce,
Charles Dyer,
James R. Chase,
James F. Macomber,
Matthew Russell,
Edward Lawton,
John Linton,
Frederick Miller,
Thomas Sweet,
Perry G. Potter,
David Potter,
George Devoll,
H. M. Kempton,
Thomas Manley,
C. A. Richmond,
George Maxfield,
Horace Macomber,
Daniel Babcock,
Peleg Blake,
John Tew,
Charles C. Hall,
Asa Buffington,
G. M. Maxfield,
George Chadwick,
Edward Osgood,
Abel Snell,
Abm. Hathaway,
Luther Atwood,
Alonzo Tripp,
William Hested.

PIONEER HOOK AND LADDER CO., NO. 1. (Purchase street.)

Foreman, Robert A. Dillingham.
First Assistant, Whitman Vinal.
Clerk, Nathan B. Gifford.

Holder Brownell,
David Hatch,
Lot T. Sears,
Elias Knowles,
James McKenney,
Benj. F. Fisk,
Christian Dantsizen,
James A. Davis,
John Hiland,
George Hatch,
George G. Peck,
David Palmer,
Stephen Wilber,
Frank Hews,
Jesse A. Palmer,
Russell Wood,
William Manley,
B. F. King, Jr.,
Wm. Goodnow,
M. L. Buffington,
C. W. Andrews,
Benj. Clifton,
John Savage,
Alden Brightman,

YOUNG AMERICA, NO. 8. (North Second street.)

Foreman, L. B. Ellis.
First Assistant, Matthias C. Pease.
Second Assistant, James W. Lawrence.
Third Assistant, James Kent.
Clerk, Alfred Osgood.

James C. Hitch,
George Walden,
Alex. H. Ellis,
Wm. H. Peacock,
B. F. Lowden,
Haile R. Luther,
Charles Bunker,
William B. Allen,
Chas. E. Maxfield,
George Allen.

C. E. Perry,
R. W. Murphy,
Benj. F. Lewis,
Edward B. Wilson,
Joseph C. Austin,
Charles Barnard,
Edward T. Wilson,
James Smith,
Alex. Doty.

THE VETERAN ASSOCIATION OF FIREMEN.

This company was composed of a number of persons who formerly belonged to different engine companies in the city, and now acted as a resevve. They had charge of the engine Mechanic, formerly belonging to company No. 6.

PROTECTING SOCIETY.

The members were special policemen when at fires or when alarms of fire occurred.

President, Henry P. Willis.
Vice-President, Charles Chandler.
Secretary, William C. Macy.
Directors, E. D. Mandell, Henry C. Kelley, J. F. Dearborn, William Tallman, Jr., Edward Russell.

George F. Barker,
Abm. Russell,
W. P. S. Cadwell,
Edmund Rodman,
Edward Knights,
George F. Kingman,
Charles Almy,
Henry Childs,
James P. Macomber,
Nathan Lewis,
Lemuel M. Kollock,
C. D. Stickney,
L. P. Ashmead,
Joshua C. Hitch,
G. D. Gifford,
C. W. Seabury,
Cornelius Davenport,
Jos. Buckminster,
W. G. Baker,
J. A. T. Eddy,
Charles Taber,
George Knights,
James Durfee, Jr.,
Jos. Plummer,
Sanford S. Horton,
Abm. Taber,
Nathaniel S. Cannon,
F. L. Porter,
Edwin Munson,
Gilbert Allen,
J. P. Knowles, 2nd,
Joseph Knowles,
William Leverett,
William Howe,
B F. T. Jenney,
Albert B. Corey,
J. W. Macomber,
R. W. Raymond,
Dennis Wood,
W. G. Wood,
M. A. Covell,
N. Lincoln, Jr.,
J. Barrell,
Charles H. Nye,
C. B. H. Fessenden,
W. H. Bartlett,
Alden Wordell,
Charles E. Hawes,

Alfred Wilson,	Ivory S. Cornish,
Thomas Russell,	Z. S. Durfee,
George W. Choate,	W. F. Durfee,
George L. Brownell,	Charles H. Gifford,
Stephen P. Haskins,	John J. Hicks,
W. K. Tallman,	J. F. Delaney,
George W. Howland,	Reuben Howland,
Taber Bowles,	Edward R. Gardner,
Ebenezer Hervey,	L. H. Morrill,

Sylvander Hutchinson.

The apparatus for blowing up buildings was under the control of the Board of Engineers. A red staff was the distinguishing badge of the engineers.

In 1856, the firemen were requested to wear at all fires badges made of white metal, with the designating figure of the company. Locks were put on all the engine houses, and each member of the department furnished with a key.

In 1857, rules were adopted to the effect that all companies should keep to the right when going to a fire, and no running was allowed in returning.

In 1858, the companies were frequently reminded from headquarters to more strictly obey orders.

Our readers will see the significance of the above extracts from the records of the Board of Engineers. They all reveal the excitement that prevailed.

TILLINGHAST P. TOMPKINS.

(Chief Engineer, 1858–1871.)

CHAPTER X.

THE Board of Engineers for 1856 consisted of:

Chief Engineer, Joshua B. Ashley.
Assistant Engineers, Tillinghast P. Tompkins, George Hinckley, Israel F. Bryant, Tilson Wood.
Secretary, J. Augustus Brownell.

1857.

Chief Engineer, Joshua B. Ashley.
Assistant Engineers, T. P. Tompkins, Thomas C. Allen,
Moses H. Bliss, John Mathews.
Secretary, J. Augustus Brownell.

1858-1859.

Chief Engineer, Tillinghast P. Tompkins.
Assistant Engineers, John Mathews, Moses H. Bliss,
George Hinckley, Thomas P. Swift.
Secretary, Charles M. Pierce, Jr.

1860.

Chief Engineer, T. P. Tompkins.
Assistant Engineers, John Mathews, George Hinckley,
Moses H. Bliss, Henry H. Fisher.
Secretary, C. M. Pierce, Jr.

On the evening of April 19th, 1856, occurred the celebrated Howland street riot, an event that must carry us back to the years 1826 and 1829, to find any parallel occurrence. It is somewhat remarkable that the conditions that brought about the riot are kindred to those of the two riots above mentioned. Our readers will remember in our description of those events that we found certain sections of our town infested with a dangerous class of citizens, occupying dwellings that were moral pest-houses, and with surroundings detrimental to the dignity and good order of our community. In each case a murder had been the prime cause that brought into existence the organized mob. In the riot we are now discussing we find a simple repetition of the same condition of things. So that we may have an intelligent knowledge of this affair, let us take a general survey of the place and the peculiar circumstances of the event.

Howland street is a short thoroughfare in the south part of the city, running east and west, parallel to and situated between Grinnell and Griffin streets, beginning at Acushnet avenue and running east to the river front. In the years gone by, and especially at the time of the riot. the eastern section was a noted resort for drunken sailors and evil-disposed persons.

Nor was this confined to Howland street, for South Water and other intersecting streets partook of the generally bad reputation. They abounded in dance halls, saloons, gambling dens and brothels. When our ships came in from their long voyages, these abodes of iniquity were in high carnival, fights and brawls were of frequent occurrence, and it was dangerous to pass through this section after nightfall. It was no uncommon circumstance for persons to be knocked down and robbed in this vicinity. Matters grew steadily worse and more uncontrollable, when the climax was reached in a murder.

Early on a Sunday morning a man coming out of Benj. Baker's fish market, then located at the foot of Howland street, discovered the body of a man close to the water's edge. Supposing that he was drunk, he called the attention of the bystanders to the danger of the incoming tide. What was their horror, on approaching the spot, to find the man dead; an ugly wound on his head showed with certainty that he had been foully dealt with. The investigation that immediately followed, under the direction of William O. Russell, coroner, revealed several startling facts: That the man had been murdered: that the crushing blow on the top of the head was the immediate cause of death: that the man had been seen in the house No. 17 Howland street the night before: that the track of blood from the spot on the shore where the victim was found was traced in direct and unbroken line to this same house. All this was brought out clearly and positively; but who did the deed, and under what circumstances, was never found out, at least by any official investigation. The name of the unfortunate man was Rogers, and he was a resident of the northwest section of the city.

Not long after this event, another body of a dead man was found in the "Long House," and, though no bruises were found showing violence, it was deemed necessary to have an inquest. The body was removed to the boat-builder's shop of R. C. Topham, where an investigation was held, but without any satisfactory results. My readers can easily understand how intense the feeling became after two such tragedies.

A thrill of terror went through the community as these dreadful occurrences became known, and they became the all-absorbing topic of conversation. But few days elapsed after the fruitless investigations, when the preliminary arrangements were commenced which ended in a most complete organized mob. Several meetings were held in which the plans were matured A triangular piece of white paper pasted about the city was recognized as a call to these gatherings. Whenever a red paper was posted it signified danger. The date first selected for the demonstration was April 5, but the affair was postponed because of the delay of the engineers in moving the old hook and ladder truck to the Second street house. The new truck, built by Joseph Brownell & Co., was to be placed in the engine house on Market street.

Let it be understood that the municipal authorities, with His Honor George Howland, Jr., at the head, were not lax in their efforts to maintain order; indeed his administration was conspicuous for the vigorous enforcement of law. And let me say in passing that the Howland street of 1890 is not the Howland street of 1856: far from it. A stroll through this thoroughfare one lovely evening recently revealed another scene than that of early days. With vivid pictures in mind of its condition in the rioting days, when the rookeries and gin shops were in full blast and the streets thronged with tipsy sailors and bold women, when the air was filled with sounds of ribald jest and profanity—deviltry, degradation and dirt reigning supreme,—with this panorama of the past before me, I walked leisurely through this street. New houses, new stores, good sidewalks; cleanliness and thrift everywhere; well dressed, well behaved, courteous people all along as I strolled down to the shore, crossing Water street to the noted "Marsh," where Mormon hall and the lesser temples of vice held high carnival in by-gone days. A group of good natured boys, who were having a jolly good time talking and laughing on the street emphasized the impression that it is comparatively sweet and pure. To be sure, here and there is a saloon with its suspicious surroundings, but even this seems compelled to have an air of decency and good order.

Just east of the house on the northeast corner of Howland and Second streets was a small, two-story house, No. 17. It was here that the murdered man, Rogers, was last seen alive. The occupants of the house were of the worst class, and the place was noted for being one of the vilest on the street. Through an alleyway on the east of the house and standing in the rear directly northeast stood what was known as the Long House, a large building occupied by similar characters and used for kindred purposes. On these two houses centred the demonstrations of the mob.

Several weeks before the riot the streets were filled with rumors in regard to something that was going to happen. At first it was not even hinted where or when. Not many days elapsed, however, before Jerry was announced as having arrived in town. That this character was no myth was soon demonstrated. My information regarding him and the organization of which he was the acknowledged head is of the most reliable character, and the facts relating to the finding of the murdered man on the shore were told me by the very man who made the discovery.

One morning our citizens were greeted with bits of red paper, posted everywhere through the city, bearing the significant words: "Fire! Fire! On Howland street! Paint your faces and look out for the police." This was an appeal to the more than three hundred members of the organization that the attack was to take place on the following Saturday night, April 19th. They met that evening on City Hall square, and, at an early hour, a party of the rioters took the old truck from the Second street house, proceeded to Howland street, and undertook to pull down the house, No. 17. Their efforts were unsuccessful, until about 9 o'clock, when a false alarm of fire was raised and brought the whole force and an immense crowd of people to the scene. The rioters now were in their greatest strength. They proceeded to the vicinity of the house, quickly stripped the carriage of the long hooks, and the work of demolition commenced. One of these hooks was thrust into the front window, another to the roof, the rioters manning the ropes, and surging, with heavy strain, the house began to come down. The Long House, in the rear, was the first to be set on fire, though both were soon in flames, and burning fiercely, while dense volumes of smoke filled the heavens. Jerry mounted the ridgepole of No. 17 and directed the operations.

A thrilling episode occurred when this building was entirely wrapped in smoke and flame. The roof fell in with a tremendous crash, carrying Jerry with it, and it was for some time supposed he had perished in the seething furnace. But he soon put in an appearance and continued to direct operations. The fire soon spread to the next building east, called the Block, but the damage here was slight. Any attempt on the part of the engines to play on either of the first two buildings was defeated by cutting the leading hose. The fire department was promptly on hand, but its operations were distinguished by its apparent stupidity and want of efficiency.

The Franklin, No. 10, was the first to arrive. Singular as it may seem the engine stopped directly over the reservoir cover and not a man could find it. Nos. 5 and 6 came tearing through the streets, anxious, of course, each to beat the other in getting first water, shoved their suctions under No. 10, got water and played on—no they didn't play on the fire, for the reason above stated. All the engines of the department were hindered from doing any service. The only instance where they were at all effective was in putting out the fire in the Block. The crowds of people were great, for the papers of the day mention the number as at least three thousand. The police were present, but were helpless in preventing the work of the mob; indeed, the mischief had been accomplished before they were present in any force.

The City Guards, Capt. Timothy Ingraham, were ordered out by the mayor, and marched to the scene, fully armed and equipped for serious work. They halted on Second street, near Howland, and awaited orders. By this time the rioters had dispersed, evidently satisfied with the work accomplished, and the Guards were not called upon for service. At midnight the crowds of people retired, and thus ended the famous Howland street riot. Several persons were arrested, but their cases never came to trial. The denizens of other notorious sections of the city were badly frightened, and during the night outposts were stationed to give the alarm should the mob be seen approaching. The city government took vigorous action to prevent further demonstrations of this character. The military were under arms for several weeks, and many of the engine companies were sworn in for special duty, but fortunately their services were not required.

I clip several items from the records of the companies:

April 26, 1856.—Oregon, No. 11.—False alarm of fire. Proceeded to Howland street: found no fire but plenty of police.

October, 1856.—Franklin, No. 10.—A beautiful pennant was presented to the company by Weston Howland, Esq. Resolutions of thanks were passed.

Jan. 21, 1858.—Fire at Fairhaven. Depot of the Fairhaven & Boston Railroad Co. burned. Engines 5, 7 and 9 went over and rendered effective service.

April 9, 1858.—William B. Cooke, Esq., presented Philadelphia, No. 7, a splendid gold-clasped Bible. The gift was received by Capt. Clark, who made an appropriate speech. The company passed a vote of thanks and also a resolution that a chapter should be read at every regular meeting. [The records show that this was faithfully carried out at this time. Church going seemed to be popular with the firemen.]

On Sunday, April 11, 1858, engine companies Nos. 1, 3, 5, 6, 7, 9 and 10 attended service at the Elm Street M. E. church, and listened to a sermon by the pastor, Rev. Henry S. White.

May 16.—Franklin Co., No. 10, attended Trinitarian church. Second sermon preached to firemen by Rev. Wheelock Craig. The Franklins mustered 62 men, including their volunteers. On June 10th they went to Allen Street church: sermon by Rev. John Howson.

In November, 1859, the Board of Engineers took the hose reel of the Franklin, No. 10, out of service for some slight repairs, supplying them with a spare reel for temporary use. At an alarm of fire on Nov. 26th the engines responded, and to the genuine surprise of the Franklins the Young Mechanics, No. 6, appeared with their hose reel. This raised their ire; and on returning to their house they appointed their officers a committee to wait on Acting Chief Hinckley for an explanation of the affair. They were informed that as the No. 6 reel was off for repairs the engineers ordered the Franklin reel to be attached to No. 6; and as the service was only a temporary one they declined the request of the committee to make any change. The sequel to this affair is given in the following extracts from No. 10's records:

Nov. 27th.—Alarm of fire at 9.30 o'clock P. M., caused by a fire in the Market street school-house. Not much damage done. No. 6, first water. No. 10 was on hand and put down at the corner of Union and Fourth streets. The company, seeing their reel at the fire, took it and, assisted by their friends, succeeded in taking it to their engine, although No. 6 tried their best, assisted by the engineers and the Protecting Society, to prevent them. Some of the tallest specimens of pulling and hauling on record was witnessed at this fire. The reel was afterwards given up to the engineers and placed again with No. 6.

Nov. 28.—The company's hose reel was returned this afternoon and placed with the engine.

At half past one on the morning of April 18, 1859, fire broke out in the carriage factory of William A. Nash, in Mechanics lane. It spread with great rapidity and the building was soon enveloped in flames. The fire spread to the two stables of John M. Hathaway & Brother, on Elm street, thence to that of Messrs. Bailey & Hathaway. Our readers may well imagine the fearful condition of matters when these four buildings, filled with combustible materials, were in a raging, uncontrollable blaze. The heat was intense and almost unbearable. Fortunately the horses, 67 in number, were saved by cutting the halters and driving them from the buildings. They went prancing about town, free to go at their own pleasure. They were corralled when their owners had more leisure, in the morning. The fire worked rapidly to the west, and Andrew J. Dam's billiard saloon and bowling alley on Elm street was soon ablaze, as was also the two-story house next west, owned by Seth R. Thomas; also, Joseph Linton's blacksmith shop, L. G. Carpenter & Son's blacksmith shop, and the building west occupied by the same firm, second story by G. Tuckwell and Pierce & Co.—all these on the north side of Mechanics lane. On the south, Mechanics Hall, occupied by the City Guards and Union Boot & Shoe store, took fire and was badly injured, though not destroyed. The city library was in great danger, and the window casements on the north side were badly burned. The granite walls of the North Congregational church, on the east, stayed the progress of the fire in that direction. The entire loss of property was $27,000, on which there was an insurance of $9500. The conflagration was the work of an incendiary, who chose a place and time for one of the most disastrous fires our city ever experienced. The combustible nature of the buildings, with their contents, made favorable material for the terrible fire, and the only wonder is that the department was able to stop it when it did; for at the moment when the flames were fiercest the reservoir on City Hall square gave out, and four of the engines had to be moved to other points for water.

The Pioneer Hook and Ladder Company did great service at this fire in pulling down sheds, (there were a number that connected the stables) and in removing fences. Thirteen buildings in all were destroyed in this conflagration. The newspapers of the day speak in commendable terms of the work done by the fire department.

At noonday on August 24, 1859, the greatest fire in our local history, involving an immense loss of property, occurred on Water street, north of Middle. It was past twelve, an hour when the shops and streets were deserted, and the workmen were at dinner, when fire broke out suddenly in the engine room of William Wilcox's planing mill, on the east side of Water street, on the same spot where now stands Tillinghast & Terry's mill. The structure was of wood and, in an instant, was enveloped in flames. A strong southeast wind was blowing at the time, and the fire spread with great rapidity to the buildings north, leaped across the street, even before the alarm was given, taking all the shops on the west side of Water street clear to North street, and worked its way steadily westward to Second street.

Meanwhile, along the wharves the flames made steady progress, taking in their path all the buildings and their contents. Wilcox's lumber yard was now one dense mass of flame, and the condition of things at this time was appalling. But when the cargoes of oil stored in the vicinity of Richmond & Wilcox's wharf took fire, and the ship John & Edward, lying at the head of the dock, was absorbed in the destruction, the flames enveloping the entire vessel, and leaping upward to the top of the masts, the scene was one of awful impressiveness. The oil, at this point, as it ran from the wharf into the dock, took fire, and at one time the water for some distance out into the dock was covered with burning oil, forming literally a sea of fire. Several ships in this dock tied to the wharf had to be pushed out into the river in order to save them from destruction. At this juncture the writer took a boat and sculled up the river, through a sea of oil, for the vast numbers of oil casks had burst, and the contents ran into the river, covering it for a long distance to the depth of several inches.

The spectacle now presented was one of sublime grandeur. At the north, mountains of black smoke were rising, tinged at the lower edges, with the forked flames that rose from the burning oil, while in the foreground was the burning ship—at this moment in the last stage of destruction. At the south the burning lumber had reached its intensest heat, and solid masses of flame shot high into the heavens. In the intervening space were the standing chimneys, grim monuments of the frightful disaster, and the burning ruins of what but a few hours before had been hives of industry. Here and there might be seen groups of firemen at their work, defying the danger that beset them on every hand.

The houses on Second street were now in flames and the fire was spreading with fearful certainty to the north, promising to cut a path through the northwest section of the city: and without doubt it would have done so but for the decision of the authorities to blow up the building on the northwest corner of Second and North streets. This was quickly accomplished, and the stunning explosion that was heard in every part of the city was the announcement to the affrighted citizens that danger from that section was over. On the northwest corner of North Water and North streets were stored under seaweed 14,000 barrels of oil, valued at $200,000. To save this from destruction a number of citizens, armed with big brooms made of brush, thrashed out the burning cinders as they fell in great clouds. The fearful heat made this task almost unbearable, and yet pluckily they stood to the work and saved this large property. They were aided by the fire department who kept the seaweed wet.

The bursting of so many oil casks sent rivulets of oil in all directions, much of it into the river, much into every sunken spot, and ponds of pure spermaceti were formed in many directions. When the conflagration was under control the gathering of this oil became a lively business. Empty oil casks were at a premium and every sort of vessel that would hold liquid was brought into requisition. "Dipping ile" was a very profitable business and was well followed for a time, some persons getting as much as 40 barrels. It was subsequently bought by the oil refining factories at about 25 cents a gallon.

At nightfall the fire had spent its fury and apprehensions of any further disaster were allayed. Several engines were at work all night playing upon the ruins.

When the Daly building on Second street was blown up, Chief Engineer Tillinghast P. Tompkins was struck on the head by a falling timber, that cut a terrible gash through the scalp. It was feared for a time that the accident would prove fatal, but Mr. Tompkins soon recovered. He still walks our streets, vigorous in mind, though scarcely capable of standing the fearful strain of an equal responsibility to the one of that dreadful day. He was ably assisted in the arduous duties of the day by his assistants, Messrs. John Mathews, Moses H. Bliss, George Hinckley and Thomas P. Swift. Our readers can understand how strong the wind was blowing, when I mention the fact that burning embers were found two miles away to the northwest.

An "oil dipper" fell off the floating logs at Beetle's spar yard and, as the oil was several inches deep on the surface of the water, he was pretty well "done in oil" before he could be slid to a place of safety.

Ships Illinois, Congaree and Cowper, lying in the docks, were slightly damaged by fire, but were towed out of danger by tugboat Spray. The occasional explosion of the bomb-lances was terrific and the reports were like those of artillery on the battle-field.

The following buildings were destroyed: William Wilcox's steam planing mill, loss $14,000, no insurance; Thomas Booth's sash, door and blind manufactory, upper story, loss $1500, no insurance: Ryder & Smith's building and spar yard, totally destroyed, loss $3000, no insurance: Thomas Booth's carpenter shop, loss $1000; all these were on the east side of Water street. The flames now crossed the street and burned Hayes & Co.'s mill for dressing staves, loss $2500, no insurance; the second story was occupied by Charles and Edward Bierstadt, turning and sawing shop, loss $1000, no insurance; the building next north was Warren Hathaway & Son's,

JOHN MATHEWS.

(Assistant Engineer, 1857-1871.)

manufacturers of whaling apparatus, mincing machines, etc., loss $7000, insurance $2600; in the rear was a blacksmith shop, entirely destroyed. In these buildings was a large lot of bomb-lances that exploded during the progress of the fire, creating much alarm among the people: next north, building occupied by Howland & Coggeshall, storage of casks: second story, carpenter's shop, G. & C. Brownell, loss $400. The flames then attacked the lumber yard, sheds and buildings belonging to Thomas Booth, loss $8000, no insurance: John D. Hursell, paint shop, in upper story of building, loss $1200, no insurance. Next in order came the large three-story building on the corner of North and Water streets, occupied by Nathaniel H. Nye, ship chandler; second story, counting rooms of Messrs. Wilcox & Richmond, B. B. Howard, Edmund Maxfield, Russell Maxfield and David B. Kempton; third story occupied by Charles Searell, rigger; loss on building $3000, Mr. Searell $500, no insurance. To the west of the machine shop of Messrs. Hathaway was the cooperage of Howland & Coggeshall. Their entire loss was $3000, no insursurance. Near this were two other small dwellings that were destroyed.

The fire still continued to spread to the west. The engineers blew up the building on Second street at 1.30 o'clock belonging to Dennis Daly. This effectually stopped the fire from going southerly. The next building destroyed north of Daly's was the house belonging to Stephen N. Potter, loss $3000, no insurance. Then came the large cooperage of Hayes & Co. It was entirely destroyed, loss $8000, no insurance. Following this a dwelling house owned by Wilcox & Richmond, loss $1200, no insurance. Next, southeast corner of Second and North streets, fish market of Gardner & Estes, loss $400, insured. The fire then extended to the west side of Second street and destroyed a dwelling owned by Mrs. Ezra Smith, loss $3000. Next, on the same side, a house on the southwest corner of North and Second streets, owned by D. R. Greene, loss $4000, insurance $2200. At 2 o'clock the engineers blew up the dwelling house of Mrs. Joseph Maxfield on northwest corner of North and Second streets, loss $1500.

The above, embracing about twenty buildings, were destroyed, and a large number of sheds, etc., and 8000 barrels of oil. The entire loss, as recorded in the books of the Board of Engineers was $254,575, with but $6975 insurance.

This was the most disastrous conflagration our city ever experienced: and what made it especially sad was that the loss fell with such terrible force upon a class of our most industrious and worthy citizens, many of whom saw all the hard earnings of years in a few hours entirely obliterated. Some not only lost their business, but their homes even were sacrificed in the great disaster.

Columbian Engine Co., No. 5, was in Newport on an excursion when this fire took place.

Hardly had the embers died out before there came an imperative demand by the citizens for a more adequate protection of our city. The newspapers took up the appeal, and "steam" became the popular cry. The hand engine service fought the battle for all it was worth, but without avail; the beginning of the end had come. The scoffs and jeers of the multitude of friends of the fire department under the old regime could not stay the tide of progress. The steam fire engine rolled into town one day, only a few months later. In less than a year following its advent, the hand engines began, one after another, to go out of service, and the number of steam fire engines increased.

CHAPTER XI.

WE have now reached the period (1860) when a new departure was made, and new methods introduced, that effectually overturned and displaced the service that had been held in high esteem, and around which had clustered the all-absorbing interest and public spirit of generations: a service that had brought within its sphere the very best elements of our community. Admitting all the weaknesses and blemishes peculiar to the hand service, our citizens cannot but be proud of the record. Its history is the history of the personality of New Bedford. Mention the name of any citizen distinguished in his day for enterprise, business capacity, broad common sense, and sterling character, and the chances are more than even that his name will be found recorded among the firemen.

What changes have taken place since the primitive machine, built by Newsham, in London, in 1772, was brought to the village of Bedford! How amused we are to read of the Bucket Brigade; but was it not equal to the demands of its day? Indeed, has not every improvemant been called into existence by the peculiar demand of the age? Was not the appalling conflagration of Aug. 24, 1859, the voice that cried aloud for advance in protective methods? Did not steam come to the front from the imperative demand of the exigencies of that experience?

In less than ten days after this awful calamity an order passed the city government—not without fierce opposition—for the purchase of the first steam fire engine, Onward, No. 1. It was built by the famous Amoskeag Mfg. Co., of Manchester, N. H.; it had rotary pumps and was equipped with the best inventions of its day, but would compare unfavorably with the machines of the present.

A company was organized Jan. 2, 1860, as follows:

Foreman, Tilson B. Denham.
First Assistant, William H. Sherman.
Second Assistant, Gideon Wing.
Clerk, Edward S. Taber.

Atwood Holmes,
Joseph G. Dean,
Ephraim Chaney,
Caleb T. Jenney,
William Cook,
Robert T. Barker,
Lewis C. Rodgers,
Charles H. Wood,
Charles Burbank,
Thomas J. Gifford.

It was arranged, in case of fire, to use horses from the city stables. The steamer arrived in February and was placed in the brick building on the northeast corner of Pleasant street and Mechanic's lane.

But a few days following the arrival of the Onward, a fierce fire broke out on the northwest corner of Middle and North Second streets, burning Pollard & Myrick's cooperage and several other buildings, entailing a loss of $8400, with an insurance of $2200. The fire department responded with its usual promptness. Much interest was centered upon the Onward, which was worked for the first time. It was taken to Parker's wharf and, after some delay in furnishing leading hose, put a stream on the fire that soon made havoc with the flames and proved an eye-opener to many who had heretofore been prejudiced against the new invention. The service of the engine was powerful and steady, revealing to a marked degree the staying quality of its work when once in operation.

In October the following permanent organization was completed and entered into regular service:

Foreman, William H. Sherman.
First Assistant, Gideon Wing.
Second Assistant, William Cook.
Clerk, George Kempton.
Engineer, Charles H. Wood.
Hostler, Benj. F. King.

Thomas J. Gifford,
Henry T. Southwick,
T. M. Grew,
Richard Bennett,
J. S. Southwick,
J. L. Luce,

C. W. Brownell,	W. O. Sullivan,
T. D. Dexter,	C. E. Doty,
J. B. Tripp.	George G. Gifford,

Robert T. Barker.

On the afternoon of March 17 the first contest and trial between hand and steam occurred. The Columbian, No. 5, built by Button, and Young Mechanic, No. 6, built by Jeffers, were selected to champion the hand engine service. The steamer Onward was stationed on the wharf at the foot of North street and drew water from the river. The two hand engines were placed at the corner of North and North Second streets. Two lines of hose, each of 500 feet length, were laid from the steamer, the open butts being placed in the hand engines. The latter played through $1\frac{1}{8}$ inch nozzles.

The preparations for the struggle had been made with great care, both companies striking hands in this competition to bring victory. Each appeared with a full complement of men, all imbued with an earnest desire to beat their common enemy. At the command of Chief Tompkins the steamer commenced work, the hose began to fill, and the water began to flow. The Columbian and Young Mechanic, with their brakes filled with their most athletic men, began to "break her down" in good earnest, and the contest was now under way. The streets were blocked in all directions with an immense crowd of people, all having an intense interest in the issue of the hour. The partisans of the Fives and Sixes for once united their voices in the common cause, and our readers may well imagine that matters were decidedly exciting. The steamer let on its power gradually until the fullest capacity was entered; and such torrents of water flowed from the butts as to suggest a miniature Niagara broken loose. The boys, meanwhile were paying strict attention to business, and the rapidity of stroke increased. "Wake her! Shake her!" was the cry. Wake and shake her they did to their utmost power. Could the steamer wash both engines? was the important question to be decided.

The contest continued for 30 minutes without cessation. The result was that the Columbian was washed, and while the Young Mechanic once or twice drained the supply, yet the struggle was on the whole decidedly in favor of steam.

The next trial was to place the No. 6 on Purchase street, the steamer to be supplied through 1100 feet of hose, and the Young Mechanic to play through 500 feet and to use 1¼ inch nozzle.

Steamer and hand engine entered the contest with vigor, which resulted in the latter using up the supply several times and then calling for more. How the boys yelled with delight, threw their hats in the air, cheered each other, cheered themselves, and made the welkin ring with their noisy demonstrations! The Fives were as pleased as the Sixes, and the Sixes were wild with joy. After the trial they took their machine to the Pleasant street reservoir and played a stream above the church steeple. They cheered themselves hoarse and took their machine home, proud of their achievements. The Columbians took their engine to the Fourth street reservoir and played three solid streams over Pierian Hall. This performance was deemed much more satisfactory than any previous trial. The Columbians rolled their machine home, more proud of it even than when it made such a splendid record in Salem. Both companies were deservedly proud of their engines. They were alike fine representatives of the best manufacturers in the land.

But let us turn our attention to the second ringing of the fire bell, and see what was the practical result of the contest between hand and steam. We found that the Amoskeags had sent us an engine whose drawing and forcing powers were immense, surpassing anything ever shown before; that under ordinary demands it could furnish ample water supply from the river for two engines easily, and drive it to any part of the town; that in doing this work it didn't get tired; only give the engine plenty of food of the right sort, and it was good for an unlimited period of service. Our citizens saw a fire apparatus that, had it been available at the Kempton lumber-yard fire, would have furnished water in such quantity as to have saved enough property from destruction on that night alone to have paid for itself and all its equipments. They saw an engine that, could it have been in service at the Mechanics lane fire, would have without doubt kept the conflagration to the first four buildings destroyed. It was easy to see that this steamer would not require so large a force of men, and therefore in its economical bearing the advantages were in its favor. Slowly but certainly the conviction fastened itself upon the community that this new method of dealing with the fire fiend was to be the method of the future. Before many months passed the boys themselves began to read the hand-writing on the wall.

It is a significant fact that from the year 1860, when steam entered the city, we have had no extensive conflagrations within our limits. The experiences of 1859 have never been repeated. Fierce fires have occurrred, but they have been in almost all cases confined to the limits of one or two buildings. I do not overlook the Wall street fire April 1, 1887, when Kirby's paint mill was destroyed, when I make this statement. There never was a grander exhibition of the power of steam than at that wild conflagration.

June 6, 1860, occurred a stubborn and scorching fire in Nathan Chase's building, 141 Union street, extending northeast to building on Purchase street, occupied by Thomas C. Allen, and Little & Allen.

Nov. 5, 1860, the building on the corner of Union and Purchase streets, occupied by Thornton & Gerrish, was partially burned. Loss, $3000.

May 21, 1860, Philadelphia Engine Co., No. 7, was disbanded by the City Government, and the machine withdrawn from service. It was also ordered that the Columbian, No. 5, should be removed to the house on Fourth street, vacated by the Philadelphia. The company did not relish this action, and on the evening of Sept. 24th voted to disband.

The Board of Engineers proposed to use the Central House for the steamers, arranged to remove Young Mechanic, No. 6, to the north of Maxfield street on Purchase, to the house of Ohio, No. 3, and also to change its name. The latter was not done, but the company disbanded Oct. 1st.

While speaking of the hand-engines I will relate a true story regarding one of our old machines. In the days of the excitement following the gold discovery in California in 1849, many of our citizens joined the great army that went from all sections of the country to the Land of Gold. I well remember a meeting of a party of these adventurous spirits being held in my father's cooper shop on Sixth street, one summer evening, to make their arrangements to go on the voyage round the Horn in the ship Pleiades. What wonderful stories they told of that marvellous country; what visions of wealth possessed the whole party; how easily fortunes were to be realized. As I listened to the discussion, my youthful imagination pictured their return laden with nuggets of gold as big as pumpkins. It was easy to believe that the casks they were to fill with bread and meat, and the boxes packed with mining utensils, would be returned filled with sparkling gold. How I wished that I were a man, that I might join the expedition! Somehow my imagination didn't include a long, tedious voyage, dreadful seasickness, privations and want, bitter disappointment at the last, and heart-sickness, that brought many of these brave men to a final resting-place on the Pacific slope. No, I thought only of a pleasant voyage, smooth seas, piles of gold strewn by the wayside, a few months away from home, then to return loaded down with riches. I doubt whether my boyish fancies were much wilder than those of the men who gathered that evening in the old cooper shop. But I started out to tell a story. One evening a fire broke out in the then primitive city of San Francisco, and as every man in those days was bound to perform the duties of a fireman, a citizen who was from New Bedford rushed out of his house and took his place on the brakes of a little hand-engine that had found its way from the Atlantic coast. After a long spell at the work it occurred to him that the working of the machine seemed familiar, and as the flames from the conflagration would occasionally lighten up the streets, it dawned upon him that he had seen the engine before. His curiosity prompted him to leave the brakes and look at the engine. What was his pleasant surprise to read on the tower "Phœnix, No. 4." Our old machine with its tail cut off, just as it had been when a part of the New Bedford Fire Department; and he had been a member of the company before he left home. For Auld Lang Syne, he took his place again at the brakes and rather surprised his companions with the vim he put into his work for a while. It was like meeting an old friend.

The disbandment of these companies practically closed the interesting career of the hand-engine service. New companies were formed in their new locations for the Nos. 5 and 6. I give the full roll of membership when organized. With Nos. 10 and 11, they continued in commission for a few years, but were retired when the steam force became sufficiently strong to protect the city.

COLUMBIAN ENGINE CO., NO. 5. (Fourth street.)

Foreman, Lysander W. Davis.
First Assistant, Allen Almy.
Second Assistant, John Colwell.
Clerk, Charles H. Bisbee.

Sylvester Paul,	John W. Footman,
George W. Hunt,	Clarfaus Vansant,
Edward Dugan,	Alfred Weaver,
James H. Hood,	Charles Brightman,
Daniel Pollock,	Rufus Randall,
Patrick McDonald,	John E. Brown,
Patrick Carroll,	Barney Kenney,
Luther S. Brownell,	Charles Parker,
William P. Howland,	Robert C. Topham,
Charles Thomas,	Frederick B. Davis,

Isaac H. Barrows,
George M. Ennis,
John W. Ennis,
Davis Standish,
Peter Gobell,
Richmond M. Taber,
Joseph Vincent,
Nathan Brooks,
Lewis H. Cable,
Edward Cavanagh,
John Duffy,
Hugh McDonald,
Patrick Murphy,
Jesse V. Lake.

The company continued in active service until June 19, 1866, when it was disbanded. The engine was afterwards sold, and is now in Galesburg, Ill.

YOUNG MECHANIC ENGINE CO., NO. 6. (Purchase street, north of Maxfield.)

Foreman, George W. Paine.
First Assistant, John A. Gifford.
Second Assistant, William H. Dammon.
Third Assistant, Job H. Gifford.
Clerk, George P. Reed.

Alexander C. James,
Robert Allan,
Alonzo Whitney,
Joseph Haffords,
Isaac Jennings,
James Thompson,
Charles H. Booth,
Edward J. Thomas,
J. H. Wilcox,
George T. Haskins,
Gideon L. Taber,
Ephraim G. Kempton,
Andrew Donahue,
Nathaniel Baker, Jr.,
John Clemons,
William T. King,
Clark Leavitt,
William Gifford,
James G. Harding,
Philip H. King,
Thomas S. Pierce,
Sabin P. Chamberlain,
Cyrus Taber,
Stephen E. Parker,
Robert McKay,
Corban B. Lucas,
S. E. Gabriel,
Henry Watson,
Jâmes Chase,
Fred. A. Mickel,
Samuel H. Mitchell,
A. McDonald,
James L. Warren,
Palmer Brown,
David D. Almy,
Thomas L. Bryant,
Samuel Barker,
Michael Sheehy,
James Duddy,
Benjamin Hillman,
William James,
Philip Tripp,
Henry B. Almy,
Robert Nelson,
Davis Kelley,
John Sawyer,
Bradford Sherman.

The new organization continued in service till Feb. 1, 1866, when the company was disbanded by the Board of Engineers, and the Mechanic taken out of commission. It was soon after sold to the town of Middleborough, and at the present time is owned in Mattapoisett.

Progress Steam Fire Engine, No. 2, was soon ordered, and a company was organized Oct. 27, 1860, as follows:

Foreman, Joseph Hammond.
First Assistant, James Dwyer.
Second Assistant, Francis Currier.
Clerk, Leonard B. Ellis.
Engineer, Lewis Rogers.
Fireman, David W. Howland.
Hostler, Charles F. Allen.
Driver, George W. Jenkins.
Torchmen, Stephen Hammond, John Fuller.

John E. Brown, Charles A. Washburn,
Martin J. Lewis, Benjamin F. Lewis,
William P. Sowle, Warren W. Parker,
James P. Prior.

The Onward and Progress were placed in full commission—in the Central engine-house—at the close of the year 1860, and the beginning of the age of steam commenced. Its growth was rapid and but few years elapsed before the force was ample to protect the city thoroughly in any emergency. The remnants of the hand service soon disappeared and vanished forever. But for the presence of Hancock, No. 9, in our Fourth of July processions, the present generation would have little to remind them of that most interesting period in our local history, when the hand engine service was in its greatest glory.

During the year 1858 the department was called out 79 times; there were 42 fires: 37 false alarms.

1859—Called out 72 times: 32 fires; 38 false alarms; 2 fires out of the city.

1860—Called out 87 times; 51 fires: 26 false alarms: 10 fires out of the city.

1861—Called out 29 times: 26 fires: 3 false alarms.

1862—Called out 31 times; 29 fires: 2 false alarms.

1863.—Called out 23 times; 23 fires; no false alarms.

1864—Called out 32 times; 30 fires; 2 false alarms.

The above statistics, taken from the official records of the Board of Engineers, are very significant, and tell their own story. My readers will see how rapidly the whole fire service merged into another atmosphere from that which had characterized it under the old regime. Business methods at the very outset were put in operation, and were improved upon as time advanced, until the system was quite as perfect as that of any of the important business corporations of our city.

The Board of Engineers for 1861 consisted of:

Chief Engineer, Tillinghast P. Tompkins.
Assistant Engineers, John Mathews, Moses H. Bliss,
Henry H. Fisher, William Cook.
Clerk, Charles M. Peirce, Jr.

1861–63.

The same, with William H. Mathews, Clerk.

1864–65–66–67.

Chief Engineer, Tillinghast P. Tompkins.
Assistant Engineers, John Mathews, Moses H. Bliss,
Henry H. Fisher, Frederick Macy.
Clerk, Charles M. Peirce, Jr.

Jan. 18, 1861, Hancock, No. 9, was transferred to the Head of the River, and the Citizen, No. 2, that had done service in this part of the town, was withdrawn and sold.

Late in the afternoon of Jan. 2, the city was startled by a terrific explosion, soon followed by the cry of "fire" and ringing of bells. From Fish Island arose dense clouds of smoke and flame that proceeded from the buildings of the Petroleum Oil Co., which were totally destroyed. A sad feature of this conflagration was the tragic death of two of the employes—David Welch and Michael Downey, and the injuring of several others. One of these men was lighting the factory and passed through one room into the other leaving the door open. At this moment naphtha was being run from the stills, and it is supposed that a draft of air brought gas in contact with his light, and the explosion took place, blowing up the buildings, and setting everything instantly in flames. The bodies of the victims were found terribly burned. The loss of property was $5350.

May 18, about quarter past eight in the evening, the carriage sheds of the Friends' meeting-house were set on fire. Damage slight. No. 10, first water.

At 6 o'clock, July 4, 1861, a trial took place on Market square between Franklin, No. 10, and Oregon, No. 11. Each played through 150 feet of hose with the following result: Franklin, No. 10, 180 feet, 10 inches; 185 feet, 9 inches; 170 feet, 4 inches. Oregon, No. 11, 166 feet, 5 inches; 165 feet; 164 feet, 8 inches. A large crowd witnessed the trial.

Sept. 21, a big blaze took place in East Fairhaven, near the railroad, in which the Keystone oil works were destroyed.

The records of the fire department during this and the following year show many withdrawals of members who enlisted in the army for the war of the rebellion.

Jan. 29, 1862, a large fire broke out in the building 111 Union street, occupied by Almy & Swain, hardware dealers, and Warren W. Parker, sheet iron worker. The flames extended to the next building west, occupied by Joseph Hicks' clothing store, the building at the east, occupied by Israel F. Parsons' book store and printing office, Davenport & Mason's express and Peleg Howland's hardware store. Loss, $16,380; insurance $12,880.

April 3, 1862, a fire broke out at twenty minutes of five in the morning in Nathan Chase's building, on Purchase street, opposite the Stone church. It originated in the armory, on the third floor and burned down into the dressmaking rooms of Miss Cordelia Raymond. The rooms in the second story, occupied by Dr. C. L. Spencer and Charles E. Fales, ambrotypist, were deluged with water, as were the stores on the first floor, occupied by B. W. Pierce, books and stationery, E. Wilson, confectioner, and H. Wilkinson, auctioneer.

Sunday afternoon, April 6, 1862, Simeon Doane's house, on the Point road, was destroyed. At this fire the hand engines Nos. 10, 6 and 11 rendered the only service. Capt. George Wilson, of the Franklin, who was on his way to church when the alarm was given, lost his best suit of broadcloth because of his plucky action in performing service that one of his officers hesitated to do. Capt. Wilson was thoroughly drenched with water and ruined his best clothes.

Several funny things happened at this fire that may be told now. Among the neighbors who responded to the call for assistance was Mr. Nathan S. Ellis, an old fireman, for many years a member and clerk of Philadelphia, No. 7, an enthusiastic citizen and kind neighbor. At this fire he paid especial attention to details in removing the goods. Some of his acts served as a permanent subject for joke for many years, and are not laid entirely on the shelf to-day. Mr. E. rushed into the pantry, carefully emptied a number of earthen dishes filled to the brim with milk, and threw every one of them out of the window, each being broken in its fall; but the milk was saved anyhow. In the front hall stood a massive hall rack, built of iron, so solid that it would have required the intense heat of the furnace to melt it. Among the many pieces of valuable furniture he was instrumental in saving from destruction, Mr. E. didn't neglect this rack, but heroically tugged it across the lawn to a place of safety. None would laugh more heartily over these episodes than did neighbor Nathan. The family cat, a great favorite with the children, was thrust hastily into a capacious apron, the ends gathered up, and was transported in quick time to a neighbor's. No catastrophe happened to that cat.

April 7th, 1862, a fire in the brick building of the Cordage Co. on Court street. Loss, $4000. Insured.

There were eight fires during the month of April,—three of them of incendiary origin.

Oct. 5th, 1862, at 1 o'clock A. M., a fierce fire occurred on Purchase street just north of Middle, in William G. White's carriage factory, which was destroyed, with James M. Tripp's blacksmith shop. Several other buildings were partially burned. There was a strong gale from the southwest blowing at the time, and but for a heavy rainfall the conflagration would have been much more disastrous.

Early on the morning of Oct. 24th. 1862, a fire broke out in the clothing house of John Cunningham, 45 Union street, spreading rapidly to the adjoining buildings on the west, occupied by Charles Taber & Co. The inflammable character of the buildings made an intensely hot fire, and the upper stories were quickly destroyed. A most distressing accident occurred, resulting in the death of a well-known citizen and in the injury of several others. A number of the members of the Protecting Society were engaged in the removal of goods from one of the upper rooms in the Taber building, when without warning the blazing roof and the attic floors fell in with a crash. In a moment the whole kindled into a seething mass of flames. It is a marvel how any of the firemen were able to clear themselves from this frightful situation, but all escaped without serious injury except Mr. Henry C. Kelley, vice-president of the Protecting Society, who was rescued in a most appalling condition, his face and hands being burned in a frightful manner, besides internal injuries. He was at once removed to his home, and everything done to alleviate his sufferings. He lingered for two weeks, and died on Nov. 9th. The Protecting Society furnished a corps of watchers, made generous gifts of a practical nature, and performed many acts of kindness that were highly creditable to themselves. Mr. Kelley was father of the present president of the society, Mr. Charles S. Kelley. He was held in high esteem and respect by all who knew him, and his untimely death was regretted by the entire community.

The year 1863 was an unfortunate one for the soap manufactories, two being burned: one on May 14th, belonging to Richard Wilson, at Jesseville, with a loss of $3550; insurance $3200. On Sept. 15th, Burgess' soap works, on Ray street, were destroyed, with a loss of $5500; insurance, $4000.

This year was remarkably free from serious conflagrations, the entire loss being but $14,985, with an insurance of $10,950.

At 1.30 A. M., on Feb. 10, 1864, fire was discovered in the west end of Liberty Hall, which was quickly communicated

HENRY C. KELLEY.

(Vice-President of the Protecting Society. Died from injuries received at C. Taber & Co.'s fire, Oct. 24, 1862.)

to every part of the building, and the interior was quickly destroyed, with all the hall furniture, scenic properties, etc. The occupants of the stores, which were all burned out, were: Peleg Allen, merchant tailor; William Little, carpet dealer;

Hathaway & Keith, eating house; B. G. Wilson, undertaker; City liquor agency; Edward Wing, restaurant; Chas. Dehn, billiard rooms. In the third story, Messrs. Eaton & Smith, architects; William B. Topham, albumen paper manufacturer. The entire loss was $32,190; insurance $25,000. The fire raged with great fierceness and, at one time, promised to spread to the surrounding buildings. Immense clouds of smoke, flame and burning cinders rose into the sky, and illuminated the heavens for miles around. It was a stubborn fire and required consummate skill and pluck on the part of the fire department to keep it within the limits of the building. The wooden building on the southeast corner of William and Purchase streets took fire on the front cornices and would have been quickly in flames, but for the prompt service of Mr. Geo. S. Hoyt, late local manager of the Western Union Telegraph Co., who climbed to the roof and put it out himself. The steamers were kept in continual service for twenty hours before the fire was pronounced out. There is no question but the services of the steamers Onward and Progress at this conflagration saved a vast amount of property from destruction.

Hardly had the firemen rested from the exhausting labors of this fire, when the alarm sounded at 2.30 o'clock on the morning of Feb. 13th. William G. Blackler's barn on Anthony street had caught fire, and was speedily destroyed. The conflagration promised to be a serious one, for the flames spread to the barn of ex-Gov. John H. Clifford. The fire was soon under control, though the latter building was much injured. The spacious dwelling was in great danger from burning cinders which were carried from the burning barns.

I shall be pardoned if I relate an incident that occurred at this conflagration. It so happened that a masquerade party was being held that night at ex-Gov. Clifford's, in honor of one of his sons, who was at home for a few days from college. A number of his student friends were present at the entertainment. When the fierce conflagration broke out the festivities were suddenly brought to a stop, and all lent their willing aid to save the building from the flames. The exigencies of the hour called for prompt service, and there was no time for change of raiment. So they were soon carrying water to the roof, and laying wet blankets on the most exposed portions of the building. There were devils in red, devils in black, devils with forked tails, devils with horns, demons and hobgoblins, witches and spirits of the night, all eagerly at work. Here one with a pail of water mounted the ladder, passed it to a goblin, who threw its contents on the burning roof and then tossed the empty vessel to the ground, only to be caught on the fly by a mysterious witch, filled again by a red devil and returned. There may have been seen a party of goblins and witches tugging with a carpet, which they soon spread over the roof, furnishing more work for the mysterious water carriers to keep it wet. Now look and see a troop of these wild masqueraders, who, leaping into an open window, appear suddenly on the roof, prancing and dancing about as if the carnival were prepared purposely for their enjoyment. The bright flames from the raging fire were throwing their brilliancy upon the scene, giving it a supernatural effect, and suggesting a glimpse of the infernal regions. It had this effect upon Clerk Paisler, of the steamer Onward, who, running along Cottage street, passed the residence of Capt. J. C. Delano, which in those days was surrounded by a high fence, back of which was a tall and almost impenetrable hedge. This shielded from his view the vividness of the flames, till he suddenly emerged from under the hedge into open space. Here before him were rolling clouds of flame and smoke, mounting high into the heavens, below them the burning buildings, now one solid mass of fire. To the sound of crackling timbers and falling walls, the fantastic group of hobgoblins, witches and devils, were cavorting about the roofs of the Clifford mansion. The scene,—weird, wild and wanton,—was too much for our friend, though his education had been among the mysticisms of German folk lore. He brought himself to a sudden stop and involuntarily exclaimed, "Gracious Heaven, I've run myself into sheol!" (This word was not in use in those days, and so he used its equivalent.) Slowly he recovered from his surprise; the

CHARLES S. PAISLER.

(State Commissioner of Firemen's Relief Fund, 1890.)

approach of the Onward brought him fully to himself, and, as he said, he entered into the duties of the hour and soon mingled with devils, demons and witches of the night, with as much familiarity as though they were kindred spirits.

In 1864 the Excelsior steam engine, No. 3, was ordered, and held as a reserve for some time. The Young Mechanic Co., No. 6, was disbanded Jan. 29, 1865, and a company for the Excelsior was formed from her ranks.

Foreman, Joseph Hafford.
First Assistant, Job H. Gifford.
Second Assistant, William T. King.
Clerk, George P. Reed.

John C. Damon,	Samuel Thompson,
John W. Walker,	Martin Blanchard, Jr.,
Henry K. Paine,	Joseph T. Hafford,
Isaiah Wilcox,	Henry M. Gifford.

The brick buildings formerly occupied by Oregon, No. 11, and Young Mechanic, No. 6, were taken down, and the material was used in the new building and stable for the Excelsior on the northwest corner of County and Hillman streets.

April 23, 1864, a disastrous fire occurred in Fairhaven, the paint shop of Messrs. Purrington & Taber, and some twenty other buildings, being wholly or partially destroyed, the loss amounting to about $10,000. Many valuable volumes of the early town records were burned in this fire.

Dec. 10, a large fire occurred on Cheapside, corner of William street, buildings owned by the Cummings estate.

Nov. 10, another large fire occurred in Snell's Bakery, northwest corner of Water and William streets.

The annual report of the Board of Engineers for 1864–5 showed the department as being prosperous, well organized, and very efficient. The fire loss was $13,630: insurance, $5650.

Feb. 5, 1865, the Congregational church at the Head of the River was burned. Loss, $2500.

April 24, the works of the New Bedford Oil Co., foot of South street, were burned. Loss $3000.

July 8, fire in Josiah Dexter's store, 40 Purchase street. Loss $1700.

Oct. 26, still house and stock of the New Bedford Oil Co., Fish Island, burned. Loss $1780.

Nov. 18, Kirby's paint mill, on Eddy's wharf, burned. Loss $2200: insurance $2000.

The Contest Steam Fire Engine Co., No. 3. of Fairhaven, was organized April 5, 1865, with the following membership:

Foreman, Andrew M. Braley.
First Assistant, George Clark.
Second Assistant. John A. Dexter.
Clerk, Nathaniel P. Fish.

James G. Card,	John P. Ellis,
Calvin Hackell,	E. Eldredge,
George Miller,	G. F. Eldred,
William E. Eldred,	C. Grinnell,
John Dexter,	Thomas Hanna,
Martin Westgate,	Robert Hanna,
Thomas H. Bowen,	Alfred Jones,
Patrick Quirk,	John Quirk,
Edwin Jenney,	William Rounsville,
Stephen Westgate,	John Sampson,
James Severance,	James D. Stetson,
William Bowen,	Joseph Smith,
B. H. Butler,	J. P. Perry,
John Brown,	David Jenney,
Ebenezer Boyden,	William Webb,
Luther Cole,	Henry Waldron,
Charles Cannon,	B. Wilcox, Jr.
E. Copeland,	Philip Westgate,
Charles F. Stetson,	Benj. Westgate,
C. F. Perry,	David Shepherd,
William Macomber,	Stephen Hutchins,
Alexander Pierce,	Edward Manchester,
John Wilcox,	B. Wilcox,
James E. Card,	E. H. Sears.

Their engine, built by Jeffers, side brake, was exchanged for a steam fire engine May 1, 1869.

May 11, 1866, Seamen's Bethel partially destroyed. Loss $600.

Sept. 13, Greene & Wood's planing mill, Leonard's wharf, destroyed, with loss $4800.

Dec. 2, Trinitarian Church partially destroyed by fire. Loss $1225.

The annual report for 1865–6 speaks in praise of the harmonious action and zealous devotion of the department. Fire losses, $12,675; insurance, $6035.

HENRY H. FISHER.

(Assistant Engineer, 1861.)

CHAPTER XII.

THE following is a list of members of the fire department in 1867:

BOARD OF ENGINEERS.

Chief Engineer, Tillinghast P. Tompkins.
Assistant Engineers, John Mathews, Moses H. Bliss, Frederick Macy, Henry H. Fisher.
Clerk, C. M. Pierce, Jr.

Onward, No. 1.

Foreman, Charles H. Church.
First Assistant, Charles H. Brownell.
Second Assistant, Samuel H. Rulon.
Clerk, Charles S. Paisler.

James Devine,
James G. Harding,
Ephraim G. Kempton,
Clark Leavitt,
Peter Nelson,
Edward G. Tallman,
Abram R. Wood,
Albert P. Winslow,
James D. Allen.

Progress, No. 2.

Foreman, Franklin Shaw.
First Assistant, John E. Brown.
Second Assistant, William P. Sowle.
Clerk, Philip E. Colby.

John Downey,
Michael Dugan,
Charles L. Gifford,
Joseph Hammond,
Thomas B. Rowe,
William H. Miller,
Charles H. Phinney,
Loring T. Parlow,
Edward A. Sowle,
John Duffy.

Excelsior, No. 3.

Foreman, Joseph Hafford.
First Assistant, Job H. Gifford.
Second Assistant, M. Henry Gifford.
Clerk, George P. Reed.

Martin Blanchard, Jr.,
John C. Damons,
James Duddy,
Joseph T. Hafford,
William T. King,
Samuel Thompson,
John W. Walker,
Isaiah H. Wilcox,
Horace M. Plummer.

Cornelius Howland, No. 4.

Foreman, Abraham H. Howland, Jr.
First Assistant, Samuel C. Hart.
Second Assistant, Michael F. Kennedy.
Clerk, Giles G. Barker.

Andrew J. Brown,
George L. Jennings,
Charles E. Jennings,
James A. Murdock,
John Murdock,
Hugh McDonald,
James M. Tripp,
Clarfaus Vansant,
Charles F. Briggs.

HANCOCK, No. 9.

Foreman, Reuben Washburn.
First Assistant, Charles E. Howland.
Second Assistant, Edward C. Spooner.
Clerk, George A. Cobb.

Arthur C. Brooks,
Seth Hoard,
James H. Hathaway,
Joseph H. Lawrence,
Thomas W. Pierce,
William D. Perry,
David Turney,
Alfred Williams,
Leander Perry,
Reuben Ellis,
John Silva,
Jireh B. Gifford,
Charles H. Hathaway,
Thomas R. Hawes,
Samuel T. Patterson,
Sylvester Pratt,
Asa Reynolds,
Frank P. Washburn,
Charles Skiff,
Howard Pittsley,
William R. Washburn.

THE PROTECTING SOCIETY.

President, F. L. Porter.
First Director, Charles Chandler.
Second Director, Edward Russell.
Third Director, Edmund Rodman.
Fourth Director, Dennis Wood.
Fifth Director, George R. Phillips.
Sixth Director, David S. Bliss.
Secretary and Treasurer, William C. Macy.

William H. H. Allen,
Gilbert Allen,
Gideon Allen, Jr.,
Edward H. Allen,
Charles Almy,
Francis T. Aiken,
Samuel P. Burt,
William H. Bartlett,
George L. Brownell,
T. Frank Brownell,
Joseph Buckminster,
William P. S. Cadwell,
Charles S. Cummings,
Nathaniel S. Cannon,
Wendell H. Cobb,
Leonard B. Ellis,
C. B. H. Fessenden,
H. A. Gifford, Jr.,
F. L. Gilman,
Edward R. Gardner,
Cornelius Howland, Jr.,
John P. Knowles, 2d,
Humphrey S. Kirby,
Edward Knights,
L. M. Kollock,
William Leveritt,
Charles H. Lawton,
Edward D. Mandell,
John W. Macomber,
Obed C. Nye,
Bethuel Penniman, Jr.,
Andrew G. Pierce,
Otis N. Pierce,
George F. Parlow,
William F. Potter,
Abraham Russell,
James H. C. Richmond,
James Robinson,
William R. N. Silvester,
William T. Smith,

Charles H. Gifford,
George D. Gifford,
William L. Gerrish, Jr.,
Ebenezer Hervey,
Joshua C. Hitch,
Charles B. Hillman,
Charles M. Haskell,
Jonathan Handy,
Sylvander Hutchinson,
Ezra Holmes,
Cyrenius W. Haskins,
William Howe,
Samuel C. Hart,
William C. Taber, Jr.,
Charles Taber,
Abraham Taber,
Robert B. Taber,
Henry J. Taylor,
E. P. Taylor,
Alden Wordell,
William H. Willis,
Alfred G. Wilbor,
William G. Wood,
James DeWolf,
Alfred Wilson,
George F. Kingman,
Joseph Knowles.

PIONEER HOOK AND LADDER, NO. 1.

Foreman, Charles H. Walker.
First Assistant, Christian Dantsizen.
Second Assistant, Edward M. Durfee.
Clerk, George C. Hardy.

Horace Aiken,
Stephen W. Booth,
James Doull,
John P. Ellis,
William B. Hardy,
Martin L. Hathaway,
Charles J. Johnson,
Revere G. Lindsey,
Leander Luce,
Alexander G. Myrick,
Barnabas H. Packard,
Charles Ruberg,
Asa R. Sherman,
Francis H. Slocum,
Philip M. Tripp,
Joseph Wheeler,
Peter Lynch,
William H. Harp,
Charles E. Pierce,
James W. Warren,
Nathaniel Booth,
Griffin T. Cornell,
Alexander Doull,
Herbert Gardner,
William W. Hatch,
Samuel A. Hardy,
William H. Knights,
Abraham Luscomb,
Thomas Manley,
Timothy O'Neil,
Warren W. Parker,
Philip H. Shepherd,
Henry Shiverick,
Stephen H. Shepherd,
Charles West,
Josiah W. Gardner,
Reuben Corson,
Charles Wood,
William Clymont,
John H. Judson.

Steam fire engine Cornelius Howland, No. 4, built by the Amoskeag Mfg. Co., was placed in commission Feb. 1, 1867. A company was organized, the membership being largely from the Franklin Engine Co., No. 10, Capt. A. H. Howland, Jr., which had been disbanded but a few days before. An elegant gold headed cane was presented to Capt. Howland by the Franklins on the evening of January 31.

The following is the roster:

Foreman, Abraham H. Howland, Jr.
First Assistant, Samuel C. Hart.
Second Assistant, Michael F. Kennedy.
Clerk, Giles G. Barker.
Torch Boys, Augustus A. Wood, William H. Coffin.

James M. Tripp,	Clarfaus Vansant,
Andrew J. Brown,	Hugh McDonald,
James A. Murdock,	George L. Jennings,
Charles E. Jennings,	John Murdock.

The engine was located on the corner of Bedford and South Sixth streets. It was named after one of our most energetic and esteemed citizens, who had been an important factor in the establishment of the steam service in our fire department. April 20th a fine photograph of him was presentsd to the company by Mrs. Cornelius Howland.

The Cornelius Howlands are proud of their record, and well they may be, for they have furnished from their ranks Mayor and Chief Engineer Abraham H. Howland, Jr., Chief Engineer Samuel C. Hart, Assistant Engineers Michael F. Kennedy, Augustus A. Wood and Hugh McDonald.

The first pair of horses attached to this steamer were named Mike and Red Jacket, and were much petted by the company, for they were very intelligent. After long and faithful service Red Jacket was sold to a farmer, and entered upon a career of ordinary hard work. He chafed under the change, and one night broke out of the barn, trotted to the engine house, and whinnied for admittance. The door was opened by one of the company; he plunged in with manifestations of real joy, and place being made for him, he took possession of the stall in a manner that plainly said he knew he was at home. Curious to see if he had forgotten his old duties, the alarm was struck. With a dash he flew from the stable and took his place at the pole, ready for the harness to be put upon him. The faithful creature was liberally fed and led back to his new home. Another intelligent horse attached to this company was General, and he was assigned to the hose-reel. He, too, becoming old and past effective service, was sold to a farmer in a neighboring village. He nearly bothered the life out of Mr. Farmer

CORNELIUS HOWLAND, JR.

whenever he was in town, if the fire alarm sounded. At the ringing of the bells General would at once become uncontrollable, run away with his owner and his load of wood and make a bee-line for No. 4's house.

It would be generous treatment for such faithful creatures to pension them with good living and tender care, with the privilege of running to all fires as volunteers. Why not have an organization of veteran horses of the New Bedford fire department? What a feature they would make in a Fourth of July parade.

At the great Boston fire in 1872 the Cornelius Howland, No. 4, was sent from this city and performed effective service in that fearful conflagration.

At two large fires at Padanaram this steamer went out, and rendered aid to the citizens that called out their gratitude in a substantial way, for the firemen report such glowing accounts of the bountiful spreads made for them that one is tempted to join the force when next they go to Padanaram just before the dinner hour.

It should be said that our fire department always receives generous treatment whenever it renders service to the surrounding towns. At a fire in Fairhaven, where No. 4 performed excellent work, some of the company were thoroughly wet through. One of them happened to have members of his family living in town, and they furnished him with a dry suit of underclothing. Nor did it belong to his brother either.

On July 27, 1867, Nehemiah Leonard & Co.'s candle works were entirely destroyed by fire, the work of an incendiary.

At 4 o'clock on the afternoon of Sept. 4, 1867, a fire broke out in the works of the New Bedford Oil Company on South street. One of the members of the firm was exhibiting to several persons present the non-explosive qualities of the oil manufactured by the company. He threw a lighted match into a large tank containing 100 gallons of oil. It took fire, and in a moment the entire contents were in a blaze, which communicated rapidly to eight other tanks of equal capacity. About 13,000 gallons of oil were destroyed, making one of the hottest conflagrations in the history of our city. At 9 o'clock in the evening one of the tanks exploded with a fearful report, and the oil flowed into a shed on the west side of the works, containing some 500 barrels of petroleum. The condition of affairs at this moment was critical and it was feared that the fire would get beyond the control of the fire department: but the steady work of the steamers in concentrating their powerful streams, held the flames in abeyance, and finally drove the fire back to the tanks. The engines were in continuous action for eight hours. The loss was $10,000, on which there was no insurance.

May 18, 1868, at 12.30 o'clock A. M., Henry Rider's manufactory of candles and lubricating oil was nearly destroyed.

At 3 o'clock, on the afternoon of May 28, 1868, Watson Rider's petroleum oil manufactory, at the foot of Howland street was burned. An employee, Mr. Samuel Peckham, was engaged in pumping water into the condenser. The monotonous action incident to working the pump-handle had brought him to an exhausted condition of body. A happy thought struck him. He would smoke. He filled his pipe with Durham, and lighted it. The lighted match did double service. It ignited the stream of oil running through an open conduit to a large vat near by. When

HOOK & LADDER TRUCK, NO. 1.

well afire the oil smoked cheerfully: so did the buildings in similar condition, rolling up immense clouds of smoke that soon attracted the attention of the whole city. The fire department put in an appearance to see the sight. Loss $800, which did not include Peckham's pipe and tobacco. He saved these, and smoked when he had more leisure, and didn't feel so tired. All ended in smoke, for there was no insurance.

An exciting race occurred at this fire between the Onward and Progress, both engines leaving the house together. I copy from the Onward's records:

> "The Onward and Progress started from the house at the same time, and while proceeding to the fire, a splendid and exciting race took place. The Onward reached the wharf first, and then ensued an equally exciting race between the hose reels. At one time the Progress reel passed the Onward's, and we would probably have been beaten, but good and faithful Flatfoot, evidently feeling that his honor and reputation were at stake, made an extra exertion, shot in ahead of the Progress reel, carried his reel nearest the fire, and thus secured first water for the Onward. Chunk and Ned, the horses attached to the engine, proved themselves equal to the emergency, and showed that on an even start, and everything else being equal, the horses that pass them must get up and get."

These horses were noted for their keen understanding of the duties for which they were trained. They were retained at the Central House for many years, and were attached to the Progress after the Onward was located at the north end.

At 12.10 P. M., June 27, 1868, the building owned by Albert Shaw, and occupied by James H. Lamb, manufacturer of planes, 115 Purchase street, was destroyed. The fire was undoubtedly the work of an incendiary. An explosion in the building first attracted the attention of passing watchmen, and was quickly followed by flames issuing from the windows in the second story. When the building was entered, varnish was discovered dripping through the scuttles from the second story, where it had never been kept. The rapidity with which the fire developed after the explosion made the fact unquestionable that the incendiary had made careful plans for a successful blaze. The fire department was occupied nearly two hours in extinguishing the flames.

Aug. 7, 1868, Caleb Maxfield's furniture warehouse on Union street was set on fire about 9 o'clock in the evening. It was a scorching conflagration, made so by the highly combustible material of the stock. Loss, $5500; insurance, $3500.

Sept. 9, 1868, a lively fire occurred in Wales & Co.'s candle works, on South street. Loss $3000.

Oct. 18, 1868, the old candle works of Thomas S. and Francis S. Hathaway, corner of School and Fifth streets, were nearly destroyed. Loss, $2500.

Oct. 27, 1868, Hayes & Co.'s stave mill was badly damaged by fire. Mayhew & Hayes, wood turners and fancy sawyers, in the same building, lost $200.

Jan. 13, 1869, at 3 P. M., Benjamin Ryder's stable, and C. W. Dyer's grocery store adjoining, both on Kempton street, were set on fire. Mr. Ryder lost two valuable horses worth $1200; one other saved his life by pluckily holding his nose to a small window till rescued. Mr. Ryder lost also a large number of fowl, twenty of which were roasted in the wagon.

Feb. 17, 1869, Wales & Co.'s paraffine works, First and South streets, were burned. Fire commenced in the press room, and like a lightning flash the whole room was in flames. The building was thoroughly saturated with oil, and though torrents of water were thrown, it was of little avail: the fire soon burned out the interior. Loss, $15,000.

May 20, 1869, there was a fire at Taber's plane factory. Loss, $7500.

The steamer Onward, which had the distinguished honor of being the first of its kind in the department, and had done royal service since Jan. 2, 1860, was deemed so far used up as to require a new machine to take its place. During 9½ years the engine had been called out 252 times. On Aug. 25, 1879, the new Onward, No. 1, arrived in the city. The event was one of great pleasure to the company, and it was recognized by a grand banquet on the evening of the 26th. Among the guests were the Board of Engineers, Mr. Batchelor, of Manchester, N. H., and several other gentlemen. Speeches were in order after the supper, and a good time was enjoyed by all. A letter from Mr. Charles S. Paisler, clerk, then in Germany, was read on the occasion. The machine proved to be highly satisfactory, and is now in service at the North End. At the trial it played 240 feet through 1⅛ inch nozzle.

Steam fire engine of the present day. Built by the Amoskeag Mfg. Co., builders of Nos. 1, 2, 4, 6, 7.

Sept. 28, 1869, Wales & Co.'s paraffine works were entirely destroyed.

Dec. 20, 1869, J. & W. Lamb, plane manufacturers, First and School streets, were burned out. At this fire the Acushnet water was used for the first time by the department.

Sept. 13, 1870, the New Bedford Flour Mills were burned. Loss, $116,000; insurance, $85,000.

Sept. 21, H. Ryder & Co.'s paraffine candle manufactory, 114 North Water street, burned. Loss, $26,379; insurance, $21,379.

Jan. 7, 1871, Walter F. Clark's stable, 21 South Second street, burned. Five horses lost their lives. Loss, $9000; no insurance.

Jan. 13, 1871, a fire occurred in dwelling 126 Summer street, occupied by David J. Shepherd. The house was filled with a dense smoke, and Mr. James Shepherd was found dead near an attic window. Though badly burned about the face and hands, it was evident he died from suffocation.

Feb. 8, 1871, building owned by Nathan Chase, 28 Purchase street, and occupied by Mrs. B. Allen & Co., milliners, was burned. Loss, $10,400; insurance, $5300.

In 1871, Mr. Tillinghast P. Tompkins, who had occupied the office of Chief Engineer since 1858, resigned his position, which he had filled in a manner honorable to himself and to the entire satisfaction of the citizens. His career was one of great usefulness. To him must be credited the honor of carrying the fire department through a most important period, when the old hand service came to its end and the steam service was introduced in our city. He did this well; and on his retirement he was honored with a banquet by the entire fire department, in City Hall, March 4, 1871, and was presented a beautiful gold medal valued at $100. Henry F. Thomas made the presentation speech. Among the guests present were Assistant Engineers Mathews, Bliss, Fisher, and Macy, Mayor Richmond, Aldermen Gifford and Hart, Joseph H. Cornell, Charles M. Pierce, Jr., Chief Engineer Abraham H. Howland, Jr., William H. Sherman, and others.

June 9, 1871, T. W. Cook's paint mill was destroyed. Loss, $6000.

June 16, 1871, a stubborn fire occurred at the Mansion House. Loss, $5000.

The city government, having built a new engine-house at the north end, decided to remove the Onward from the central house. This action necessitated the organization of a new company, whose members resided in the north part of the city. The old company disbanded, escorted the engine to its new quarters, and delivered it to the new company in fine style. To the credit of all concerned it may be said that the change was made in a courteous and gentlemanly manner. The officers of the new company were:

Foreman, W. J. Marr.
First Assistant, Loring T. Parlow.
Second Assistant, G. G. Broadbent.
Clerk, E. C. Milliken.

The new organization has always maintained a fine reputation for efficiency and public spirit. Captains Marr and Parlow have since served as assistant engineers.

In Sept., 1871, the fire alarm was introduced into our fire service, during the adminstration of Chief Engineer Abraham H. Howland, Jr. It became one of the most important and effective features of the department. The first alarm rang out on the evening of Sept. 25, from box 18, H. H. Fisher's bakery. I copy from the Onward's record:

"The fire department was promptly on hand, but fire there was none. The veteran fireman and the firemen's friend, H. H. Fisher, had conceived a plan for testing the alarm service in a practical manner, and at the same time show his appreciation of the fire department. Mr. F. invited them into his building, where they found a bountiful collation spread for them. The firemen were not backward, but showed themselves equal to the emergency. A pleasant evening was passed in a social manner, and the company departed with three hearty cheers for Henry H. Fisher, and with the hearty wish that the fire fiend might never come to his doors."

Daniel E. Webb, the clerk of the Board of Engineers for 1871, died in September, and the entire fire department attended the funeral.

BOARD OF ENGINEERS.

1871–72.

Chief Engineer, Abraham H. Howland, Jr.
Assistant Engineers, John E. Brown, George P. Reed,
Charles W. Dyer, Alfred M. Chapman.
Clerk, Alfred M. Chapman.

1872-73.

Chief Engineer, Abraham H. Howland, Jr.
Assistant Engineers, John E. Brown, Alfred M. Chapman,
Charles W. Dyer, William H. Sherman.
Clerk, A. M. Chapman.

1873-74.

Chief Engineer, Abraham H. Howland, Jr.
Assistant Engineers, Moses H. Bliss, Freeman C. Luce,
Charles H. Taber, Loring T. Parlow.
Clerk, Moses H. Bliss.

The Franklin Hose Carriage, No. 1, built by the Amoskeag Manufacturing Co., was put in commission, Jan. 1, 1872.

FRANKLIN HOSE CO., NO. 1.

Foreman, Pliny B. Sherman.
First Assistant, Herbert B. Gardner.
Second Assistant, Clarfaus Vansant.
Clerk and Treasurer, James S. Hathaway.

Benjamin F. King, Joseph W. Spooner,
Peter Nelson. Jeremiah L. Cavanaugh.
David W. Howland.

October 17, 1872, the Excelsior Steam Engine Co., No. 3, made an excursion to Taunton, where the members were handsomely received by the Edward Mott Engine Co., of that city. The Excelsiors were allowed to take their engine with them, the only instance of the kind on record since steam was introduced in the department. Dec. 13, 1873, the company attached to the Excelsior, No, 3, was disbanded, and the engine placed in reserve. The company was reorganized and took possession of the new steam fire engine named Zachariah Hillman, No. 5, built by Clapp & Jones, Hudson, N. Y. This engine on its test trial threw a stream 280 feet, through 150 feet of hose, using 1¼ inch nozzle. The Excelsior was placed in reserve, and is still held valuable for service.

Sept. 15, 1872, Cornelius Howland, No. 4, visited Fall River and were the guests of Metacomet Steam Fire Engine Co., No. 3, and Cascade Engine Co., No. 1. They were the recipients of much attention, and brought home as mementoes the "pipe of peace" and a historic broom.

Feb. 22, 1873, a destructive fire occurred at 1.20 A. M. Concert Hall building was destroyed, and also the building south. Macomber's building, on the corner of Purchase and Union streets, was badly damaged, as was also Knights' furniture warehouse at the north. A terrible snowstorm prevailed at the time, with a heavy gale of wind. But for the immense body of snow on the roofs the conflagration would have been fearful in extent. Loss about $35,000.

The Firemen's Mutual Aid Society was organized in our home department in 1872. Its object is to assist members who may receive injuries while performing fire service. At the death of a member his family receives $50. At the annual meeting in October, 1890, the society was reported in a highly prosperous condition, entirely free from debt, and $1836.18 in the treasury. The Firemen's Beneficial Association is another noble organization connected with our fire department. On the death of any member, every fireman contributes $1.00, which amount is paid to the family within 30 days of the death. As the entire membership is about 190, our readers will see the beneficent character of this society.

In 1873, the Protecting Society was rendered more useful by being furnished with tarpaulins, rubber blankets, etc. During the following year, 1874, the society furnished themselves with badges, to be worn at fires. In 1877, the society was re-organized with a limited number of 50. Its efficiency had steadily increased from year to year, but in 1878 radical rules and regulations were adopted, new apparatus added, and, under the energetic management of President Charles S. Kelley, the importance of the Protecting Society became more manifest. Mr. Kelley induced the agents of the insurance companies to donate $350, which was at once expended in a large supply of rubber blankets. The society is well organized, and no branch of the service is more effective and useful. Thousands of dollars have been saved by their prompt and systematic work. In 1885, the plan of distributing the members in time of fire was adopted. It worked well and is still in operation at the present time.

CHARLES S. KELLEY.

(President of the Protecting Society.)

The fire departments of the State are united in an organization which holds annual conventions, where matters of vital interest are discussed, and much valuable information is obtained by the firemen. The Massachusetts State Firemen's

Association is held in high esteem by our local firemen. It was organized in 1880.

Feb. 3, 1873, a fire was discovered in the attic of house 188 Middle street, owned by Nathan Chase, and occupied by Rev.

SAMUEL C. HART.

(Chief Engineer, 1874-1875.)

Ensign McChesney. Loss on building about $1000. The reverend gentleman's household effects and library were safely removed. He and his family found kindly shelter with a near neighbor. Soon after the flames were extinguished their host's door bell rang and a well dressed, benevolent-looking gentleman handed in a small bottle of ink, which he said belonged to the clergyman. Had it been a bottle of gold he could not have guarded it with more care, or have held it more upright for fear of its precious contents being spilled.

April 27, 1873, Gerrett Geils' furniture store, 148 Purchase street, was destroyed. A fierce gale was blowing at the time and grave fears were entertained that the fire would sweep to the river.

Board of Engineers.

1874-75.

Chief Engineer, Samuel C. Hart.
Assistant Engineers, Alfred M. Chapman, Loring T. Parlow, Charles H. Taber, Michael F. Kennedy.
Clerk, Charles S. Paisler.

1875-76.

Chief Engineer, Moses H. Bliss.
Assistant Engineers, Alfred M. Chapman, Freeman C. Luce, Loring T. Parlow, John H. Judson.
Clerk, George H. Bliss.

Nov. 26, 1873, was a gala day in the history of our fire department. Not since the famous parade of 1844 had there been such a pageant as was seen in our streets on that November day. Nature seemed to give its benediction on the event, for the day was one of rare clearness, just the bracing air for comfortable marching.

The firemen made extensive preparations for the event, and they were all carried out on a grand scale, and successfully. Three fire companies from other cities were in the procession. The fire engines were beautifully decorated with wreaths and flags, the horses decked with plumes and gold mounted harnesses. Without question this parade was the finest ever made in our city. I give the entire list and order of the grand procession as it moved from City Hall square at 1.30 o'clock:

First Division.

Platoon of Police.
New Bedford Band, 20 men, George Hill, leader.
Chief Engineer Abraham H. Howland, Jr., and Aids.
Chief Holmes, of North Bridgewater; Chief Cozzens, of Newport; Chief Green, of Providence.
Pioneer Hook & Ladder Company, No. 1, P. M. Tripp, foreman, with apparatus, 14 men in red shirts, black pants, navy blue fatigue caps.
Volunteer Hook & Ladder Company, No. 1, of Taunton, Joseph T. Haynes, foreman, 13 men, in dark blue shirts, black pants, and navy blue caps with white band, blue belts, on which was inscribed Taunton Fire Department.
Onward Steam Fire Engine Company, No. 1, William J. Marr, foreman, 20 men, in red shirts and black pants, black belts, fire hats and white worsted neckties.
Quequechan Steam Fire Engine Co., No. 1, Fall River, Lot T. Sears, foreman, 18 men, in red shirts, black pants, white belts, fire hats and navy blue fatigue caps with gold bands.

Second Division.

Smith's American Band, Israel Smith, leader.
Progress Steam Fire Engine Company, No. 2, with apparatus, Franklin Shaw, foreman, 19 men, in blue shirts, dark pants, white belts and navy blue caps.
Excelsior Steam Fire Engine Company, No. 3, with apparatus, Job. H. Gifford, foreman, 20 men, with fire hats, red shirts bound with blue, white belts, black pants and fatigue caps.
Cornelius Howland Steam Fire Engine Company, No. 4, with apparatus, John Murdock, foreman, 20 men with black fire hats, dark blue shirts trimmed with red, white belts, dark pants, fatigue caps.
Zachariah Hillman Steam Fire Engine Company, No. 5.

Third Division.

Acushnet Band, 15 men, E. M. Swift, leader.
Hancock Engine Company, No. 9, from Head of the River, with apparatus, Reuben Washburn, foreman, 25 men, in red shirts, dark blue pants, white belts, and blue caps.
Alert Engine Company, No. 4, of Taunton, N. H. Rankin, foreman, 12 men, in blue shirts, dark pants, white belts, navy blue caps.
Franklin Hose Company, No. 1, with apparatus, Pliny B. Sherman, foreman, 8 men, in blue shirts, black pants, black belts, and fire hats.
Old Colony Steam Fire Engine Co., No. 6, of East Taunton, H. N. Robinson, foreman, 10 men, in red shirts, dark pants, white belts and glazed caps.

The streets along the route were lined with immense crowds of people, and many compliments were showered on the splendid show. The fire engines were brilliant with polished metal, and, set with abundance of flowers, made a dazzling display. One interesting feature of the procession consisted of a number of pet dogs belonging to the companies. The animal belonging to the Progress weighed only five pounds.

At the conclusion of the parade a fine banquet was served in City Hall, provided by William A. Searell. A large number of guests were present. Among them were the following gentlemen who had served the city as engineers: Messrs. George Wilson, George G. Gifford, Benj. B. Covell, Caleb L. Ellis, T. B. Denham, Joshua B. Ashley, Oliver M. Brownell, Israel T. Bryant, T. P. Tompkins, James Durfee, George Perry, John Mathews, Thomas P. Swift, Henry H. Fisher, William Cook, Frederick Macy, John E. Brown, George P. Reed, Charles W. Dyer, Alfred M. Chapman, W. H. Sherman. Henry H. Fisher furnished an appropriate feature of the banquet—loaves of firemen's cake, each inscribed with the name of an engine company delicately lined with sugar. Another loaf, given by the same donor, inscribed "To the Press," was stolen by some hard-hearted thief. Invocation was made by Rev. O. A. Roberts, and the dinner was then discussed. There was music by the band, and Mayor George H. Dunbar was introduced by Chief Engineer Howland. His speech abounded in compliments to the fire department.

James B. Congdon followed with an interesting speech and read the poem given at the celebration in 1844. Rev. Dr. Quint amused the audience with remarks comparing the past with the present.

One of the musical features of the occasion was given by Smith's Band and was called "Fireman's Polka." The *Standard* describes it as introducing an alarm of fire at the prelude, a vocal song and three cheers in the coda.

Then followed a succession of toasts, Chief Howland acting as toastmaster:

"Quequechan Steam Fire Engine Co., of Fall River, the veteran steam fire engine of Bristol county. May their record be such that all may feel honored in following them."

"Onward Steam Fire Engine Co. The first in the field of our steam department. With an honorable record of the duty done and work accomplished you are justly entitled to the emblematic name your steamer bears."

Responded to by E. C. Milliken.

Tilson B. Denham, the first foreman of this company, made a few remarks.

"'Ever ready and on the *alert*, that fires may be quenched in their incipiency,' is the motto of our visitors from Whittenton, the Alert Engine Company."

Response by Capt. Rankin.

A song entitled "All Together," was sung by a glee club connected with the Cornelius Howland, No. 4.

"Progress, No. 2. The special protectors of the central portion of our cherished city. Ever ready when duty calls to give battle to the fire fiend."

Response by Charles S. Paisler, clerk, who read a selected poem, "The Song of the fireman."

Music by Smith's Band, "Paisler Polka."

"Volunteer Hook & Ladder Co., of Taunton. The pride, yet the terror, of the citizens, for 'Say the word and down comes your house.'"

Response by Capt. Haynes.

"Excelsior Steam Engine Co., No. 3. Whenever called into action on the performance of your duty may your aim, like your name, be Excelsior."

Response by Capt. Gifford.

Music by the Acushnet Band, "Mollie Darling."

"Hancock, No. 9. Like the illustrious statesman, whose name you bear, may each member of the company be firm in the resolve that 'freedom's fire' shall never go out."

Response by Foreman Washburn.

Music by the New Bedford Band, "Magnetic Polka."

"Pioneer Hook & Ladder Co., No. 1. The Pioneer at the sound of the alarm bell may ever lead the way."

Response by Assistant Foreman Judson.

"Cornelius Howland Steam Engine Co., No. 4. Always on the alert for the first sound of the fire alarm, active and efficient in the discharge of duty, may your honorable record of past service reflect its brilliancy upon your future career."

Response by Foreman Murdock.

"Franklin Hose, No. 1, the youngest born, yet bearing a venerable name: may your record be worthy of your illustrious namesake."

Response by James S. Hathaway, clerk.

The final toast was:

"To all friends present or absent: here is good health to everybody, lest somebody should feel slighted."

The exercises were closed with rounds of cheers for the Mayor and City Council and the past engineers, and the whole company then joined in singing "Auld Lang Syne," led by the bands. The festivities of the day closed with the Firemen's levee, in Pierian Hall, in aid of the Firemen's Mutual Aid Society. The hall was finely decorated with flags and bunting and presented a fascinating appearance. An immense throng of people were present, and the affair resulted in a handsome sum being added to the treasury.

The celebration was a success in every particular and may be appropriately designated as the second grand parade of the New Bedford fire department.

Roster of the Fire Department for 1876-77.

Chief Engineer, Moses H. Bliss.
Assistant Engineers, Alfred M. Chapman, Freeman C. Luce,
William J. Marr, John H. Judson.
Clerk, George H. Bliss.

Onward, No. 1. (House on Purchase street, foot of Franklin.)

Foreman, Charles H. Church.
First Assistant, Julian A. Sweet.
Second Assistant, Allen W. Tinkham.
Clerk, E. C. Milliken.

E. K. Dollard,
C. R. Hathaway,
Irving Smith,
George H. Pierce,
George Tripp,
Henry O'Neal,
H. N. Tinkham,
J. Harrington, Jr.,
H. C. Pierce, Jr.,
George H. Parker,
Charles S. Stratton,
James L. Bryant,
Henry S. Webb.

PROGRESS, No. 2. (House corner Purchase st. and Mechanics lane.)

Foreman, Charles S. Paisler.
First Assistant, John Downey.
Second Assistant, Eugene R. Leverett
Clerk, James D. Allen.

Edward C. Spooner,
James G. Harding,
S. H. Mitchell,
Charles F. Dean,
John Dollard,
A. T. Kendrick,
A. B. C. Davenport,
Moses Dean,
John C. Taber,
Fred. H. Wood,
George B. Russell,
Lemuel W. Hayes,
W. P. Sowle,
Michael Conway.

CORNELIUS HOWLAND, No. 4.
(House corner South Sixth and Bedford streets.)

Foreman, Hugh McDonald.
First Assistant, Joseph B. Wing.
Second Assistant, John Gillis.
Clerk, Giles G. Barker.

James M. Tripp,
John B. Peckham,
Augustus A. Wood,
James A. Murdock,
Frank Wood,
William A. Gibbs,
Henry A. Gray,
Arthur Baylies,
Charles L. Wing,
Henry A. Barker,
Daniel D. Briggs,
George H. W. Tripp,
Charles W. Borden,
Charles G. Taber.

ZACHARIAH HILLMAN, No. 5. (House cor. Hillman and County sts.)

Foreman, William A. Russell.
First Assistant, Orlando F. Bly.
Second Assistant, E. R. Bentley.
Clerk, Charles W. Wheeler.

Joseph Hafford,
I. H. Wilcox,
William T. King,
Martin J. Murphy,
George W. Parker,
Joseph H. Wheeler,
Jethro Hillman,
George H. Chadwick,
Louis Myers,
Frank Wood,
Martin Blanchard, Jr.,
Charles L. Davis,
Benj. F. King,
Reuben Taber.

FRANKLIN HOSE CO., NO. 1.
(House corner Purchase street and Mechanics lane.)

Foreman, Pliny B. Sherman.
First Assistant, Clarfaus Vansant.
Second Assistant, Daniel W. Howland.
Clerk, James S. Hathaway.

Peter Nelson,
C. A. S. Sherman,
John F. Snow,
William H. Perry,
W. H. Drescott.

PIONEER HOOK AND LADDER CO., NO. 1.
(House cor. Purchase street and Mechanics lane.)

Foreman, Philip M. Tripp.
First Assistant, Lysander W. Davis.
Second Assistant, James Conway.
Clerk, Charles E. Pierce.

Abraham R. Luscomb,
James W. Dugan,
Eben A. Butts,
Alexander Doull,
Charles M. Hathaway,
Charles J. Johnson,
Thomas T. Manley,
Charles H. Walker,
B. F. Hinckley,
Nathaniel H. Caswell,
Thos. M. Holleran,
William Clymonts,
Chris. C. Gifford,
F. L. Hathaway,
Andrew V. Landers,
F. H. Sampson,
George T. Manley,
Squire Gifford,
Lewis G. Allen.

HANCOCK, NO. 9. (Located at Head of the River.)

Foreman, Reuben Washburn.
First Assistant, Charles E. Howland.
Second Assistant, George W. Bennett.
Clerk, George A. Cobb.

John Silva,
Frank C. Terry,
Frank P. Washburn,
Arthur C. Brooks,
Joseph Spooner,
William R. Washburn,
Howard Pittsley,
Alfred Williams,
L. A. Washburn,
Joseph H. Lawrence,
William D. Perry,
John A. Russell,
A. B. Grinnell, Jr.,
James A. Wilbour,
G. W. Paige,
Asa Reynolds,
Seth Howard,
Charles H. Hathaway.

THE PROTECTING SOCIETY.

President, Samuel P. Burt.

George R. Phillips,
Charles Almy,
Andrew G. Pierce,
Obed N. Swift,

Edward Knights,
Gardner T. Sanford,
Edward H. Allen,
William P. S. Cadwell,
Joseph Tillinghast,
William H. Bartlett,
Edward R. Gardner,
Charles A. Case,
Geo. H. Topham,
H. A. Gifford, Jr.,
Dennis Wood,
E. Kempton Taber,
Charles S. Cummings,
George F. Kingman,
Joseph Buckminster,
F. L. Gilman,
John P. Knowles, 2d,
L. M. Kollock,
Nathaniel S. Cannon,
Charles H. Gifford,
George L. Brownell,
Gilbert Allen,
Gideon Allen, Jr.,
Morgan Rotch,
Humphrey S. Kirby,
George D. Gifford,
Gilbert D. Kingman,
William H. H. Allen,
Alfred G. Wilbor,
Jonathan Handy,
Wendell H. Cobb,
S. H. Cook,
W. A. Robinson, 2d,
George F. Parlow,
Joshua C. Hitch,
Charles S. Kelley,
Alfred Wilson,
Alden Wordell,
Francis T. Aiken,
John W. Macomber,
James H. C. Richmond,
A. W. Hadley,
Bethuel Penniman,
Otis N. Pierce,
Charles B. Hillman,
H. C. Denison,
Ezra Holmes,
William H. Willis,
Joseph Knowles,
Cyrenius W. Haskins,
Edward D. Mandell,
William G. Wood,
Leonard B. Ellis,
Wm. Wood,
Wm. Anthony,
Henry J. Taylor,
Charles M. Haskell,
Charles M. Taber,
Charles H. Lawton,
William R. N. Silvester,
George R. Gray,
W. O. Woodman,
William T. Smith,
William C. Taber, Jr.,
Eben Perry,
William F. Potter.

CHAPTER XIII.

THE following are the lists of the Board of Engineers from 1877 to 1884:

1877–78.

Chief Engineer, Frederick Macy.
Assistant Engineers, Michael Kennedy, Nathan M. Brown,
John H. Judson, William J. Marr.
Clerk, Luther G. Hewins, Jr.

1878–79.

Chief Engineer, Frederick Macy.
Assistant Engineers, Michael Kennedy, Nathan M. Brown,
John H. Judson, Augustus A. Wood.
Clerk, Luther G. Hewins, Jr.

1879–84.

Chief Engineer, Frederick Macy.
Assistant Engineers, Michael Kennedy, Nathan M. Brown,
Pliny B. Sherman, Augustus A. Wood.
Clerk, Luther G. Hewins, Jr.

Thursday, Oct. 13, 1876, the P. H. Raymond Engine Co., of Cambridgeport, made a visit to our city and were the recipients of unexpected hospitalities from the Cornelius Howland Engine Co. No. 4. A firemen's ball at Pierian Hall, a clambake at Peckham's Grove, and other festivities, made the occasion one of rare enjoyment to all participants.

Aug. 23, 1877, a return visit was made. The Cornelius Howlands were accompanied by Chief Engineer Macy, Assistant Engineer Judson, ex-Assistant Engineer Chapman, Councilman Taylor, and the Union Cornet Band. The excursion lasted three days, and our firemen had a good time. They were received by the entire fire department of Cambridgeport, and a round of festivities was kept up to the last hour. On their return to the city they were agreeably surprised by an escort of our whole department from the station. The Raymonds entertained their guests in such a manner as to astonish the boys, so lavish and bountiful were the pleasures arranged for them. Clerk Barker's record of the event is very entertaining.

The year 1877 was remarkably free from fires. In December the first sleigh reel was added to the department.

Feb. 19, 1878, William Sanders' clothing house and Frederick Coffin's box manufactory, 112 Union street, were burned out. William Sanders' loss was $13,735; insurance, $10,000. F. Coffin's loss, 10,000; insurance, $3775.

July 7, James Doull's carpenter shop, South Front street. Loss, $2600; insurance, $2000.

July 28, Monroe Holcomb's stable, corner of Howland and Grinnell streets.

Jan. 26, 1879, a dwelling house belonging to Hiram H. Goff, corner of Pope and State streets, was burned. Loss, $2388.

July 13, Hersom & Bryant's soap factory was burned. Loss, $3000; insurance, $11,000.

July 16, Mosher & Brownell's sash and blind manufactory was struck by lightning. Loss, $1300.

The steamer Progress, which had done faithful service, was disposed of, and a new engine built by the Silsby Manufacturing Co., Seneca Falls, N. Y., was placed in commission Sept. 4, 1879.

During the year 1880 the permanent force of the department was uniformed, so that the regulation uniform is worn at all times when on duty.

April 11, a fire in William street Baptist church. Trivial loss.

July 8, a fire occurred at the Mansion House.

Jan. 27, 1881, fire in the works of the New Bedford Copper Co. Loss, $2750.

April 16, fire in steamer Albatross, lying at the wharf of

the B. C. F. & N. B. R. R. Co. The steamer was laden with merchandise belonging to various parties. Loss on steamer, \$4825; on merchandise, \$26,579.

DAVID W. HOWLAND.
(Foreman Franklin Hose, No. 1, 1879–90.)

The Frederick Macy Steam Fire Engine, No. 6, was put in commission Nov. 1, 1882. It was built by the Amoskeag Manufacturing Co., Manchester, N. H. A company was organized Oct. 31:

Foreman, George W. Parker.
First Assistant, Herbert B. Gardner.
Second Assistant, Felix Cavenaugh.
Clerk, George S. Hoyt.

Marshall S. Greene,	A. G. Howland,
Thomas Wood,	Lavello I. Pierce,
William H. Barnes,	Charles R. Cornell,
Jason L. Ballou,	Charles K. Wood,
Frank Greene,	Frederick Nelson,
Charles G. Taber,	Edward Dugan,
Frank T. Perry.	N. Herbert Green.

The engine-house on Fourth street, head of Potomska, was built specially for the new engine, and it is very complete in all the appointments and supplied with every convenience for the comfort of the firemen, as well as for efficiency.

Two of Ryan's four-wheel hose carriages for Nos. 5 and 6 were added this year.

During the year 1882, private alarm boxes were introduced into many of the important manufacturing establishments.

June 7th, a destructive fire occurred at Head-of-the-River. A grist mill and ice houses, belonging to Mr. Simeon Hawes, were burned. Loss, $12,817.17; insurance, $7900.

June 25, fire in cotton storehouse of Wamsutta Mills. Loss, $990.

Aug. 30, fire in H. J. Taylor's crockery store, Purchase street. Loss, $3947.24.

Feb. 3, 1883, Elbridge G. Turner's box board and shingle mill at Plainville was burned. Loss, $3000.

June 15, fire at Wamsutta Mills. Total loss, $9371.78; insurance, $22,000.

Dec. 30, fire in dwelling house, on County street, of George S. and F. A. Homer. Loss, $1689.37.

Roster of the Fire Department for 1884–85.

Board of Engineers.

Chief Engineer, Frederick Macy.
Assistant Engineers, Michael F. Kennedy, Loring T. Parlow, Pliny B. Sherman, Augustus A. Wood.
Clerk, Luther G. Hewins, Jr.

Onward, No. 1.

Foreman, Allen W. Tinkham.
First Assistant, George A. Tripp.

Second Assistant, Edward M. Durfee.
Clerk, E. C. Milliken.

Hosemen.
Julian A. Sweet,
Charles A. Wilson,
Charles H. Brown,
F. W. Brightman,
Nathaniel J. Stone,
Edgar F. Tripp,
John Whitehead.

Engineer, Frederick H. Wood.
Driver, James L. Bryant.
Reel Driver, Samuel C. France.
Stoker, Harris J. Tinkham.

Torchmen.
Thomas Larkin,
George H. Snow.

PROGRESS, No. 2.

Foreman, James G. Harding.
First Assistant, John Downey.
Second Assistant, John Dollard.
Clerk, James D. Allen.

Hosemen.
E. C. Spooner,
E. R. Leverett,
Charles F. Dean,
Allen T. Kendrick,
Moses Dean,
George M. Crapo,
Wm. R. Sherman,
Samuel W. Mitchell.

Engineer, George B. Russell.
Driver, William P. Soule.
Stoker, Lemuel W. Hayes.
Reel Driver, Michael Conway.

Torchmen.
James R. Goddard,
Wyman D. Jacobs.

CORNELIUS HOWLAND, No. 4.

Foreman, Henry A. Gray.
First Assistant, Edgar S. Gilbert.
Second Assistant, Benjamin F. Hinckley.
Clerk, Wm. A. Gibbs.

Hosemen.
James M. Tripp,
Hugh McDonald,
John H. Backus,
Charles H. Card,
Charles S. Wing,
Samuel Watson, 2d,
William C. Hiscox,
Roland W. Snow.

Engineer, Daniel D. Briggs.
Asst. Engineer, Alonzo V. Jason.
Driver, George H. W. Tripp.
Reel Driver, Horace D. Bradley.

Torchmen.
Wilson A. Tripp,
James J. Donaghy.

ZACHARIAH HILLMAN, No. 5.

Foreman, R. S. Lawton.
First Assistant, Charles C. Gifford.
Second Assistant, Squire A. Gifford.
Clerk, Jerrie B. Taber.

Hosemen.
E. R. Bentley,
G. H. Chadwick,
Isaiah H. Wilcox,
William T. King,
Charles W. H. Potter,
D. S. R. Durfee,
Charles R. Hathaway,
Martin S. Nelson.

Engineer, M. Blanchard, Jr.
Driver, B. F. King, Jr.
Stoker, Charles Jones.
Reel Driver, Reuben Taber.

Torchmen.
Walter Bates,
George H. Cook.

FREDERICK MACY, NO. 6.

Foreman, George W. Parker.
First Assistant, Herbert B. Gardner.
Second Assistant, Felix Cavenaugh.
Clerk, George S. Hoyt.

Hosemen,
Marshall S. Greene,
Robert N. Allen,
Thomas Wood,
Joseph Jackson,
William H. Barnes,
Charles R. Cornell,
Jason L. Ballou,
Charles K. Wood.

Engineer, Charles G. Taber.
Driver, Edward Dugan.
Stoker, Frank T. Perry.
Reel Driver, N. Herbert Greene.

Torchmen.
Frank Greene,
Frederick Nelson.

PIONEER HOOK AND LADDER CO., NO. 1.

Foreman, Lysander W. Davis.
First Assistant, Charles J. Johnson.
Second Assistant, James Conway.
Clerk, Charles E. Pierce.

Laddermen.
James W. Dugan,
Charles H. Delano,
Selmer Eggers, Jr.,
Edward D. Francis,
Henry R. Gidley,
Charles M. Hathaway,
Edward F. Jennings,
John L. Olstein,
Philip C. Russell,
Frank Spooner,
Philip M. Tripp,
Clarfaus Vansant,
Charles W. Vining.

Axemen.
Nathaniel H. Caswell,
Abraham R. Luscomb.

Torchmen.
Alfred M. Gifford,
Wm. A. Hamer.

Lewis G. Allen, Driver.

FRANKLIN HOSE CO., NO. 1.

Foreman, Daniel W. Howland.
First Assistant, Philip R. King.
Second Assistant, Daniel H. Burns.
Clerk, James S. Hathaway.

Hosemen,
A. B. C. Davenport.
James B. Drew,
Bradford D. Tripp.

Driver, Henry R. Meigs.

Torchman,
Wm. H. Maxfield.

HANCOCK, No. 9. (Located at Head of the River.)

Foreman, John A. Russell.
First Assistant, George W. Randall.
Second Assistant, Israel Peckham.
Clerk, Allen Russell, Jr.

Joseph H. Lawrence,
William T. Gifford,
Eli W. Reed,
A. B. Grinnell, Jr.,
James A. Wilbour,
Charles R. Gifford,
Frank P. Washburn,
F. E. Wellington,
John Silva,
Herbert M. Spooner,
Joseph Spooner,
L. A. Washburn,
George R. Little,
George W. Hawes,
John G. Whalon.

Torchmen.
Walter H. Darling.
Isaac Reed.

THE PROTECTING SOCIETY.

President, Charles S. Kelley.

Directors.

Jonathan Handy,
W. A. Robinson,
Charles H. Lawton,
Edward T. Pierce,
Charles M. Haskell,
Edmund F. Maxfield,
Edmund Wood.
John H. Lowe.

Secretary and Treasurer, Edward H. Allen.

Francis T. Aiken,
Gilbert Allen,
Gideon Allen, Jr.,
George H. H. Allen,
O. Frank Bly,
Standish Bourne,
George E. Briggs,
Thomas Boardman,
Charles A. Case,
R. C. P. Coggeshall,
Edwin Dews,
H. C. Denison,
John H. Denison,
Ernest A. Dunham,
Joseph Dawson,
Heman Ellis,
Willis M. Fiske,
Edward R. Gardner,
William F. Potter,
Arthur E. Perry,
James N. Parker,
William H. Pitman,
Charles L. Paine,
William F. Read,
Morgan Rotch,
William A. Russell,
Arthur E. Robbins,
Louis H. Richardson,
Gardner T. Sanford,
R. W. Swift,
Frederick Swift,
William T. Smith,
Leander H. Swift,
Edward S. Shaw,
Robert Snow,
Charles M. Taber,

Edmund Grinnell,
Frank H. Gifford,
A. W. Hadley,
Charles B. Hillman,
John J. Howland,
Charles M. Hussey,
Henry F. Hammond,
Thomas H. Knowles,
Gilbert D. Kingman,
Edgar R. Lewis,
Philander F. Manchester,
Willard Nye, Jr.,
Charles W. Plummer,
George F. Parlow,
Henry J. Taylor,
Joseph Tillinghast,
William T. Taylor,
Henry W. Taylor,
Francis C. Terry,
Alfred G. Wilbor,
William H. Willis,
Horace Wood,
W. O. Woodman,
Frederick A. Washburn,
Edward L. Wilde,
Thomas F. Wood,
William R. West,
Frederick D. Wade,
Mark T. Vincent.

May 30, 1884, a new engine, built by the Amoskeag Mfg. Co., for the Cornelius Howland Steam Fire Engine Co., No. 4, was placed in commission, the old engine being placed in the reserve.

Feb 9, 1884, fire in Liberty Hall building, with an explosion in the store of O. G. Brownell & Sons. Loss, $9000.

Feb. 13, fire in Charles Taber & Co.'s frame manufactory, corner of Water and Spring streets. Loss, $3750.

Feb. 14, fire in dwelling house of John W. Cornell, Middle street; incendiary. Loss, $775; insurance, $2800.

March 1, fire in Elijah Gifford's brass foundry. Loss $2000.

June 25, fire in E. D. Mandell's residence, Hawthorn street. Cause, lightning. Loss, $3000.

July 4, 10 P. M., fire on North Christian church. Cause, fireworks. Loss, $600; no insurance.

Aug. 22, a fire occurred which entirely destroyed F. A. Sowle & Son's planing mill on Elm street. Several other buildings were damaged. Loss about $16,000.

Nov. 6, 1884, the engine now in commission as Progress Steam Fire Engine, No. 2, built by Amoskeag Manufacturing Co., was placed in commission; the Silsby engine was placed in reserve.

Dec. 15, 8.15 A. M., a fire in Haskell & Tripp's dry goods store, corner of Purchase and William streets. The whole fire department was called out. Contest steam fire engine from Fairhaven rendered valuable aid. B. H. Waite's dry goods store badly injured. Haskell & Tripp's loss, $73,104.03: insurance, $60,500. B. H. Waite, $5500; insurance, $18,000. J. Dexter, jeweler, $1144.50; insurance, $4000. Cause of fire, a pile of blankets falling on a gas jet.

The year 1885 was marked by its freedom from fires of any magnitude, the fire loss being less than $7000.

March 25, 1886, fire in Potomska mills. Loss, $6447.

On the 5th of July, 1886, the fire department contest for a series of prizes offered by the city occurred. The following record was made:

Onward, No. 1,	253 feet, 11-2 in.
Old Progress, No. 2 (Silsby),	252 feet, 6 in.
New Progress, No. 2 (Amoskeag),	255 ft., 21-2 in.
Cornelius Howland, No. 4,	263 feet, 8 in.
Zachariah Hillman, No. 5,	222 feet, 6 in.
Frederick Macy, No. 6,	242 feet, 11 in.

Pioneer Hook and Ladder Co., No. 1, and Franklin Hose, No. 1, also took part in the contest.

Oct. 20, fire in house on Arnold street, owned by Hon. William J. Rotch. Cause, "rats and matches."

Oct. 23, fire in Smith Brothers' decorative establishment, William street. Loss, $5109.08.

Jan. 31, 1887, fire in Myrick's cooperage, Water street. Loss, $900.

April 1, Kirby's paint mill and Job Wade's currier establishment, with several dwelling houses on Willis Point, destroyed or badly damaged by fire. Whole loss about $30,000.

Oct. 24, fire on Tarkiln Hill road in G. A. Cobb's fire kindling factory. Loss, $1300.

Aug. 1, 1887, the Franklin Hose Co., No. 1, made an excursion to Oakland Beach, on the invitation of the Fall River Firemen's Association.

Henry R. Meigs, an esteemed member of Franklin Hose Co., No. 1, died Nov. 15, 1887. During a long and painful illness, he received the faithful and tender care of his brother firemen. His funeral was attended by the entire fire department. The services were in charge of Rev. M. C. Julien, and were of a very impressive character.

The only serious fire that occurred in 1888 was that of Greene & Wood's planing mill on the evening of Aug. 8.

First Assistant Engineer Michael F. Kennedy died June 27, 1888. He had been a member of the fire department for about forty years, was a charter member of the Cornelius Howland Co., No. 4, and had served twelve years as First Assistant Engineer.

During the year 1887, the department responded to 41 bell alarms, 36 still and telephone alarms; 1888, 47 bell alarms, 45 still and telephone alarms; 1889, 34 bell alarms, 54 still and telephone alarms.

July 13th, 1889, Progress Steam Fire Engine Co., No. 2, made a visit to East Weymouth, and were the recipients of the generous hospitality of Z. L. Bicknell Hose Co., No. 2.

At the great fire in Boston, Nov. 28, 1889, the Cornelius Howland, No. 4, rendered valuable service.

Roster of the Fire Department for 1889–90.

Board of Engineers.

Chief Engineer, Frederick Macy.
Assistant Engineers, Loring T. Parlow, Pliny B. Sherman, Augustus A. Wood, Hugh McDonald.
Clerk, Luther G. Hewins, Jr.

Onward, No. 1.

Foreman, Allen W. Tinkham.
First Assistant, George A. Tripp.
Second Assistant, Edward M. Durfee.
Clerk, E. C. Milliken.

Hosemen.
Julian A. Sweet,
F. W. Brightman,
John Whitehead,
W. O. Brightman,
Charles A. Wilson,
Edgar F. Tripp,
James F. Powers,
Roland A. Hatch.

Engineer, Frederick H. Wood.
Driver, James L. Bryant.
Reel Driver, Isaac Dawson.
Stoker, Harris N. Tinkham.

Substitutes.
John T. Aghen,
A. D. Milliken.

2d Assistant Pliny B. Sherman. 1st Assistant Loring T. Parlow.
Chief Engineer Frederick Macy.
4th Assistant Hugh McDonald. 3d Assistant Augustus A. Wood.
Luther G. Hewins, Jr., Clerk.

PROGRESS, NO. 2.

Foreman, George M. Crapo.
First Assistant, John Downey.
Second Assistant, Charles F. Dean.
Clerk, James D. Allen.

Hosemen.
James G. Harding,
E. C. Spooner,
Moses Dean.
William K. Wagner,
Wyman D. Jacobs,
E. R. Leverett,
Samuel W. Mitchell,
E. Kempton Peirce.

Engineer, George B. Russell. (deceased.)
Driver, William P. Soule.
Stoker, Lemuel W. Hayes.
Reel Driver, Michael Conway.

Substitutes.
Alex. J. Aiken,
Jas. L. Crowley.

CORNELIUS HOWLAND, NO. 4.

Foreman, Edgar S. Gilbert.
First Assistant, James J. Donaghy.*
Second Assistant, Charles H. Card.
Clerk, Wm. A. Gibbs.

Hosemen.
James M. Tripp,
Samuel Watson, 2d,†
Roland W. Snow,
Henry J. Marshall,
Benjamin F. Hinckley,
Charles S. Wing,
Wm. E. Watson, Jr.,
Frank C. Jennings.

Engineer, Alonzo V. Jason.
Stoker, John H. Backus,
Driver, George H. W. Tripp.
Reel Driver, W. C. Kennedy.

Substitutes.
Leander Reed,
John W. Donaghy.

*Elected Foreman June 1, vice Samuel Watson, 2d, resigned.
†Elected Foreman May 1, vice E. S. Gilbert, resigned.

ZACHARIAH HILLMAN, NO. 5.

Foreman, Charles C. Gifford.
First Assistant, John F. Gifford.
Second Assistant, Squire A. Gifford.
Clerk, Joseph C. Forbes.

Hosemen.
George H. Chadwick,
Charles H. Brown,
Obed S. Cowing,
W. H. Knowles,
I. H. Wilcox,
Henry C. Stubbs,
George H. Cook,
Thomas H. Forbes.

Engineer, Martin Blanchard.
Reel Driver, Martin S. Nelson.
Driver, Benjamin F. King, Jr.
Stoker, Charles Jones.

Substitutes.
Arthur Forbes,
Henry Jones.

FREDERICK MACY, No. 6.

Foreman, George W. Parker.
First Assistant, Edward O'Neil.
Second Assistant, Robert N. Allen.
Clerk, Herbert B. Gardner.

Hosemen.
Thomas Wood,
Joseph Jackson,
Jason L. Ballou,
James Harrington Sherman,
Marshall S. Greene,
Charles R. Cornell,
Charles K. Wood,
Henry M. Mosher.

Engineer, Charles G. Taber.
Stoker, Benj. C. Groves.
Driver, Frank A. C. Greene.
Reel Driver, N. Herbert Greene.

Substitutes.
Frederick Nelson,
Walter Almond.

HANCOCK, No. 9.

Engine built by John Agnew, Philadelphia, 1843. Removed to Acushnet January 18th, 1861.

Foreman, John A. Russell.
First Assistant, Francis P. Washburn.
Second Assistant, Joseph W. Spooner.
Clerk, Allen Russell, Jr.
Steward, John Silvia.

Israel H. Peckham,
William T. Gifford,
John G. Whalon,
James A. Wilbur,
Eli W. Reed,
George W. Hawes,
John F, Parker,
Nathan C. Briggs,
Job T. Haskins,
Herbert M. Spooner,
Andrew B. Grinnell, Jr.,
George W. Randall,
Lemuel A. Washburn,
James L. Haskins,
John G. Dawson,
Wm. P. Reed.

Substitutes.
George H. Gifford,
John B. Wilbur.

HOOK AND LADDER, No. 1.

Carriage built by La France Steam Fire Engine Co., Elmira, N. Y. Put into service August 30th, 1888.

Foreman, Charles J. Johnson.
First Assistant, Frank Spooner.
Second Assistant, Loren N. Mosher.
Clerk, Charles E. Pierce.

Charles B. Allison,
Nathaniel H. Caswell,
Edward D. Francis,
Andrew V. Landers,
William R. Russell,
Philip C. Russell.

John W. Cannavan,
Lysander W. Davis,
Alfred M. Gifford,
Abram R. Luscomb,
Philip M. Tripp,
Clarfaus Vansant.

Driver, George S. Allen.

Tillerman, Charles W. Vining.

Substitutes.
William A. Hamer,
William L. Fletcher.

Hook and Ladder, No. 2.

Carriage built by Joseph T. Ryan of Boston. Put in service August 4th, 1877. Present company organized September, 1888. House on Weld street.

Foreman, Henry W. Kenyon.
First Assistant, Edward F. Dahill.
Second Assistant, Albert W. Moore.
Clerk, Peter F. Sullivan.

James Slater,
John W. Bannister.
David Warren,
Edward T. Ryan,
Martin H. Sullivan,
John S. Harrington,
William McCann,
Alfred Chausse.

Substitutes.
Jeremiah T. Haggerty,
Sylvester Budlong.

Driver, Lewis G. Allen.

Hose, No. 1.

Wagon built by Brownell, Ashley & Co., and put into service December 1st, 1888.

Foreman, David W. Howland.
First Assistant, Charles T. Maxfield.*
Second Assistant, John B. Oliver.
Clerk, James S. Hathaway.

Hosemen.
John W. Baker,
William H. Maxfield,
Aug. G. Mitchell.

Driver, William H. King.

Substitute.
William Young.

*Elected Foreman May 1st, vice D. W. Howland, resigned.

Hose, No. 2.

Carriage built by the Amoskeag Mfg. Co., Manchester, N. H. Present company organized December 3d, 1888. House on Weld street.

Foreman, Samuel C. France.
First Assistant, Joseph Dawson.*
Second Assistant, Mark Watson.
Clerk, George C. Hewins.

Hosemen.
Stephen L. Finnell,
Frank E. Foley,
Bartholomew P. Fury.

Driver, Reuben Taber.

Substitute.
William Wolfenden.

*Elected Foreman September 30th, vice S. C. France, transferred to Engine No. 7.

Steam Fire Engine, No. 7.

Engine built by Amoskeag Mfg. Co., Manchester, N. H. Put into service September 1st, 1890. House on Durfee street.

Foreman, Samuel C. France.
First Assistant, James Slater.
Second Assistant, S. C. Lowe.
Clerk, Thomas Mack.

Hosemen.
C. A. Gallagher,
J. D. Manseau,
J. A. Ryan,
Edward H. Booth,
James McDonald,
W. Sinister,
Wm. Crocker,
Maurice Dahill.

Reel Driver, E. H. Coggeshall.
Stoker, Andrew Tripp.

New Bedford Protecting Society.

President, Charles S. Kelley.

Directors.

Jonathan Handy,
William A. Robinson,
Charles H. Lawton,
Edward T. Pierce,
Charles M. Haskell,
Edmund F. Maxfield,
Edmund Wood,
John H. Lowe.

Secretary and Treasurer, Edmond L. Wilde.

Francis T. Akin,
Gilbert Allen,
Gideon Allen, Jr.,
George H. H. Allen,
O. Frank Bly,
Standish Bourne,
George E. Briggs,
Thomas Boardman,
Charles A. Case,
R. C. P. Coggeshall,

Clifton H. Cornish,
Edwin Dews,
Henry C. Denison,
John H. Denison,
Fred. C. Dunham,
Joseph Dias,
Walter F. Field,
Edward R. Gardner,
John E. Gibbs,
Edmund Grinnell,
Frank H. Gifford,
Charles H. Gifford,
A. W. Hadley,
Charles B. Hillman,
John J. Howland,
Charles M. Hussey,
Henry F. Hammond,
Henry Howard,
Thomas H. Knowles,
G. D. Kingman,
Edgar R. Lewis,
Philander F. Manchester,
Willard Nye, Jr.,
Otis N. Pierce,
William F. Potter,
Arthur E. Perry,
James N. Parker,
William H. Pitman,
Charles L. Paine,
William F. Reed,
Morgan Rotch,
William A. Russell,
Arthur E. Robbins,
Louis H. Richardson,
Gardner T. Sanford,
R. W. Swift,
Frederick Swift,
William T. Smith,
Leander H. Swift,
Edward S. Shaw,
Robert Snow,
Charles M. Taber,
William T. Taylor,
Henry W. Taylor,
Francis C. Terry,
Alfred Thornton,
Alfred G. Wilbor,
William H. Willis,
Horace Wood,
Frederick A. Washburn,
Thomas F. Wood,
William R. West,
Mark T. Vincent.

Roll of the Fairhaven Fire Department for 1890.

Chief Engineer, George R. Valentine.
First Assistant, John A. W. Burgess.
Second Assistant, James M. Allen, Jr.

Contest Steam Fire Engine Co., No. 3.

Foreman, Thomas R. Brownell.
First Assistant, Nathaniel B. Dunn.
Second Assistant, Wm. K. McLane.
Third Assistant, Dennis D. Holmes.
Clerk, Henry Spiller.

Hosemen.

Wm. H. Bryant,
Thomas F. Morse,
Harry W. Delano,
Joseph A. Gifford,
John J. Brownell,
Henry Reed,
Wm. A. Hanna,
Wm. Asten,
Oliver S. Gurney,
Silas H. Rounsevelle.

Torchmen.
Thomas D. Brownell,
Frank E. Dunn,
Walter S. Harding.

Engineer, Charles F. Dillingham.
Stoker, Walter L. Rounsevelle.
Drivers, George L. Bauldry,
Edward Manchester, Jr.

Hook and Ladder Co., No. 1.

Foreman, Davis Sherman.
First Assistant, John E. Thompson.
Clerk, Joseph B. Peck.

Joshua R. Delano,
Thomas W. Nye,
George C. Mathewson.
Driver, Charles S. Dunham.

Protecting Society.

President, Isaac N. Babbitt, Jr.
Secretary and Treasurer, John T. Hanna.
First Director, Horace K. Nye.
Second Director, Charles F. Brownell.
Third Director, Herbert D. Burke.

Herman H. Hathaway,
John S. Howland,
E. L. Shurtleff,
Frank A. Hanna,
F. A. Keith,
B. Taber, Jr.,
Louis N. Baudoin,
Fred. R. Fish,
Wm. Card,
Joseph K. Nye,
James L. Gillingham.
Charles H. Gifford,
Lyman C. Bauldry,
George D. Hammond,
Wm. H. Taylor,
Henry L. Card,
Thomas Dahl,
David A. Kelley,
Arlington Craig,
Charles D. Waldron.

Driver of Chemical Wagon, Benj. F. Tripp.

CHAPTER XIV.

THE great feature of the Fourth of July celebration in 1890 was the contest between the old time hand engines. The very suggestion of such an affair served to awaken a flood of memories among the veterans in the fire service, and to arouse the curiosity of the present generation, many of whom had never seen a hand engine in operation. The weeks preceding the natal day were busy ones for the firemen who were perfecting arrangements and testing the hand engines that had been secured for the contest.

The Cornelius Howland Co., No. 4, obtained the Relief, No. 5, of Fairhaven.

The City Committee secured the Young Mechanic, No, 6, of Mattapoisett, and the adherents of this famous machine were glad to avail themselves of the opportunity to work once more on their favorite engine of the past.

The Hancock Engine Co., No. 9, of Acushnet, were to handle their own machine.

The Fairhaven Veteran Firemen's Association secured the Mazeppa, No. 3, from Provincetown.

The Providence Veteran Firemen's Association with their famous hand engine, Gaspee, No. 9, were the special guests of the city.

A good natured but vigorous rivalry was developed from this combination of organizations, and it gave spice to the trial on the morning of the glorious fourth.

A procession was formed at 10 o'clock on the square fronting the Old Colony Station. The route included Pearl, Purchase, Fourth, Madison, Sixth, Market, and Pleasant streets. I give the names of the firemen who took part in the affair and marched in the line.

Mounted Police.

Hill's Band, George Hill, leader, 25 men.

Committee.	Judges.
E. C. Gardiner,	C. S. Ashley,
W. H. Rankin,	R. C. P. Coggeshall,
W. G. Kirschbaum.	L. B. Ellis.

Chief Marshal, Fredk. Macy.

Aids — Loring T. Parlow, Pliny B. Sherman, Augustus A. Wood, and Hugh McDonald.

Hancock Engine Co., No. 9.

Foreman, John A. Russell.
First Assistant, Francis P. Washburn.
Second Assistant, Joseph W. Spooner.
Clerk, Allen Russell, Jr.

George W. Randall,
Lemuel A. Washburn,
James A. Wilbour,
William T. Gifford,
Israel H. Peckham,
John G. Whalon,
William P. Reed,
John G. Dawson,
Albert K. Pool,
Richard Grinnell,
Thomas Hersom, Jr.,
Frederick Bowles,
William Ward,
Eli W. Reed,
Andrew B. Grinnell, Jr.,
John Sylvia,
George W. Hawes,
Herbert M. Spooner,
John F. Parker,
Nathan C. Briggs,
James Haskins,
Job T. Haskins,
Leonard R. Reed,
Allen Briggs,
Edwin F. Morton.

Hancock Hand Engine, No. 9.

Young Mechanic Veterans,
with guests from Columbian, No. 5, Oregon, No. 11, Pioneer H. & L. Co., No. 1, and Zachariah Hillman Steam Fire Engine Co., No. 5.

Captain, Freeman C. Luce.
First Assistant, William H. Sherman.
Second Assistant, Nathan B. Gifford.
Clerk, Haile R. Luther.

Frederick Macy,
E. B. Macy,
Henry B. Almy,
William B. Allen,
William Oesting,
Henry Southwick,
James W. Lawrence,
A. H. Hillman,
Joseph W. Lavers,
Michael Cannavan,
N. B. Mayhew,
George Bumpus,
Charles W. Dyer,
Benj. F. Lewis,
Charles W. Jones,
Thomas Forbes,
Joseph C. Forbes,
Henry K. Jones,
Josiah Macy, Jr.,
Clarfaus Vansant,
Charles H. Underwood,
T. C. Baker,
James A. Lewis,
Samuel H. Mitchell,

Abraham R. Luscomb,
Warren W. Parker,
Seth J. Sampson,
Ira S. Negus,
William McKim,
W. G. Dunham,
L. T. Parlow,
Eben J. Kempton,
Thomas Myers,
George H. Cook,
Charles C. Gifford,
Stephen E. Parker,
Wm. Rounsville,
John R. Linton,
H. M. Gifford,
J. T. Burbank,
Daniel Ripley,
David W. Holmes,
William A. Russell,
James G. Harding,
George P. Reed,
P. G. Thompson,
Isaac W. Benjamin,
Edward A. Sowle,
C. F. Smith,
L. E. Milliken,
David L. Hathaway,
Rufus H. Ellis,
E. Kempton Peirce,
Edward C. Spooner,
John Downey,
Joseph H. Lawrence.

Young Mechanic Engine Company, No. 6, of Mattapoisett:

Gideon P. Barlow,
Charles H. Hiller,
Edwin P. Gifford,
Abner Harlow,
Charles A. Bolles,
Arthur T. Hammond,
Ezra Bridgham,
Anthony S. Wilber,
Jonathan M. Clark,
Ellis L. Mendall,
Melvin Harriman,
Charles H. Robinson,
Edwin F. Barstow,
Melvin O. Downing,
George Downing,
William F. Holmes.

Young Mechanic Hand Engine, No. 6, of Mattapoisett.

Young Mechanic Juniors,
in charge of Second Assistant Robert Allen, of Frederick Macy Steam Engine Co., No. 6:

Captain, Robert E. Allen.
First Assistant, Henry M. Whalon.
Second Assistant, Ernest P. Hammond.
Clerk, William H. Allen.

Frank L. Hathaway,
Harry M. Grey,
Herbert Apsey,
Otto A. P. Benton,
James W. Gleason,
Harry L. Hathaway.

Miniature Model of Young Mechanic Engine, No. 6.

Glenwood Band of Taunton, W. F. Livesey, leader, 26 men.

Providence Veteran Firemen's Association, Edwin Hall, President, 70 men, non-uniformed men in charge of B. J. Cornell, marshal, and uniformed men in charge of John H. Kinyon, foreman.

Vice Presidents,

John H. Kinyon,
James B. Buffum,
W. I. Williams,
Edward Havens.

Albert C. Winsor, Secretary.
John K. Oakes, 1st Assistant. Pembroke S. Eddy, 2d Assistant.
Benjamin J. Cornell, Marshal.

Hosemen.

Chris. B. Little,
Geo. S. Bamford,
Jacob L. Myers,
Chas. H. Greene,
Samuel A. Brightman,
Lewis G. Messenger.

Benjamin W. Cole, Torch.
Joseph Bradbury, Banner.
Ernest Warner, Colors.
James McCord, Hydrant.

James S. Allen,
Edward Atkinson,
Oscar Bender,
William N. Bucklin,
John Church,
Pardon G. Goff,
George O. Gorton.
Daniel Grant,
Henry T. Hall,
Charles A. Henley.
Josiah Hill,
John Howland,
Charles Gardiner,
Ira D. Kelley.
James Kennedy,
C. G. Kranich.
P. A. Hern,
Clarence Niles.
C. L. Nye,
K. T. Lewis,
Frank H. Patt.
Darius Pinkham.
Albert M. Read,
Alpheus Reed,
William H. Shepard,
Benjamin W. Snow,
John E. Spencer,
William Sprague,
William H. Sprague,
Samuel W. Thurston. and Master Arthur as "Young Mose,"
Charles H. Worsley.
A. A. Gray,
John Curtiss,
Lewis Peckham.
W. R. Holmes.
Samuel G. Read,
William E. Smith,
William H. Reynolds.
Palmer C. Thurston,
William H. Aldrich,
William C. Almy,
Edward T. Angell,
James I. Mason.
James L. Warner,
Charles Harwood,
Charles Pay.
William Smith,
G. O. Westcott,
Caleb B. West,
Albion Rounds.
C. E. Edmands,
Daniel O'Brien,
Abner E. Claflin.
Charles Hill.
Henry E. Pearce,
John Wareham,

Joseph West.

Gaspee Engine, No. 9, of Providence.

F. W. Mosher, Drum Major.

Musical Exchange Band, D. J. Sullivan, leader. 21 men.

Fairhaven Veteran Firemen's Association, F. R. F. Harrison, president. 35 men, with members of Frederick Macy Company as guests.

Foreman, J. W. Lawrence.
First Assistant, F. R. F. Harrison.
Second Assistant, John F. Sullivan.
Director of Stream. William J. Marr.

Suction Hosemen, Joseph W. Cook, Fred. Rounsville, George Bumpus.

Leading Hosemen.

A. G. Braley,
N. LeB. Shurtleff,
A. Sisson,
L. M. Baudoin,
George Carpenter,
John Fish,
George W. Parker,
George A. Jenney,
John Stone,
Albert Williams,

Horace Saunders.

Levin Morse,
M. Miller,
T. Croacher,
J. Paull,
C. LeBarron,
C. Gifford,
W. Gifford,
Burt Akin,
William Marshall,
E. Wilkie,
C. K. Wood,
J. L. Ballou,
Fred. Nelson,
Abm. Hammond,
Charles Bowen,
Archie McFlynn,
Walter S. Wood,
George Baylies,
Fred. Weston,
John Clarkson,
J. McDonald,
James Corson,
Joseph Delano,
William Sawyer,
W. Pierce,
William Howland,
S. Shaw,
A. Westgate, Jr.,
George Quirk,
Robert N. Allen,
W. Almond,
T. W. O'Neil,
Charles E. Allen,
Thomas Albert,
D. McErenery,
Phil. Russell,
Henry M. Mosher,
Dan'l Mehan,
F. A. Hanna,
W. C. Gifford,
F. McKenzie,
Joseph Donaghy.

Mazeppa Engine, No. 3, of Provincetown.

Co. E. Fife, Drum and Bugle Corps, C. J. Hogan, leader, 15 men.

Cornelius Howland Engine Co., No. 4, Foreman, James J. Donaghy.

Volunteers, Guests and Members.

Foreman, Roland W. Snow.
Captain of Trial, Alonzo V. Jason.
Director of Stream, William A. Gibbs.
Pipemen, Charles A. Card, John H. Backus.
Suction Hoseman, James M. Tripp.

Wm. E. Watson, Jr.,
Benjamin F. Hinckley,
Edgar S. Gilbert,
Frank C. Jennings,
John W. Donaghy,
Spencer B. Green,
James J. Donaghy,
Charles S. Wing,
Henry J. Marshall,
Leander Reed,
Edwin F. Tripp,
Samuel Watson, 2d,

Wm. C. Kennedy.

Guests.

William Gleason,
Edwin B. Gray,
Samuel J. Russell,
Paul W. Wing.

Harry S. Hutchinson,
Wm. Carroll,
F. N. Hall,
Orrick Smalley, Jr.,
Mark T. Vincent,
Abram. Matthews,
J. Roland Macy,
Isaac L. Ashley,
Charles Sampson,
C. J. Khanser,
Henry Spiller,
Thomas Brown,
Sydney Smith,
Charles T. Ennis,
Ansel Blossom,
Henry Reed,
William H. Bryant,
William Hanna,
William Asten,
Samuel Gurney,
John I. Bryant,
M. P. Whitfield,
Joseph C. Omey,
Charles Manchester,
George S. Bucklin,
George H. Gibbs,
John Gifford,
Harry Brightman,
John Davis,
Charles Johnson,
Charles Delano,
John Marshall,
Daniel J. McDonald,
John B. Peckham,
Frank N. Lincoln,
John W. Frazier,
William Rooks,
W. K. McLane,
Nat. B. Dunn,
W. J. Gifford,
Thomas R. Brownell,
Edward D. Francis,
William Bowie,
Harry Delano,
Fred. Vinal,
John Sheffield,
John Crussell,
D. D. Holmes,
S. H. Rounsvill,
Martin J. Galvin,
Walter Brownell,
Frank Bowman,
Bert Thomas,
Zach C. Dunham,
Henry C. Swain,
Charles Baker,
Benj. W. Jones,
Sylvester Paul,
Wm. Ryan,
Henry J. Kirwin,
Fred. P. Coe,
John C. Emery,
John B. Jones,
Edward S. Baker,
Walter J. Kirwin,
Fred. Thean,
O. Frank Bly,
Jos. B. Peck,
Wm. L. Bly,
Benj. F. Drew,
Fred. Dunham,
J. A. W. Burgess,
Walter Andrews,
J. J. Brownell,
E. Briggs,
Wm. P. Booth,
Samuel Whitehead,
John H. Deane,
Crawford Dunham,
Courtland Shaw,
Henry Yound,
George A. Stetson,
Jas. R. Denham, 2d,
Roland A. Leonard,
Charles B. Riley.

The City Hall square and intersecting streets were crowded with people, and the interest was intense throughout the trial. Water was taken from a trough located on the corner of William and Pleasant streets, which furnished an ample supply from the water mains. Each engine was given fifteen minutes in which to take position, play and retire. No restrictions were made as to the size of nozzles used, nor as to the number of men engaged. Each engine could make as many trials as the time limit allowed. Positions were drawn by lot, and the engines played in the following order:

Gaspee, No. 9, of Providence.
Mazeppa, No. 3, of Provincetown.
Hancock, No. 9, of Acushnet.
Young Mechanic, No. 6, Mattapoisett.
Relief, No. 5, of Fairhaven.

As the Providence firemen rolled their engine into position, they were greeted with cheers: and when the "click, click" of the brakes announced that the trial had begun, the people were loud in their manifestations of enthusiasm. The veteran firemen were reminded of the good old days, and they stood about the Gaspee, watching every movement with interest.

The boys of the city, and there was a large delegation of them present, filled every space of standing room near the engines. They ornamented the electric poles, fences and sheds which gave a view of the contest. When the Gaspees, in response to the vigorous orders of First Assistant John K. Oakes, who directed their movements from a position on the tower, began to "break her down" in earnest, the effect on the throng was electric. They gave expression to their feelings in tumultuous shouts and huzzas. The pipemen directed the streams, delivered through 150 feet of hose, to the north on Pleasant street. After repeated trials it was found that the engine had played 211 feet, 11½ inches, through a 1¼ inch nozzle. It was conceded that the Gaspee might have made a better record but for an unfortunate accident in breaking one of the working bars. The Gaspees retired, amid cheers of the multitude for their plucky performance.

The Fairhaven Veteran Firemen's Association brought up their engine, Mazeppa, No. 3, of Provincetown, and received a hearty welcome. Capt. Lawrence controlled the movements of the engine, and William J. Marr directed the stream. The tests were made with the vigor and snap that veterans know so well how to use on such occasions. The Cape Cod engine showed that it was still in prime condition, for it threw a stream 198 feet, 1¼ inches. The announcement of this result was greeted with applause as the Mazeppa was withdrawn.

Now came the opportunity for the Hancock, No. 9, the only active representative of the past; a good, reliable Agnew machine, the exact type and style of the engines of the fire department in the fifties. Would my reader like to know how the Ohio, No. 3, Philadelphia, No. 7, Franklin, No. 10, and Oregon, No. 11, looked in those times, the memories of which are called up by the events of the day? Let me suggest that he take a good look at the Hancock as the Acushnet firemen roll it into position. Let his imagination put on name, number and paint of the proper color, and he may then see a good representation of any of the above named machines. But the brakes begin to move, and we must observe what is to be done. Three times in succession the Acushnets put in their best work and a stream of 189 feet, through a ⅞ inch nozzle, is obtained.

The appearance of the Young Mechanic, No. 6, of Mattapoisett, was signalized by a most enthusiastic reception. The engine was drawn into position by a company of veteran firemen, who had been attached to it in the fifties, when the engine was a part of our own fire department. The working force was greatly strengthened by the Mattapoisett company, and by several Columbians, who, forgetting their old rivalry, rendered effective service on the brakes. This episode was one of the most delightful occurrences of the day. The engine was under the management of Chief Engineer Macy, whose early experiences were associated with it. Capt. Freeman C. Luce had charge of the general operations, and William H. Sherman served in his former capacity as pipeman. The tests resulted in a stream of 201 feet, 10¼ inches. It was an interesting feature of the trial to observe the vim and energy displayed by the gray-haired veterans as they responded to the commands of Chief Macy to "Wake her! Shake her!" It was evident that the Young Mechanic had made an exhibition highly satisfactory to the company: and this, as it subsequently proved, served to put a new valuation upon the engine in the town of Mattapoisett. It was not for sale on and after July 4, 1890.

Next, and last on the programme, came the Relief, No. 5, of Fairhaven, manned by the Cornelius Howlands and their army of adherents. It was apparent from the business-like methods adopted by the company that they had made careful preparations for the event, and that they had, by diligent practice, learned just how to get the most out of the discarded machine of Fairhaven. Alonzo V. Jason directed the working of the engine, William A. Gibbs directed the stream, and J. H. Backus and Charles H. Card served as pipemen. The repeated tests were conducted with great spirit, and on the third trial the stream measured 216 feet, 5⅞ inches. This won the first prize and with it the cordial congratulations of everybody. The bands played, the crowd cheered, and the boys shouted themselves hoarse. A banquet was served to the visiting firemen in City Hall, after which the prizes were distributed. Thus closed the hand engine trial of 1890.

Allen W. Tinkham, Foreman No. 1.
James J. Donaghy, " No. 4.
George W. Parker, " No. 6.

George M. Crapo, Foreman No. 2.
Charles C. Gifford, " No. 5.
Samuel C. France, " No. 7.

In March, 1890, George B. Russell, who had for several years faithfully served the Department as engineer of the Progress Engine Company, No. 2, died after a long illness. His funeral was attended by the entire Fire Department. Albert W. Taber is now filling the position of engineer.

Aug. 3, 1890, the Z. L. Bicknell Hose Co., No. 2, of East Weymouth, visited our city and were the guests of Progress Engine Co., No. 2. Mindful of the generous entertainment accorded them on their visit to East Weymouth in 1889, the Progress Co. arranged a liberal series of festivities, which were highly enjoyed by their guests.

Steamer No. 7, built by the Amoskeag Manufacturing Co., was put in commission September 1, 1890. It is located in a new house on Durfee street, built expressly for its accommodation, and is thoroughly equipped with all the modern conveniences for fire service. On the second floor of the building is a finely furnished hall for the use of the company.

Wednesday, Oct. 15, 1890, was observed as Muster Day by the Fire Department. The City Government had appropriated $500 to defray the expenses of the occasion, and firemen and citizens entered heartily into the festivities of the day. The weather was bright and sunny, the streets were in fine marching condition, and, with a bracing northwest wind, made the parade with which the event opened one of keen enjoyment to all.

At 11.15 A. M. the following procession moved from City Hall square, through William, Water, Union, Sixth, Madison, County, Hillman and Pleasant streets, passing in review before the City Government at the Library building, thence through Union, North Sixth and Market streets:

ORDER OF MARCH.

Police skirmishers Wing and Moynan.
Chief Engineer, Frederick Macy.
Assistant Engineers, Loring T. Parlow, Pliny B. Sherman, Augustus A. Wood, Hugh McDonald.
Chief's wagon.
Hill's New Bedford Band, 26 men, George Hill, leader.

Charles T. Maxfield, Foreman Hose No. 1.	Joseph Dawson, - Foreman Hose No. 2.
Lysander W. Davis, Foreman H.& L. No. 1.	Henry W. Kenyon, Foreman H. & L. No. 2.
Daniel D. Briggs, - Supt. Fire Alarm.	John A. Russell, Foreman Hancock, No. 9

Hancock Engine Co., No. 9, 22 men, John A. Russell, foreman.
Hose Co., No. 1, 9 men, Charles T. Maxfield, foreman.
Cornelius Howland Engine Co., No. 4, 20 men, James J. Donaghy, foreman.
Onward Engine Co., No. 1, 21 men, Allen W. Tinkham, foreman.
Hook and Ladder Co., No. 1, 16 men, Lysander W. Davis, foreman.
Musical Exchange Band, 20 men, Daniel J. Sullivan, leader.
Progress Engine Co., No. 2, 18 men, George M. Crapo, foreman.
Frederick Macy Engine Co., No. 6, 18 men, George W. Parker, foreman.
Engine Company No. 7, 18 men, Samuel C. France, foreman.
Hook and Ladder Co., No. 2, 14 men, Henry W. Kenyon, foreman.
Hose Co., No. 2, 8 men, Joseph Dawson, foreman.
Zachariah Hillman Engine Co., No. 5, 20 men, Charles C. Gifford, foreman.

All along the route the buildings were decorated, and crowds of people lined the sidewalks as the fire companies marched by to the inspiring music of the bands.

The contest for prizes took place at the conclusion of the parade, Messrs. W. H. Sherman, Freeman C. Luce, Edward S. Haskell, Edgar B. Hammond and D. W. Wilson serving as judges. The first trial was between Hook and Ladder Companies Nos. 1 and 2. They were to run from the corner of Market and Pleasant streets to Mechanics lane, raise a 30-foot ladder against the Odd Fellows' building, and send a man to the top round. The time was taken from the firing of a signal gun. The following were the results:

Hook and Ladder, No. 1, - 35 1-2 seconds.
Hook and Ladder, No. 2, - 31 1-4 seconds.

The second trial was between Hose Companies, Nos. 1 and 2, and Hancock, No. 9. The latter used the reel attached to their engine. The test was to run from Market street to the hydrant at the corner of Pleasant and William streets, connect, and reel off 150 feet of hose: time to be taken from the firing of the signal gun to the moment when water came through the nozzles. The following were the results:

Hose Co., No. 1,	32 1-4 seconds.
Hose Co., No. 2,	42 seconds.
Hancock, No. 9,	29 seconds.

At this point a clambake was served at the Manhattan House to the City Government, Fire Department and invited guests.

Then followed the contest between the steamers. They were to play through two lines of hose of 150 feet each with a Siamese connection and a 1⅛ inch nozzle. Each steamer was allowed 100 lbs. pressure, and Supt. D. D. Briggs adjusted the safety valve to that point in each case; 20 minutes were allowed for each trial. The following results were reported by the board of judges:

Progress, No. 2.	276 feet, 1 inch.
Cornelius Howland, No. 4,	270 ft., 8 inches.
Engine No. 7,	262 feet, 10 3-4 inches.
Onward, No. 1.	251 feet, 10 inches.
Frederick Macy, No. 6,	216 ft., 2 1-4 inches.

The Zachariah Hillman was out of order and did not enter the contest. A grand ball in Co. E's armory, in aid of the Firemen's Mutual Aid Society, closed the festivities of the day.

One of the saddest events in the history of our Fire Department was the death of Edward C. Spooner, a member of Progress Engine Co., No. 2. Mr. Spooner lived in the family of Mr. William B. Bird, 107 Cedar street. On Tuesday evening, Oct. 14, 1890, while at the supper table, he was startled by a loud explosion in the tenement above. Hastily proceeding upstairs and entering the kitchen, a frightful scene greeted his eyes. There, in the middle of the room, stood his neighbor, Mrs. William L. Cobb, completely enveloped in flames. A can of petroleum had exploded in her hand, and the contents was distributed on her garments and on the carpet, which quickly ignited and were burning fiercely when Mr. Spooner entered the room. Seizing Mrs. Cobb in his arms and shutting his eyes and mouth, to shield them from the fire, he bravely carried her down stairs to the room below. A bed-quilt thrown about her body soon extinguished the flames, and she was then removed to the residence of Mr. Squire A. Gifford, across the street. Everything was done to alleviate the sufferings of the unfortunate woman, but without avail. She died at 10 o'clock. Mr. Spooner was shockingly burned about the head and hands, and his sufferings were intense dur-

EDWARD C. SPOONER.

ing the weary days that followed. He received the loving care of his brother firemen and friends, and nothing was left undone to relieve him in his distress; but he passed away on the morning of Nov. 1. Forgetful of himself, he sought to save the life of another; and his name will go down into history among those of the noble men who have sacrificed themselves for helpless humanity.

The funeral was held in the County street M. E. church, Monday afternoon, Nov. 3. Rev. Charles W. Holden, pastor of the church, and Rev. Matt. C. Julien, officiated. The chancel was filled with floral tributes from the family and fire companies. The fire alarm bells tolled mournfully, as the Fire Department and a delegation from the Street Department, of which Mr. Spooner had been a member, accompanied by the Musical Exchange Band, escorted the remains to the church. The services were of a most impressive character and formed a worthy tribute to the memory of one who had been faithful unto death. The burial took place at Acushnet, the escort accompanying the funeral cortege to Weld street on Acushnet avenue. Here the firemen were drawn up in line and, with bowed heads and lifted caps, bade farewell to the dead hero. All the companies were then dismissed except those of Progress, No. 2, and Hancock, No. 9. The following graphic account of the interment, written by Mr. Charles S. Kelley, is taken from the *Evening Standard:*

"Chief Macy, Assistant Hugh McDonald, and the President of the Protecting Society, the members of the two companies, the delegation from the street department and the band boarded four horse cars, which had been provided for them, and proceeded to Lund's Corner, arriving there when it was quite dark. Lighted lanterns were procured from the house of Engine No. 9, and, alighting from the horse cars, the procession formed and proceeded on its way in the darkness to Pine Grove Cemetery, a half mile distant, on the Tarkiln Hill road, the band playing dirges. The procession passing between the open gates of the cemetery, upon the two posts of which were hung lighted lanterns, but poorly dispersing the intense darkness, the quiet broken only by the tap, tap of the muffled drum and the tramp of the men, added solemnity to the occasion. At the grave the scene was even more impressive and touching. The firemen were drawn up in line and, by the light of three or four lanterns, the remains were removed from the hearse and deposited by the roadside, firemen with lanterns being at the head and foot of the casket. The carriages containing the mourners passed by, the bearers lowered the remains into the grave, the Chief Engineer stepped forward, cast a flower into the grave upon the casket, and, with trembling voice, said "Farewell Comrade." He was followed by the members of Progress, No. 2, who, each casting in a flower, said feelingly, "Farewell Brother," and the President of the Protecting Society, who, dropping in a flower, said "Farewell Brave Fireman." A few drops of rain fell, as if the heavens would also weep, and the firemen march sadly away into the darkness. It was at about the same hour that the brave fireman carried the woman from the flames and thereby lost his life."

LINES

In memory of EDWARD C. SPOONER, a member of the
New Bedford Fire Department, who died
Nov. 1, 1890, aged 55 years:

Oh! ne'er again the "fire alarm" will wake him,
  His slumbers now are peaceful and secure,
The jars of earth no more have power to shake him,
  Nor worldly snares his footsteps to allure.

Another's life to save he gave his own,*
  Thus, with the good of every land and clime,
His soul from earth to higher realms hath flown,
  The happy guerdon of an act sublime.

Louder than preaching hath our lost friend spoken,
  The "Good Samaritan" he proved to be:
And gave to us a far more blessed token
  Of human goodness than poor words foresee.

Safe in the hands of Him who rules above,
  A martyr to the noble cause he served,
A true exemplar of devoted love,
  Whose memory with the just will be preserved.

Nov. 2, 1890. D. R.

---

*In an interview with the deceased, during his illness, on the writer's observing that he had done a noble deed, he feelingly replied: "*I could not help it.*"

CHAPTER XV.

THE New Bedford Veteran Firemen's Association, a legitimate outgrowth of the hand engine contest on the 4th of July, 1890, was permanently organized on Monday evening, Nov. 10, 1890. The objects of the Association, as expressed in the constitution, are to "collect and preserve records, papers, relics and sayings pertaining to the New Bedford Fire Department, and to foster good will and friendly intercourse by occasional meetings." The officers of the association, who will serve until the annual meeting in January, 1891, are as follows:

President, Charles S. Kelley.
Vice-Presidents, Frederick Macy, James Delano.
Directors, Samuel C. Hart, Leonard B. Ellis, Haile R. Luther, William G. Kirschbaum.
Secretary, William G. Kirschbaum.
Treasurer, Haile R. Luther.

The following members have been elected:

Charles S. Kelley,
Samuel C. Hart,
Leonard B. Ellis,
Wm. G. Kirschbaum,
Haile R. Luther,
Frederick Macy,
James Delano,
William G. Taber,
Charles H. Gifford,
Charles H. Lawton,
Obed C. Nye,
I. W. Benjamin,
Edwin Dews,
Charles S. Paisler,
William Baylies,
John P. Knowles, 2d,
Augustus A. Wood,
Loring T. Parlow,
Ira S. Negus,
Pardon G. Thompson,
Alfred M. Gifford,
Thomas W. Cook,
Martin S. Nelson,
Charles W. Jones,
John Downey,
James A. Lewis,
Robert H. Taber,
Charles A. Case,
William A. Hamer,
Charles E. Pierce,
George T. Bumpus,
S. H. Mitchell,
George H. Gifford,
David L. Hathaway,
Oliver P. Brightman,
S. A. Tripp.

James C. Hitch,
E. C. Gardiner,
John Mathews,
Jireh Swift,
Charles F. Smith,
Philip E. Colby,
A. H. Akin,
Edward A. Sowle,
Philip H. King,
J. H. Lawrence,
Thomas Albert, Jr.,
William L. Fletcher,
Charles P. Johnson,
Charles F. Briggs,
Henry W. Kenyon,
Henry F. Hammond,
Arthur E. Perry,
Thomas Wood,
Willard Nye, Jr.,
Charles B. Hillman,
Francis P. Washburn,
Edmond L. Wilde,
William H. Maxfield,
Stephen E. Parker,
Eugene R. Leverett,
William G. Dunham,
Wyman D. Jacobs,
B. W. Harrison,
John H. Lowe,
Leopold Bartel,
James Ferguson,
F. C. Jennings,
Augustus G. Mitchell,
Charles T. Maxfield,
Alonzo V. Jason,
Stephen H. Shepherd,
Charles H. Delano,
Frank Spooner,
Samuel C. France,
William E. Macomber,
James L. Wilber,
A. R. Luscomb,
Freeman C. Luce,
Edward F. Dahill,
Henry M. Mosher,
Charles R. Cornell,
John B. Oliver,
Mark T. Vincent,
Charles W. Vining,
Henry C. Stubbs,
Samuel Watson, 2d,
E. C. Milliken,
William T. Taylor,
William R. Sherman,
Charles K. Wood,
W. K. Wagner,
William A. Church,
Charles W. Dyer,
J. J. P. Zettick,
Allen Russell, Jr.,
Moses Dean,
Robert T. Barker,
Francis T. Akin,
George H. Cook,
John J. Howland,
Nathan C. Briggs,
Andrew V. Landers,
Jesse Allen,
William H. Rankin,
Harry C. Jenney,
N. H. Caswell,
John R. Linton,
Benjamin C. Graves,
Amos F. Lovejoy,
J. Harrington Sherman,
William H. Sherman,
Charles F. Dean,
Roland W. Snow,
O. Frank Bly,
David W. Howland,
Charles M. Taber,
Edmund Grinnell,
Joseph W. Lavers,
Alexander H. Hillman,
E. Kempton Peirce,
Fred. H. Wood,
Samuel W. Mitchell,
George S. Bowen,
Arthur E. Robbins,
Henry H. Fisher,
James H. Pease,
H. M. Spooner,
William A. Russell,
Seth J. Sampson,
Joseph W. Robertson,
John A. Russell,
Eugene H. Gifford,
William B. Allen,

B. F. King, Jr., Amos W. Hadley,
Benjamin F. Lewis, Michael Canavan,
Lemuel W. Hayes.

It is the purpose of the Association to purchase a hand engine of the older type, to furnish a hall for meetings, and to adopt such methods of usefulness as shall put the society on a substantial basis.

The following is the amount of losses by fire in this city for the past thirteen years, together with the amount of insurance:

Year.	Loss.	Insurance.
1877.	$26,063.66	$21,528.36
1878.	28,154.46	66,025.00
1879.	9,163.19	54,950.00
1880.	7,609.13	49,450.00
1881.	26,624.96	86,979.00
1882.	23,169.64	692,950.00
1883.	17,398.14	77,450.00
1884.	134,729.82	310,950.00
1885.	6,982.41	148,025.00
1886.	26,786.03	1,108,800.00
1887.	45,141.50	708,150.00
1888.	32,881.87	125,927.00
1889.	48,285.71	182,772.00

I have spoken of the wonderful intelligence and aptitude of the horses attached to the steam department. Their training partakes of the same rigid discipline that pervades every other feature of the fire service. The permanent members of the department are in reality what their name suggests. The engineers who superintend the practical working of the machines, the hostlers, who care for the horses, and the drivers, who handle the ribbons so gracefully and safely when on a rapid pace to the scenes of conflagration, all live in the engine-houses and are present day and night. Their sleeping rooms are arranged with due regard to prompt response to the call of the alarm bell. I am telling no secret when I say that so systematically arranged are the details that when the fireman springs from his bed, he lands in his boots and trousers in one movement, and is down stairs attending to business before the first round of three strokes has been tolled off. I am assured this is the rule and not the exception.

Have any of my readers ever visited one of our engine houses and seen the practical working of the wonderful system in vogue in our department? If not, let me invite you to accompany me, and you may as well take your friends along with you. It will not matter much which one we select, for we shall be sure of a courteous reception from any of them. Suppose, however, we go down to the Frederick Macy engine house on Fourth street. This structure is one of the latest built, and is well modelled for the practical use of our fire service. No need of knocking, for the doors are open wide in the summer days. The handsome engine stands abreast of the large doors, beside it the hose reel, both brilliant in polished brass and steel. The spacious room is as neat and clean as a parlor. The walls are finished in hard wood, and upon them are hung the telephone and other apparatus connected with the fire service. We go upstairs into the hall. Here we find a reception room worthy of any gentleman's house. The walls are of a delicate tint and are hung with fine pictures; Brussels carpet on the floor, handsome furniture placed about the room, comfortable chairs inviting us to rest—everything bears an air of refinement and good taste.

Shall we visit the stables where the well-drilled horses are kept? From the parlor to the stable! Well, yes, it is a change, but we want to see the whole thing, so to the stable we will go. Down the spacious stairway, we cross to the west side and enter. And is this the stable? Why, barring a carpet, we might imagine it a boudoir; for the pet horses in the stalls are clean, and everything is scrupulously neat; no fear of soiling your clothing anywhere. And the horses are plump, handsome and good natured, and they answer to their names by unmistakable manifestations of intelligence. Kind treatment and patient instruction have developed a degree of intelligence truly wonderful in the horses of our fire department. We shall soon see an illustration, for we will accept the courteous invitation to witness "ringing in an alarm." We take our station near the main doors, where we may better see the operations and give any nervous member of our party a chance to escape up the street if affrighted at the commotion. Now, listen, clang goes the gong, presto! the double doors of the stalls open instantly, out leap—yes, leap is the word—the three horses. Without halter or guide they rush to their places at the pole of the engine and shafts of the hose reel, take position exactly under the overhanging harness, which at once drops upon their backs, a pull here, a strap fastened there, and the drivers are on their seats, reins in hands. Doors all open, out of the house moves the whole apparatus with lightning speed, fires all lighted, clouds of black smoke rolling out of the smoke stack, steam up in a moment, and all in readiness for instant work, all this in 18 seconds, and frequently in less time. And this thing is done in every engine house at every alarm, without fuss, friction or confusion.

Do you wonder that we have so few extensive fires? Is it not a rare thing to have a fire extend beyond the building where it originated? With such promptness in response to the magical fire alarm—giving the firemen and citizens alike correct information as to the exact locality—an ordinary fire has little chance of making headway, and if, by any accident, it should get a good start, the entire resources of the fire service would be quickly brought into action and the fire speedily extinguished.

The fire alarm system, under the immediate care of Assistant Superintendent D. D. Briggs, has become a most important feature of our fire service, and much credit is due him for the perfection to which he has brought it after so many years of faithful service. The Board of Engineers, in their last report, say "the utmost care is observed, and the result is that the lines have been ready to perform their remarkable work. There are now 61 fire alarm boxes, 35 miles of wire, 9 bell-strikers, 8 15-inch engine-house gongs, 7 7-inch engineer's gongs, and three small tappers, operated by a battery of 191 cups."

The telephone has also become an important feature in our fire service. A telephonic communication with an engine-house at any time, day or night, calling for immediate help, will be answered by experienced firemen, with apparatus for prompt and effective use.

The La France Hook and Ladder Truck [see illustration on page 182], fitted with all the latest appliances, is another very useful arm of the department. The extension ladder, with lever attachments, furnishes ready facilities for reaching the highest buildings.

I have described as best I can all the important elements which go to make our efficient department, and I have reserved the closing lines to speak of the commanding officers of the whole service. It must be frankly admitted that to Chief Macy and his able and experienced assistants belongs much credit for its present healthy condition. Their long service has been of great benefit to our city; and the people of New Bedford can feel assured that our fire department has no superior in New England for efficiency and completeness.

INDEX.

For the names of the officers and members of the fire companies see rosters of the Department.

www.ingramcontent.com/pod-product-compliance
Lightning Source LLC
Chambersburg PA
CBHW020848270326
41928CB00006B/605